Museum Websites and Social Media

Museums and Collections

As houses of memory and sources of information about the world, museums function as a dynamic interface between past, present and future. Museum collections are increasingly being recognized as material archives of human creativity and as invaluable resources for interdisciplinary research. Museums provide powerful forums for the expression of ideas and are central to the production of public culture: they may inspire the imagination, generate heated emotions and express conflicting values in their material form and histories. This series explores the potential of museum collections to transform our knowledge of the world, and for exhibitions to influence the way in which we view and inhabit that world. It offers essential reading for those involved in all aspects of the museum sphere: curators, researchers, collectors, students and the visiting public.

Volume 1. *The Future of Indigenous Museums: Perspectives from the Southwest Pacific.* Edited by Nick Stanley

Volume 2. *The Long Way Home: The Meaning and Values of Repatriation.* Edited by Paul Turnbull and Michael Pickering

Volume 3. *The Lives of Chinese Objects: Buddhism, Imperialism and Display.* Louise Tythacott

Volume 4. *Colonial Collecting and Display: Encounters with Material Culture from the Andaman and Nicobar Islands.* Claire Wintle

Volume 5. *Borders of Belonging: Experiencing History, War and Nation at a Danish Heritage Site.* Mads Daugbjerg

Volume 6. *Exhibiting Europe in Museums: Transnational Networks, Collections, Narratives, and Representations.* Wolfram Kaiser, Stefan Krankenhagen, and Kerstin Poehls

Volume 7. *The Enemy on Display: The Second World War in Eastern European Museums.* Zuzanna Bogumił, Joanna Wawrzyniak, Tim Buchen, Christian Ganzer, and Maria Senina

Volume 8. *Museum Websites and Social Media: Issues of Participation, Sustainability, Trust and Diversity.* Ana Luisa Sánchez Laws

Museum Websites and Social Media

Issues of Participation, Sustainability, Trust and Diversity

Ana Luisa Sánchez Laws

berghahn
NEW YORK • OXFORD
www.berghahnbooks.com

Published in 2015 by
Berghahn Books
www.berghahnbooks.com

Library of Congress Cataloging-in-Publication Data

Sánchez Laws, Ana Luisa.
Museum websites and social media: issues of participation, sustainability, trust and diversity / Ana Luisa Sánchez Laws. — First edition.
pages cm. — (Museums and collections)
Includes bibliographical references and index.
ISBN 978-1-78238-868-5 (hardback: alk. paper) —
ISBN 978-1-78238-869-2 (ebook)
1. Communication in museums. 2. Social media. 3. Museums — Social aspects. 4. Museums and the Internet. I. Title.
AM125.S36 2015
0.69.02854678—dc23
2015003125

British Library Cataloguing in Publication Data

A catalogue record for this book is available from the British Library

ISBN: 978-1-78238-868-5 (hardback)
ISBN: 978-1-78238-869-2 (ebook)

Contents

Illustrations

Tables

Figures

Acknowledgements

I wish to thank Professor Katherine Goodnow and Associate Professor Stephen Barrass for their comments and suggestions on previous versions of this manuscript. Thanks also to Dr Heng Wu for allowing the use of her interviews with Museum of London staff. Chapter 8 describes a project developed in collaboration with Stephen Barrass from University of Canberra, in liaison with Catherine Styles from the National Museum of Australia. Chapter 9 is about a comparative study conducted in collaboration with Professor Katherine Goodnow. Chapter 10 describes a project developed in collaboration with Kamilla Bergsnev, and with the participation of Bernard Finucane (Questacon National Science Centre) and Stephen Barrass. Stephen O'Connor and Geoff Hinchcliffe (University of Canberra) took part in the conceptual stages of research and development.

Thanks to the anonymous reviewers whose comments and careful reading helped improve and bring to final form this volume. And thanks to my colleagues at Media Arts and Production at University of Canberra for a period of great professional growth.

Most importantly, thanks to my partner Kamilla for her love and support, and to my family for always being there, even when I call them on Skype at 3 A.M. because I forget that, in spite of the wonderful ways in which the Internet has changed our lives, the fact remains that Australia, Norway and Panama are still physically thousands of kilometres apart.

Introduction

The past decades have seen a number of transformations and expansions in uses of the web in museums. In the late 1990s, museums used websites to expand the outreach of museum education, conservation and marketing, to provide information about opening hours, tours, location, and new and past exhibitions, and to give access to specialized collection databases and learning resources (Marty and Jones 2012; Parry 2007).

For example, museums such as the University of California Museum of Palaeontology, whose website was launched in 1994, used the web to provide information about the museum, to present an online exhibition about fossil records, and to allow access to the museum's collections database (Bowen 2010; Paleontology 1994). In the UK, 1994 also saw the birth of the country's first web museum, hosted by the Natural History Museum (Bowen 2010).

The community of museum visitors was also creating their own online versions of well-known museums, as in the case of the WebLouvre, a virtual museum launched by a student, Nicolas Pioch. This virtual museum was later renamed as the WebMuseum for legal reasons (Bowen 2010). And in 1997, acknowledging the growing importance of the web for museums, David Bearman and Jennifer Trant started what would become one of the biggest museum technology conferences in the world, the Museums and the Web conference series. In the introduction, the conference presented what continue to be the great ambitions and challenges museums have faced since:

> Museums still have much to learn about the potential for using the Web. Move beyond institutional presentation of static page, to enable uses of museum information that are more than just browsing and looking. Truly lively Web sites will reflect an understanding of what people do with museum data. Our next generation of web sites need to create spaces that support activities such as comparison and analysis, and that provide means to integrate information provided by many institutions into packages defined by museum visitors. We also need to ensure that the communication enabled by the network is not one way. Museums can capitalize on the potential of the Web by using it as a means to discover how to become more relevant. (Trant and Bearman 1997)

In 1999, museums such as the National Museum of Science and Technology Leonardo Da Vinci in Italy were experimenting with creating virtual worlds (Alonzo, Garzotto and Valenti 2000). Many other museums across the world opened web portals during these years, and slowly but surely online activities became integrated into the more traditional activities of museums.

From 2000 onwards, new functions began to emerge. Museums started to use websites to facilitate social activities and debate, and to provide access to collection databases as well as avenues for the public to contribute to the interpretation of these collections. Major digitization projects were well under way around the globe at the time, as well as the deployment of these digital collections in publicly accessible databases. Museum blogging became a popular workshop topic in the Museums and the Web 2006 Conference. Its potential to deliver two-way or even many-to-many modes of communication featured in the agenda of the NODEM 2006 conference (Russo et al. 2006b).

Today, museums continue to explore myriad new forms of public engagement and participation. Museums are currently experimenting with hybrid physical–digital combinations enabled by mobile technologies (as we will see in one of the cases discussed in this book, the Museum of London, which placed its collections in the city of London via mobile applications). Learning activities have become a focus, and museums are also investing resources in the web as a space for education: social media help to create online education networks and to allow access in schools via remote sessions with museum educators. Other museums are going as far as letting visitors 'curate' whole exhibitions through social media (for example the Brooklyn Museum's 'Click! A Crowd-Curated Exhibition' exhibition). In addition, the shape of online narratives continues to evolve as new technologies develop, from interactive immersive spaces, to multi-story and multi-site mobile narratives where users are in command of story progression with varying degrees of freedom.

Scholars and museum staff address the effects of these changes in both optimistic and cautious terms. Some commentators praise the positive aspects of more enhanced participation via digital means, especially with the advent of social media (Kelly 2010; Russo et al. 2006a; Simon 2010). Lynda Kelly, Manager of Online, Editing and Audience Research at the Australian Museum, argues that

> Social media offer greater scope for collaboration, enabling museums to respond to changing demographics and psychographic characteristics of the public.

> Significantly, the tools of social media also provide new ways to learn about audiences through interacting with them directly, where curatorial and exhibition development staff can act as stimulators and facilitators. Audiences can invest in and contribute their ideas, with the subsequent interactions informing and shaping their exhibition experiences. (Kelly 2009)

She further argues that social media change museums in a positive way: they encourage the creation of exhibitions that provide richer experiences for visitors through backstage access and catering for the unexpected; they provide content that becomes more meaningful; they help connect with young audiences and bring more opportunities for socializing between museum staff and visitors and amongst visitors themselves (Kelly 2009).

Kelly's remarks show that the museum community sees great potential in these new tools. However, while remaining optimistic about the potential of these technologies, this book seeks to present more fine-grained understandings of the new forms of public engagement and participation that social media may help bring about. The time is right to reconsider the true impact social media have had on museum practice. The book's aim is to discuss how museums can truly engage with digital heritage, in contrast to the current trend of using digital technologies merely to develop a greater market share of audiences. Some assumptions about the potential of social media to foster broader public engagement and participation (and to therefore be always beneficial to museums, regardless of their type) need to be examined. Also, the sustainability of digital heritage, in terms of how the work of museums online contributes to sustainable development and how social media activities may be sustained over time, has emerged as a major concern.

Against this background, two broad questions serve as springboards for this volume:

- What new flows of information, participation and public engagement are emerging through museum websites and social media?
- How do museum websites and social media activities shape the potential of digital heritage as a tool for diversity, trust and sustainable development for the museum, its communities and its cultural resources?

Public Engagement and Participation Online

Museums are taking on new roles as brokers of culture, seeking to become sites that allow multiple interpretations of the objects they hold. As museums shift their focus from the conservation of material culture towards their role as forums for the negotiation of knowledge, the development of appropriate forms of public engagement between them and their various communities becomes a main concern. The issue is not new. New Museologists raised similar issues in the 1970s; and the topic of communication in more general terms has been on the agenda of museums since at least the 1960s. In 2000, the Third Report to the Parliament from the Select Committee on Science and Technology in the UK cited Dr Bloomfield from the Natural History Museum, who raised similar concerns:

> Public access to 'knowledge resources' is becoming increasingly important 'as people take a more democratic role . . . in the decision-making process' (Q 239). He [Bloomfield] sees putting such resources on the Internet, and achieving international standards to allow data from different sources to be searched and correlated consistently, as a major task for the next few years (p 63, QQ 239, 269). (Technology 2000)

Bloomfield's words point to public access as well as to issues of democracy and participation in decision-making. This takes us into the concept of public engagement, which is central to the discussion about the role of the Internet in helping to fulfil a museum's social mission. Public engagement can be unpacked as ranging from communication, i.e. coming from the organization towards its communities, to consultation, i.e. coming from the communities to the organization, and to participation, a two-way flow between organization and communities (Rowe and Frewer 2005). Within these forms, the public becomes involved in agenda-setting, policy-forming and decision-making processes (Rowe and Frewer 2005).

Lukensmeyer and Torres (2006) offer a critique of the effectiveness of the various forms of public engagement, pointing out that 'to simply inform and to consult are "thin", frequently pro forma techniques of participation that often fail to meet the public's expectations for involvement and typically yield little in the way of new knowledge'. They also argue that 'collaboration is an essential but often too narrow, time-consuming, and expert-driven mode of participation to achieve the level of inclusiveness and awareness necessary for reform' (Lukensmeyer and Torres 2006).

Recent museum scholarship has also investigated in more depth public engagement and forms of participation. Goodnow (Skartveit and Goodnow 2010) analyses participation and argues that it involves access, reflection, provision and structural involvement. For her, access mainly refers to the availability of channels for a given audience to reach the museum and its collections if they so wish. Reflection describes attempts made by the museum to include members of the community in its galleries by way of making their stories part of the exhibition, without this necessarily involving consultation or participation. Provision is equivalent to a flow coming from community to museum, differing from consultation in that it only has to do with collecting information or artefacts from the community (as opposed to collecting input for decisions made by the museum). Structural involvement refers to situations in which the community and the museum manage decision-making, agenda-setting or policy-forming as equal partners (Skartveit and Goodnow 2010). Applying these ideas to the digital domain, they argue that access, while seemingly limitless online, may be curtailed by issues of language and the categorization of information; reflection may be enhanced due to the bypassing of physical boundaries, but it may be shaped by the curator's interests, which will then be visible in the selection of online material; provision may be enhanced because certain material restrictions in terms of object transfer may be ignored when dealing with digital artefacts (for example, in the provision of images); and lastly, structural participation will be broader due to the fact that new communities may be able to create their own spaces, without needing support from the larger heritage institutions. In the digital domain, grassroots initiatives have as many chances of being a top hit in a web search as established organizations do (Skartveit and Goodnow 2010).

In their discussion on participation and the responsibilities of government and institutions in facilitating citizen engagement, Lukensmeyer and Torres distinguish between information exchange and information processing. For them, while exchange is necessary, it has to be conducive to allowing people to partake in information processing, which involves 'learning and involvement over the breadth and frequency of the exchange' (Lukensmeyer and Torres 2006). It is participation in information processing which will empower citizens to have a real impact in decision-making.

More specifically in the digital domain, Hoem and Schwebs (2010) present a short characterization of various kinds of user engagement with online content. They highlight three distinct roles, in growing order of influence: user-driven, user-created and user-generated. User-driven content points to the ability to customize one's online experience, for example through moving items in an interface until the user achieves a comfortable arrangement for themselves. User-created content encompasses all the media uploaded in sites such as YouTube, Flickr, etc. Users profit from existing content delivery platforms, but they have little influence upon the features offered by these platforms. However, users are able to re-contextualize (remix, share, bookmark) this content, moving it to different platforms and therefore creating new meaning. User-generated content includes both content and context, which is to say that when a message is disseminated via a platform, the message itself and the place where it was broadcasted are important for an understanding of its meaning. User-generated context leaves a single user's machine to become part of a larger conversation in the social arena online (Hoem and Schwebs 2010). It is this last use that is most relevant for discussions of public engagement online, as websites such as Facebook, Badoo, Renren and Twitter grow in popularity due to their capacity to support a feeling of community amongst their users.

Other approaches to the issue of user participation in the creation of culture can be found in the work of Henry Jenkins, who defines 'participatory culture' as one with

1. relatively low barriers to artistic expression and civic engagement,
2. strong support for creating and sharing creations with others,
3. some type of informal mentorship whereby what is known by the most experienced is passed along to novices,
4. members who believe that their contributions matter,
5. members who feel some degree of connection with one another (at least, they care what other people think about what they have created). (Jenkins 2009)

Jenkins argues that with the new interactive technologies, participatory culture 'absorbs and responds to the explosion of new media technologies that make it possible for average consumers to archive, annotate, appropriate and recirculate media content in powerful new ways' (2009: 8), but it is not possible to fully understand this culture if we only focus on the technology without taking into account the cultural knowledge that shapes its uses.

The above concepts and discussions are key for an understanding of the role of social media in museum work. Fine-grained understandings of public engagement and of participation allow us then to see the online activities of museums with more precision, and to understand when, how and why these activities may have a positive, neutral or negative result. Technology is one of the tools through which museums, upon trying to achieve their social goals, explore how to encourage cooperative behaviour inside and outside their physical spaces. As any other tool that museums use for this task, new technologies present their own set of benefits, challenges and drawbacks. Social media technologies lend themselves to multiple uses as their features can be constantly improved or completely changed. They also provide a unique opportunity to make visible the museum's networks of social relations online. However, and departing from the above work on participation, providing increased access is not enough to claim that the creation of a museum social media service encourages public engagement.

It is necessary to distinguish between the various forms of engagement that social media may help foster.

Following Goodnow as well as Rowe and Frewer, to understand the spectrum of engagement that museum social media can support, we can categorize current digital media forms of public engagement in museums (the 'participatory culture' they are engaged in creating) into the following groupings:

- *Access*, such as the dissemination of collections via social network sites, or providing a 'behind the scenes' look at the work of museums, as well as making collection databases available to the public. One example that combines some of these features is the now closed Brooklyn Museum ArtShare Facebook application, which allowed users to create personal collections based on the museum's artworks and then share these with friends and family in the social network. This particular application went beyond access in that it let visitors have a small amount of involvement in 'curating' collections, although the user-generated selections in ArtShare were never meant to feed back into official curatorial work.
- *Communication and consultation*, such as blogs and online fora. These services encourage dialogues with curators about the inner workings of a museum or an exhibition. Museum blogs have almost become a requirement in museum websites; some blogs are about special objects, others are about the expertise of museum staff, and others are used to promote temporary exhibitions. They all share the ability to 'log', as in a diary, events around collections or the museum. As platforms for consultation, museums frequently use blogs to pose questions to the public, about their thoughts concerning an exhibition, etc. Some museums have used blogs to start a consultation process about upcoming activities, but this type of use is less common.
- *Reflection and provision*, such as digital spaces where the community might upload their own media (pictures, sounds, texts), or might annotate, rearrange, select and share favourite items. As we shall see in examples cited below, museums have started to promote the results of independent 'citizen science' websites in their own official pages, and are increasingly willing to incorporate (after some curatorial validation) material generated by the public into the metadata about collections.
- *Structural involvement*, such as systems where external individuals and communities curate digital and physical exhibitions, with the museum working as facilitator of the process. These experiments are much more radical in that the museum gives great control to the public over the functioning of the system itself. Visitors may be asked to 'vote' on

content or on features, to assess the work of other contributors, to participate as community moderators, and so on.

These new forms of online public engagement bring new layers of complexity. As Lukensmeyer and Torres argue, making information available, while necessary, is not all that is required to create the spaces for debate and engagement that museums are keen to foster. However, the move from access to structural involvement is far from straightforward. When experimenting with 'crowdsourced curatorship' and other new forms of structural involvement, voices of 'authority' are subverted. Issues of power, which have long featured in the agenda of museum scholars, surface once again as very sensitive areas: museums must rethink time and time again how to incorporate other voices while keeping their position as trustworthy institutions, as authoritative (yet not authoritarian) repositories of information, in sum, as places where communal knowledge thrives and grows.

Museum blogging is a good example of unexpected conflicts in the emergence of new forms of public engagement. On the one hand, museum blogs are praised as optimal channels to provide visitors with increased access to the work that goes on behind the scenes at the institution. Blogs are seen as places where curators and the public can engage in horizontal, open conversation about many aspects of museum work. On the other hand, blogs raise questions about the boundaries between a staff member's personal views and the institution's position. As Bilkis Mosoddik, in charge of web development at the Museum of London (MOL), points out:

> [In our blog] you are presenting MOL but is not MOL official presentation. . . Whereas press releases come from Corporate, when you go to the MOL blog it is each individual employee representing themselves . . . is their individual voices and that is why each of the persons who blogs there has a different tone or voice because it's them, the individual blogging and they have some interesting things to say and different ways of saying it. I say to people I don't moderate what people write on the blog, because to me it is their voice. . . [but] our website is our property. . . at all times yes, it is your voice, but you have to remember you are speaking as MOL employee. As long as you remember that, and remember all the core policies within the museum about communication, it's fine. (Mosoddik 2009b)

Mosoddik's comments highlight how changing informational flows challenge assumptions about the role of employees within the organization. It seems though as if these new forms of engagement challenge the traditional hierarchies of museum administration within museums (in addition to the more obvious discussions about participation from outsiders).

In addition, as Hoem and Schwebs (2010) point out, while blogs are seen as social meeting places, it is often the case that the blogosphere is most interesting for the owners of blogs themselves, since these platforms offer so many opportunities for commercialization via sponsors on the look for competent writers to endorse their products. In this case, blogs, far from being neutral forums for horizontal conversations, become highly commercial locations, perverting the aura of authenticity and independence that has been attributed to these media forms.

A second case is online museum curatorship. Radical experiments, such as 'Click! A Crowd-Curated Exhibition' by the Brooklyn Museum, place visitors in the position of curators, not only superficially as when users are offered the chance to 'make their own collections and share them with friends', but with a real power to make decisions about public exhibitions. Results are varied: while some visitors appreciate the invitation to take part in a more involved manner, others reject it, or even feel overwhelmed by the opportunity. In addition, while some curators are happy to let visitors temporarily act as curators, others are more critical about the way in which 'being an expert' is portrayed in these activities, feeling that their expertise is trivialized.

Digital Heritage and Sustainability

As was pointed out earlier, thinking about sustainability in the social media activities of museums requires a two-pronged approach. One needs to consider both the sustainable management of digital heritage and the role of digital heritage in sustainable development.

The first issue is preservation. The twenty-first century has seen an enormous growth of the generation of culture and heritage in digital format, to the extent that a large amount of contemporary culture now lives and evolves exclusively online. A pressing question for museums thus becomes preserving this emerging digital heritage. The pace of change from storing crucial information about our world in durable artefacts to storing it in the more ephemeral digital formats is fast. The call is then to understand what the sustainable management of digital heritage involves in terms of preservation.

The problem is well known. Since the early 2000s, heritage stakeholders and communities around the world have sought to address this, identifying the need to tackle the fast obsolescence of formats, data corruption, data loss due to compression, and the question of future-proofing artefacts, for example by providing hooks/metadata to facilitate future linkages and use. The issue extends to what data should be kept when moving from the material to the virtual world and how to perform the digital recording of real world objects/sites (metadata, co-ordinates, snapshot in time), and also how to preserve the usability of these artefacts and the data generated around them for future generations. In 2003, the National Library of Australia prepared the 'Guidelines for the preservation of digital heritage' for UNESCO's Memory of the World Programme (Webb 2003). Amongst the issues addressed were the ephemeral nature of digital resources and how changes in technology would mean the loss of many expressions; the inadequacy of instruments such as 'legal deposit' in this new digital context; shortcomings in storage capacity to cope with growing digitized and born-digital items; and the need for a cooperative approach (in this document primarily between institutions) to tackle these issues (Webb 2003).

A case in point is digital media content produced around existing collections: can or should it become part of a collection, and under which criteria? Currently, curators and IT staff make decisions about what data will be preserved. For example, in the case of social media content produced from outside the institution – in blogs, forums, social network sites, etc. – it is necessary to ask whose experience should be preserved. Whose point of view should museums choose to represent, and why? We return to the problem of authenticity, the authority and credibility of museums, and the emerging challenges of expert vs. non-expert input in collections.

Local, national and international bodies continue to work on criteria for preservation, often attempting to deal with digital heritage as a form of intangible heritage. Work on documentary heritage encompasses digital material. The UNESCO documentary heritage policies make provisions for the safeguarding of audio-visual and digital material in programmes such as the Memory of the World Programme. To be accepted into the Memory of the World Programme, applicants have to comply with criteria such as authenticity, uniqueness and irreplaceability, and significance. In addition, matters such as integrity, rarity, threats and management plans are also taken into account.

'Authenticity' requires an external body to certify the source of the artefact. In the Nara Document on Authenticity, UNESCO guidelines state that identifying the sources of heritage as credible and truthful is essential to establish that heritage as authentic. The document also makes provisions to acknowledge a diverse range of sources (physical, oral, written and figurative) as well as their dependence on context (Lemaire and Stovel 1994). The Nara Document provides a general framework; it does not, however, provide tools to deal with particular cases. The assumption is that each case will be unique in its challenges concerning authenticity.

In the digital preservation domain, authenticity has been defined as requiring 'multiple preservation properties: that the digital record remains unchanged, that the preservation context correctly tracks information about preservation processes performed upon the digital record, and that the chain of custody of the digital record remains unbroken' (Moore, Jaja and Chadduck 2005). Furthermore, for Moore et al. (2005), authenticity requires that content (data), contexts (databases), and the systems to associate content with context (data grids) should enable the logging of all data acquisition, processing and archiving operations, so that the way in which a given piece of information came to its present state can be examined in the future. However, this digital preservation approach does not take into account systems in which information is being supplied by heterogeneous sources through technologies such as social media. Museums are experimenting with ways of incorporating 'citizen knowledge' while maintaining the authenticity of their collections and of information about these collections, and in this case, international policies are lagging behind.

'Uniqueness and irreplaceability' demand that the artefact is a document of restricted access, that it is representative but does not have a direct equal, and that its impact in a region of the world can be proved. Again, this is a complicated issue in digital material, whose main characteristic is its easy reproducibility. In fact, it may be more appropriate for the case of digital heritage to make multiple copies of materials, and to do so often, so as to keep data in the most up-to-date format. When it comes to digital material, irreplaceability may well be a problem for preservation.

'Significance' involves comparative criteria: time, place, people, subject and theme, and form and style. Within these, there is blurriness in the type of canon to be used to determine which time or place is important for the history of humanity (whose view should prevail upon this point?). With regard to form and style, similar problems emerge. What artistic canon is to be used? Does the programme appeal to some kind of universal consensus on what is aesthetically important?

Expanding upon significance, Australian approaches to valuing heritage have provided an alternative to the built-fabric conceptions of heritage that for some time dominated the field. Specifically, Australia's 1979 Burra Charter helped to establish a set of guidelines for assessments that corrected the bias towards the built fabric (which favoured the heritage of colonizers) implicit in the 1964 Venice Charter. The Burra Charter introduced the concept of significance, and became a step in creating pathways for the recognition of Aboriginal heritage, for which criteria based on the Venice Charter had proved insufficient. Briefly, significance assessments involve the non-hierarchical evaluation of aesthetic, historical, scientific and social value (Australia ICOMOS 1988: 12, and interview with Ireland 2012). The definition of social value states that 'social value embraces the qualities for which a place has become a focus of spiritual, political, national or other cultural sentiment to a majority or minority group' (Australia ICOMOS 1988: 12). The spirit of the Australian approach is echoed in other countries around the world. In the UK, for example, the issue of more inclusive policies for heritage has recently been added to the agenda. A number of instruments have helped guide heritage policy to better address the issue of unequal power that biases in heritage protection reflect. Since 2000, the Race Relations Amendment Act has required public authority heritage institutions to promote racial equality (Cheddie 2012). According to the Greater London Authority Report on 'Delivering Shared Heritage: The Major's Commission on African and Asian Heritage' (2005), the case for more inclusive heritage policy needed to address a variety of fora: legal, ethical, human rights, intellectual, business and corporate responsibility (Cheddie 2012). The Act also included human rights principles from international frameworks (e.g. UN conventions that the UK abided to). As a result, definitions of heritage proposed by the commission 'moved away from concepts of materiality towards concepts of the ritual, memory, transmission and orality' (Cheddie 2012: 274). The resulting expanded idea of heritage 'guardianship' gave impulse to new spaces for dialogue about cultural diversity in the sector (Cheddie 2012). Speaking about significance, Mason (2003) argues that one of the things to bear in mind is why we preserve. For him, preservation has its origins in our desire to highlight the connection between memory and environment (2003: 64), and he adds that this connection is dynamic. An important point Mason makes in his evaluation of the concept of significance, however, is that it tends towards exclusion, as it leaves the task solely to experts who often fail to acknowledge community voices. Mason argues that if one wishes to undertake a complete significance assessment, it is necessary to establish a dialogue between architects, historians, city planners, community members who are experts on the site because of prolonged relations with it, and also stakeholders who may have little direct contact with a site but still value it highly (2003: 68). He calls for a more open process in which both the community and the experts engage in a dialogue in order to come to a fuller understanding of the reasons why a particular site should be preserved (2003: 66–68). In a review of the way in which the Australian NSW Heritage office was conducting its assessments of heritage value, Byrne et al. (2003) made a similar call, stating that 'the Service should encourage a culture in which the questions "Who values this heritage and how do they value it?"' should be the starting point

(2003: 141). Perhaps the collateral lesson from the Australian experience is that the task is not only to establish a clearer pathway or guidelines, but also to ensure that participation from a broad range of stakeholders is embedded in the process, and moreover, that the questions of unequal power in this dialogue are addressed.

'Integrity' involves proving that the artefact has not been manipulated or damaged. In the context of digital media, an appropriate consideration of integrity requires a distinction between digitized and born-digital material. Digital cultural resources are at times the product of digitization, at others a combination of born-digital material and digitized resources, and yet in other cases they are born-digital only. The Digital Preservation Coalition (2008: 24) provides the following definition of 'born-digital' material:

> Digital materials which are not intended to have an analogue equivalent, either as the originating source or as a result of conversion to analogue form. This term has been used. . . to differentiate them from 1) digital materials which have been created as a result of converting analogue originals; and 2) digital materials, which may have originated from a digital source but have been printed to paper, e.g. some electronic records.

When the resource is defined as the digitized material, museums tend to treat digital interpretations as temporary additions. However, when it is born-digital material, the boundaries between the artefact and other digital material added at a later stage (for example, user interpretations, tags, remixes) becomes fuzzy. Often, for digital culture resources that are the digitized version of a material object in the collection, the goals of using digital media (be it social media or other Internet services) is to make the resource available to the public while preserving its integrity.

In general, the Memory of the World Programme may be the most advanced global programme available at the moment to attempt to preserve digital heritage. However, it still has a long way to go in solving issues with its fitness for the kind of heritage increasingly seen in the digital domain. For example, irreplaceability or uniqueness may be hard to defend with regard to digital media, which as noted previously live in a kind of paradox: digital media are incredibly easy to reproduce, yet without multiple copies they run the risk of evaporating into binary oblivion. The problem of the sustainable management of digital heritage is one which the programme tries to address. However, at this point a crucial aspect in need of further development is how a decision is made to identify digital media as being worthy of conservation. Crowd-sourced consensus through social media might work for some digital heritage materials, but the voices of minorities may be muted, or worse, completely ignored.

Moving briefly away from the sustainable management of digital heritage and towards the role of this heritage in sustainable development, different questions need to be asked:

- How does involvement with digital heritage result in meaningful opportunities for participation for museum communities?
- What kinds of sociality can be seen around these media, and how do they reflect on the museum as an institution?
- What kinds of new museum community building functions, ethical, administrative and curatorial practices emerge through digital media?
- How does digital heritage reflect issues of diversity, social inclusion and sustainable development?

Museum Social Media, Inclusion and Diversity

The above questions and concerns have roots in the large body of scholarship that deals with the museum's social role and mission, in which a central question is the need to shift focus from the museum to the communities it serves. This questioning began long before the web, when, in the 1970s, the 'New Museologists' discussed the purpose of museums in society. In Australia and in the UK, Tony Bennett and Eileen Hooper-Greenhill criticized the museum 'as an ideological construct' (Moore 2000: 4) with 'regimes of knowledge' and 'constructed taxonomies' (Hooper-Greenhill 1992), an 'the exhibitionary complex' that constructed its visitors and regulated their behaviours, though perhaps, in so doing, becoming a productive force (Bennett 1995: 5–6).

Hooper-Greenhill (1992: 8) pointed out that museology had considered museums in view of their historic development, but the linear history used to explain them did not acknowledge the plurality, the historical specificity, and the political, cultural, economic and ideological contexts of the museums. In *Museums and the Shaping of Knowledge* (1992), she used Foucault's (1970) critique of systems of classification in *The Order of Things* to question the museum's orders of classification and regimes of knowledge. Hooper-Greenhill (1992: 5) asked whether museum taxonomies and documentation practices gave preference to particular ways of knowing at the same time that they excluded others, or whether these taxonomies were socially constructed rather than 'true'. Hooper-Greenhill (1992: 6) also cited Roland Barthes's statement in *Image, Music, Text* (1977) that 'there is little idea that material things can be understood in a multitude of different ways, that many meanings can be read from things, and that this meaning can be manipulated as required . . . it is not understood that the ways in which museums "manipulate" material things also set up relationships and associations, and in fact create identities'.

In her 'holistic' approach, Hooper-Greenhill (1995: 2) felt it necessary to take into account the political and economic contexts in Britain during the 1990s in order to understand changes in museums during that period. She linked changes in museums to how these institutions were 'pushed by the government to think . . . as an industry', with museums hiring marketing experts, and shifting from 'visitors' (persons who do go to museums) to 'audiences' (persons who might come to museums) as the preferred term. At the same time, Hooper-Greenhill (1995: 7, 12) pointed out how the persons or institutions establishing the collection held the power over what was viewed, an issue that needed to be problematized, and also drew attention to the need to understand the 'epistemes' (the set of relations within which knowledge is produced and rationality defined, a concept she borrowed from Foucault) in which museums operated.

In contrast to Hooper-Greenhill's (1992) genealogy of museums based on classification and display, Tony Bennett (1995: 5–6) proposed in *The Birth of the Museum* his own genealogy, which took into account the development of other cultural institutions, even those that seemed alien or disconnected from it, such as for example fairs and exhibitions. He used Foucault's theories of disciplinary power in combination with Antonio Gramsci's theory of hegemony to develop the idea of 'the exhibitionary complex'. Bennett (1995: 7) also used Foucault's critique of how man is both the object and subject of knowledge (*The Order of Things*), transferring this critique to the tensions in the museum's attempt to construct their visitors and regulate their behaviours. In the US, Karp and co-editors (Karp 1992, 2006; Karp and Lavine 1991) focused on cultural diversity and 'the politics of public culture', including the role of museums in confirming or denying identity, and in acknowledging processes such as globalization. These critiques and analyses were based on historical accounts as well as case studies where exhibitions were 'read' and interpreted as representations of identity or expressions of power. In the main, these critiques have in common a desire to challenge traditional fixations on object collection, with theorists 'de-material(izing) these objects as mere semiotic indicators or rematerial(izing) them in social, political and economic contexts, or (doing) both' (Starn 2005). The goal is to replace 'object-centeredness with experience-centeredness' as the core business of museums (Parry 2007). The critiques have also resulted in increased pressure for understanding and managing the accountability and social responsibility of the museum.

More recently, digital media have reinvigorated the debate. In the US, practitioners have written compelling volumes about participation and community building in museums, especially about activities supported by social media (*The Participatory Museum* by Nina Simon, 2010, is a prominent example). A stream of research on the making of exhibitions off- and online (the focus of the majority of research about museum technology) has contributed alternative perspectives. Researchers from fields such as Human Computer Interaction (HCI), Interaction Design, Educational Technology, Media Studies and many more have used the museum as a playground and backdrop for concerns relating to views of museums as media forms. In Norway, for example, researchers have analysed museums by combining cultural theory, film studies and new media studies, and have highlighted concerns over diversity and the representation of minorities and migrants. Goodnow et al.'s *Museums, the Media and Refugees* (2008) is a good example of mixing media and communication concerns with museum studies. Other Scandinavian research has taken into account the points of view of designers and communities, and has gone as far as to enable and investigate museum communities as core members of the exhibition design team. Pierroux, Krange and Sem (2010) have investigated mobile technologies and learning in museum contexts within a socio-cultural approach to learning, and Wagner, Stuedahl and Bratteteig (2010) have used museums as contexts for understanding the design of digital media.

Digital media are having an enormous impact on our everyday lives. This is even more true of social media, which, as Hinton and Hjorth (2013) point out, bleed across platforms (from desktop to mobile to tablets and the internet of things) and across social and media contexts, thus 'colonizing' the web. Social media represent the promise that our participation will have as much impact on the production of global culture (and heritage) as that of the stakeholders of traditional media. Instead of mostly consuming visual media, we are now able to deliver our audio-visual creations to the whole world on YouTube. To register our thoughts on a topic of interest, we will now often start a blog instead of a diary, and make it available globally. Thus, as museumgoers, we expect increased input into museum collections, for example by having online tools to group our preferred objects and share these with friends in social media sites, and we might even find the curator's blog and engage them in conversations about these objects.

Digital media have also seemingly levelled the field between individuals and institutions and all voices are now supposed to have similar access and participation on the web. For instance, institutions like the Smithsonian have launched wikis, an eminently participatory and open form of web collaboration, where they make their web design and policy process transparent to the public, and where they also embrace concepts such as ensuring that their websites are 'vast, shareable, findable, and free' (Smithsonian 2009). This marks a shift away from the idea of website design as the exclusive exercise of the museum towards the idea of community participation as a core web design value.

However, when museums join sites such as Facebook or Twitter, everything from time management to the more delicate art of community building needs to be rethought. Shelley Bernstein, Chief of Technology at the Brooklyn Museum, has described some of the dilemmas faced, in particular the difficulties of 'pulling the plug' on a social media platform. With their ArtShare application on Facebook, staff never expected the work overload involved in keeping up with the constant technical changes made to that social network, and yet were concerned that abandoning it would mean letting down the community of users they had nourished. In the end, as soon as the user base decreased, the museum discontinued the service (Bernstein 2011). Bernstein shares the Brooklyn Museum's thoughts on when to leave:

> Generally, you'll see us continue to jump into social platforms as we see our audience gathering there. We feel it's important to have a presence where people *know* they may not come directly to www.brooklynmuseum.org, but as with any technology we will watch the landscape and adjust as we go along. As audience moves from one platform to another or as platforms modify beyond recognition, we'll change with them and that can mean making difficult and carefully studied decisions about when to stay and when to go. (Bernstein 2011)

Holding a more optimistic view, Kevin Bacon, curator of the photographs at the Royal Pavilion and Museums, Brighton & Hove, states that digital media, in particular social media, are excellent channels to show people what goes on behind the scenes, and thereby thread museums into the public's imagination and build new relations, for example for funding or political support (quoted by Billings 2011).

Collaboration seems to be the key feature of the web, promising increased freedom and choice, and arguably enhancing sustainable development. However, taking into account issues of access (many communities in the world are underrepresented online), how can we assess the real potential of digital heritage for the sustainable development of communities?

In sum, in our digital age, the museum stores and nurtures heterogeneous sources of knowledge (from lay to curatorial) which both compete and collaborate to shape the legacy of contemporary societies – a topic to be developed more fully in the chapters that follow.

How This Book is Structured

The volume is intended as a resource for museum staff, students and researchers working at the intersection of cultural institutions and digital technologies. It recognizes the importance of bringing together curators, directors, educators and web designers, and is written therefore in an accessible manner for these various groups.

The volume offers extensive examples of museum web pages and the technology and thinking behind them, while discussion of the theoretical and technical issues surrounding museum websites and social media helps to outline the broad context within which technology developments take place. The aim is to provide an insight into the issues behind designing and implementing web pages and social media in this process, for the broadest range of museum stakeholders (communities of experts and non-experts engaging with museums at different levels). In so doing, the volume intends to offer a holistic picture of museum online activities that can serve as a starting point for cross-disciplinary discussion.

This introduction sets the tone of the book and provides an overview of its structure. The book is divided into three parts. Part I, History and Theory (Chapters 2 to 4), presents in more depth the three theoretical foci outlined above. Part II, Practice (Chapters 5 and 6), outlines practical considerations concerning the use of social media in museums. Part III, Cases (Chapters 7 to 9), uses the insights from the theoretical foci to discuss specific cases. Readers who are mostly interested in examples of contemporary uses of social media may prefer to go directly to the cases provided in Part III. Part IV (Chapters 10 and 11) departs from these perspectives and contemporary cases and presents emerging practices that help to portray what the future of digital heritage may be.

Chapter 2 provides our theoretical setting and offers an overview of the changing theorizations of museum communication. This overview reveals a transition in the literature from a focus on institutions to one on visitors. Previous conceptions of museums as senders of a clear and irrefutable message are contrasted with more recent calls for the inclusion of multiple voices, and the push for an ever-growing social mission for the museum. The emergence of the social web is discussed and connected to the uses of computing in museums, from early uses for cataloguing tasks to more recent experiments with visitor participation. The chapter intends to place these changes in museum websites within the context of larger shifts in the uses of the web. I briefly discuss authors such as Benkler and Bruns, who have provided the more optimistic interpretations of these changes, and contrast them with commentators from within museums who refer to the way in which the Internet may threaten assumptions about the role of museums. As a counterpoint, the last section of this chapter looks at contemporary museum websites and their use of social media. Three foci for museum websites are identified: institution-oriented, collection-oriented, and user-oriented websites and social media. These call into question how effectively museums use their websites and social media to transform themselves from repositories to spaces for debate.

Following on the issue of how to understand and measure the degree in which museums can effectively engage audiences with digital culture, a framework for Digital Heritage Sustainability (DHS) is introduced in Chapter 3. The chapter presents an analytical framework for the cases that follow, which allows us to identify how museum social media and museum websites contribute to or detract from the sustainable management of digital culture and digital heritage. The DHS framework is inspired by other frameworks that have been used in the analysis of the sustainable management of digital commons, such as Ostrom's (2005) Institutional Analysis and Development Framework. One of the ideas put forth later on in this volume is that the Internet can be seen as a common-pool resource, that is, one that is horizontally and collaboratively managed by a community (see Benkler 2006). The DHS framework also builds on previous experiences with the analysis of physical museums (Sánchez Laws 2011). The framework uses three signposts to guide analyses: contexts, stakeholders and digital practices.

Chapter 4 closes the theoretical section of the book with a consideration of trust as a pillar of the sustainable informational flow between museums and their communities. In this chapter, the impact of digital media upon the trust relationship between museum and community is examined, with a discussion of the idea that current efforts of museums to connect to users online reflect a 'radical trust' approach where the potential benefits of broad engagement are considered to outweigh the possibility of abuse.

Part II, Practice, outlines practical ways in which museum staff can build up their social media skills. Chapter 5 includes a compilation of useful resources intended to invite readers to engage in hands-on-work with museum social media. Chapter 6 is a survey of the current uses of social media in museums, and establishes a common vocabulary of the various forms of social media. Amongst the various media discussed are blogs, social network sites, mashups and media sharing sites. The broad range of examples provided is intended to give readers a sense of the possibilities available; however, the emphasis is on uses that blur the boundary between curator and audience by expanding user-access to the curatorial process with the inclusion of user-generated content, filtering and social curating. Cases include museums (Brooklyn Museum, the Museo Reina Sofia and Red de Conceptualismos del Sur, the Museu da Pessoa, amongst others), and networks that include new stakeholders as part of the institutional structure: Google Art Project, Flickr 'The Commons' and Digital New Zealand. These examples suggest that the move from museums to audiences is becoming a structural change in how stewardship for culture and heritage is institutionally organized.

In Part III, Cases, Chapter 7 is about the Museum of London's (MOL) website and social media services. The chapter examines how the MOL has attempted to strike a balance between building the image of the institution and strengthening a sense of community amongst its stakeholders online. At the MOL, this balancing involves clarifying some of the unwritten rules about how employees may represent the museum in social media such as blogs. It also touches upon the extent to which communities are invited to take part in decisions about the content and message of exhibitions, on and offline. As we shall see, while the MOL constantly creates opportunities to get involved, it does so within a well-established set of parameters that ensure the image of the museum will remain under the tight control of the organization. In this sense, the MOL is moderate in its use of social media.

Chapter 8 deals with a website and social media which focuses on diversity in knowledge about collections. The Museum of World Culture (Världskulturmuseet) uses social media to enhance user participation in provisioning, classification and interpretation. This case is of particular interest because of the mandate of the museum, which in effect demands that heterogeneous sources of knowledge are acknowledged and incorporated.

Chapter 9 is a comparative exercise where museums and galleries in Sydney and Panama City are examined for their similarities and differences in their treatment of Aboriginal, Indigenous and 'Ethnic' heritage, off and online.

In Part IV, Futures, Chapters 10 and 11 present a landscape of the future of digital heritage. The cases presented have as a recurring theme defiance in the face of boundaries between the digital and the physical. They portray a museum reality where hybrid spaces are the norm, and where the interplay between technology, audiences and contexts is much more transparent and acknowledged.

Chapter 10 presents research in co-creative digital practices, using as a case study the 'digital colonization' of the National Museum of Australia's 'Garden of Australian Dreams'. Working in collaboration with the museum's digital officers, over one hundred students and researchers from University of Canberra used Augmented Reality (AR) to produce in excess of 700 images, texts and sounds, which were displayed via mobiles and tablets to created a 3D overlay in the physical space of the museum. Shared via social media platforms, the overlay complemented official curatorial information with unique personal stories and interpretations from the student community.

Chapter 11 represents a return to the topic of sustainability, this time from the more conventional environmental perspective, with the case of the Questacon National Science and Technology Centre in Canberra. Questacon has in recent years emphasized the need to adopt sustainable energy consumption practices in its building, and in this project, it sought to communicate this story via digital means, including social media.

The Conclusion draws together the cases and theoretical insights about the impact of social media in an attempt to redefine the role of museums in the conservation and dissemination of heritage. It is argued that new flows of information and therefore of public engagement, from communication to consultation to participation, are being explored by museums online to various degrees, with the general norm being a communicational flow (from museum to community) that allows some form of participation via provision. Cases where participation (on and offline) is structural become more visible thanks to exposure through social media, but from the examples presented in the book, it is argued that when structural involvement occurs online, it is because the institutional culture of the museum would have allowed it from the start, regardless of whether it was on or offline.

In terms of digital sustainability, it is argued that the problem of authenticity and the emerging challenges of expert vs. non-expert control over the experience continue to be key elements in the longer term strategies that museums may adopt.

As for trust, the various cases discussed in this volume show that a collaborative creation of heritage has become a core activity of museums, and that the transfer of power between stakeholders will continue to create challenges and opportunities for museums and communities seeking to build their trust.

Finally, considerations of issues of diversity seem to be lagging behind in the realm of museum digital technologies. Yet as the examples provided in the book show, it is precisely in this area that small groups who were previously limited in their access and control over their heritage are successfully adopting new technologies, thus creating new networks (both off and online) where their heritage has begun to thrive.

Part I: History and Theory

Chapter 1

Museums Online, from Repositories to Forums

The twenty-first century presents us with a heightened awareness of the relationship between the inner and outer spheres of museum practice, that is, the relationship between museums and their communities. Museums are using digital media to change from 'communicating who they are' to 'establishing dialogues with their publics'. In this chapter, the discussion centres upon changes in uses of computing and concepts of communication in museums from the 1960s to the present (Sánchez Laws 2009). This history reveals shifts in who is addressed, what information is provided, and what communication relationships are intended. This evolution makes apparent assumptions behind three current types of museum website and museum social media: institution-, collection-, and user-oriented. This overview will allow us to analyse the role technological changes have had in changing the museum-community relationship.

Early Days: 1960s to 1990s

At the heart of the technological developments that have led to today's social web lay a long-held desire: to connect people with their environment, with their objects, and with each other. A well-known precedent is Vannevar Bush's 1945 idea of the Memex, a library reading desk that enabled the creation of trails between various texts and would thus help link knowledge and people across barriers of time and space. Consider also Tim Berners-Lee's key goals when he described in 1989 the implementation of a hypertext system at CERN. His approach was driven by a clear desire to enable networking and collaboration between people. In 'Information Management: a proposal', he highlighted the need to find ways to secure and store the continuously changing, dynamic and highly valuable social information that was being lost at CERN, arguing that Hyper Text Markup Language (HTML) was the key to help organizations store in a more efficient and reliable manner the constantly changing information about people and their environment (Berners-Lee 1989). Yet neither Bush nor Berners-Lee could foresee that the web would become a major platform not only for storing information but also for social interaction itself.

Computers entered the everyday world of museums long before the emergence of the World Wide Web. For instance, the Smithsonian Institution incorporated computing during the 1960s because it saw the power of automation to process the information contained in its increasingly large collections (Parry 2007). Jones-Garmil provides a rich account of these developments in the US, noting that the Smithsonian's system, the Self Generating Master (SELGEM), was the first 'open source' system for data management. Shortly after, in 1965, the University of California-Berkeley, the Lowe Art Museum at University of Florida and the Oklahoma Inventory of Ethnological Collections started to add entries to the Smithsonian SELGEM databases (Jones-Garmil 1997).

Several national committees and programmes began to form in the 1970s in North America, with the aim of promoting the use of digital technologies for collection management. Amongst them were the National Inventory Programme, created in Canada in 1972, and the US Museum Data Bank Coordinating Committee (Jones-Garmil 1997).

With the web, however, museum computing became more than an asset: it became a mandate. In 1994, the International Council of Museums (ICOM) announced that in order for museums to comply with their social mission, they should be participating more actively in the online world (Parry 2007). In response, museums started to expand the role of computing to include a concern for the dissemination of their catalogues to the public. That same year, the Natural History Museum and the Science Museum launched the first museum websites in the UK (Rellie 2006). Museums started to think of ways to make their catalogues more accessible, as a result of which the digitization of collections began to take off. In addition, one of main goals of early websites was to promote events at the physical museum (Rellie 2006). And in 1997, Macdonald and Alsford theorized that the digital museum would help overcome the limitations of physical space and would enable museums to display an unprecedented amount of objects to visitors; to break the barriers of geography in making materials accessible to wider audiences; to enhance the educational mission of the museum by making more materials available to teachers and students; and to use an array of interactive media to present and enhance their subject matter (Macdonald and Alsford 1997). However, they also predicted that the digital world would result in a levelling of the playing field, where museums would not have the monopoly on interpreting culture (Macdonald and Alsford 1997).

While museums were implementing automation and dissemination technologies, other entrepreneurs of the web started to move in a different direction: to make the web into a major platform for human relations. In 1997, SixDegrees.com was launched. It was the first service to allow the listing of friends, and one of the first examples of a website whose purpose was to harvest social relations and make this information visible to users. Meanwhile, some museums had started to pick up the trend, such as the Tate Museum in London, which in 1998 launched a website that included opportunities to chat and participate in forums (Rellie 2006).

In terms of concepts of informational flows, museums started adopting Shannon and Weaver's model of communication in the late 1960s (Hooper-Greenhill 1994b, 1994a). In this well-known model, communication was a simple linear process involving a communicator, a message and a receiver. The model took into account the intentions of the communicator, the subject of the message, whether there was a common language and shared background, and any changes in the message after the process of communication took place (Fiske 1982). Among museums, this created much debate over the role of objects in museum practice, and the extent to which objects were at the core of a museum's means of communication or were just one of many means of communicating their message. Debates over objects aside, there was a strong assumption that the originator of communication was the museum.

Voices outside the museum presented an alternative view, placing visitors at the centre. In 1967, Marshall McLuhan proposed that instead of delivering an institutional point of view of its collections, a museum could become a facilitator of the points of view of other stakeholders. McLuhan described a non-linear approach to museum communication wherein story lines should be dismissed to allow visitors to become co-producers or co-creators of history. McLuhan emphasized simultaneous rather than sequential stories.

McLuhan's ideas had little effect at the time (although digital media would rekindle them later). Instead, shortly after in 1968, Duncan Cameron presented a systematic account of museum exhibitions as communication systems, in which he argued that responsibility for the content in a museum, the transmitter, lay with the museum's curator/exhibitor, that museumgoers were the receptors, and that objects were the medium of communication (Cameron 1968). In this linguistic approach, Cameron (1968) stated that objects functioned as nouns within the museum message, relationships between these objects were verbs, and the context of the exhibition and supplementary material were adverbs and adjectives. While Cameron acknowledged that there were many transmitters, media and receivers within a museum, he argued nonetheless that curator expertise was required to properly 'transmit' the meaning of objects to audiences (1968). Supporting media such as film, photographs, audio recordings and texts were seen as necessary, though ancillary, to explain the correct meaning of objects. It was the duty (and privilege) of curators to create a museum environment that was free from distracting elements and that would help objects reveal their true meaning. When Cameron considered the audience, it was as a means to help exhibitors to improve their communication. Audience studies could be used to verify a correct understanding of the museum's message: if audiences were not able to reproduce the museum's message, then the museum would have to work harder to make the audience 'get it'.

Similar to Cameron's theory, the linear 'hypodermic needle' theory soon became popular in museums. The theory helped support a view of museum audiences as passive receivers, though more radically, it suggested that the sender (the museum) had the power to 'inject' ideas into the consciousness of receivers (the audiences) (Morley 1980).

Roger Miles criticized the hypodermic needle model in the context of exhibition production. He highlighted the problem with the narrow focus on the sender, which led to a disregard of audience feedback or of the need for preliminary research on audiences (Miles 1986). Miles wanted to bring the audience back into the communication model, and thus proposed the inclusion of extensive research for the different stages of the production process, such as market research, trial of exhibitions and summative evaluation after openings, and also noted the importance of developing accompanying literature and educational activities parallel to the exhibition. But in reality, Miles' inclusion of the audience was similar to Cameron's idea of using audiences to test whether the museum was doing a good job in transmitting the true meaning of its collections. Nevertheless, Miles also developed a typology of display techniques that contemplated the possibility of interactive dynamic exhibits requiring some sort of dialogue (Miles 1982). This means that he saw museumgoers as more than just passive receivers.

In the 1980s, within a movement known as The New Museology, scholars began to address some of the assumptions of the above communication models. Hugues de Varine, one of the New Museology advocates, declared that the 'visitor is not a docile consumer . . . but a creator who can and should participate in the building of the future – the museum's research' (Varines 1985). However, The New Museology's ethos would also be contested:

> In the political sense, the potential mission of museums according to The New Museology is enlarged, even glorified, to include the fostering of social justice. But at the same time, the potential social role of museums seems diminished by the negative tone of New Museology rhetoric. Attempts to define new missions seem riddled by doubts about the possibility of knowing in any meaningful sense, or of communicating effectively, or of presenting a message that is untainted by class or personal interests. (Stam 1993: 275)

In spite of these and other critiques, in the 1990s many theoreticians and practitioners followed up on The New Museology's calls for an overhaul of museum communication and outreach practices. Hooper-Greenhill (1991) proposed a 'holistic' approach, a model that expanded the earlier focus on exhibitions to a more far-reaching view in which museums were seen as part of their social environment. She argued that building, location, political and economic contexts were relevant to how people reacted to museum exhibitions (Hooper-Greenhill 1995). In her view, more attention had to be paid to the reasons why audiences came to museums, and to their backgrounds. She criticized Miles' idea that better museum communication models would emerge from information technology, behaviourist psychology and American mass media communication theory, because for her, museum audiences were not as naïve or prone to influence as these approaches implied. Her model reflects the slow realization that visitors had in fact autonomy.

This realization of the existence of 'visitor opinions' led to proposals about how to become more persuasive and appealing (given the acceptance of the futility of pursuing the 'injection of ideas'). Hooper-Greenhill, for example, talked about polysemy, the plurality of meanings, and described this as the ability to provide a set of well-planned meanings that could appeal to different audiences with differing interests. The basic idea was to plan exhibitions that, given a range of coexisting meanings, could attract the attention of a wider audience who would choose which meaning to engage in. Hooper-Greenhill pointed out the need to change from a linear model to 'a transactional model where messages are formulated, exchanged and interpreted in a continuous process' (Hooper-Greenhill 1995).

This was, however, still a model where the centre was the museum and its message. Thanks in part to The New Museology, visitors had been added as more active pieces of the model, but their activity was constrained to choosing from what the museum had to offer. Yet New Museologists had worked for far more than creating a broader market of museum generated interpretations: they had worked to bring into museums issues of inclusivity, participation and trust.

Many of these models were influenced by what was taking place at the time in mass media. Mass media are technically defined as broadcasting technologies and mechanical reproduction conceived as being limited to a 'one sender–many receivers' model of communication. Going back to basic media theory, mass media has also been extensively discussed as a technology that is used to transmit a uniform and standardized output directed towards passive and homogeneous consumers of cultural products, and in this way has also been used to link technology to political structure (Terranova 2008). One example of this is Nazism's massive deployment of propaganda through tightly controlled radio systems and film to build the idea of the true German national community.

According to Dennis McQuail, the study of mass media during the early twentieth century gave primacy to the technological features of the media, and the view that these technologies sustained and created the supposed masses (McQuail 2007). Later on these views changed, and the focus of study became what could be made more effective in the transmission of the message. It was assumed that the message or content was always the same, and that it was the mode of transmission that needed to be improved. Thinkers such as Harold Innis argued that technologies do not so much determine as bias human practices. The debate has for some time been settled in favour of a predominance of human agency and a disregard of anything that can point to 'technological determinism' or the thought that technology develops in an internal process and then causes changes in society (the view that Marshall McLuhan is accused of). Celia Lury points out that this debate is also concerned in part with highlighting concepts such as responsibility and accountability, or, in opposition, thinking of media as not only reproducing us but also transforming us (Lury 2008).

In museums, a departure from the 'mass media view' came in the late 1990s, when practitioners started to reflect upon some underlying assumptions that supported the museum-centrism of communication models. In the UK, talking about issues of representation in museums, Henrietta Lidchi pointed out that

> museums do not simply issue objective descriptions or form logical assemblages; they generate representations and attribute value and meaning in line with certain perspectives or classificatory schemas which are historically specific. They do not so much reflect the world through objects as use them to mobilize representations of the world past and present. (Lidchi 1997)

It began to be clear that museums were offering expert interpretations, not absolute truths. This meant a slow opening of the door for outside stakeholders (both expert and lay visitors) to participate in discovering the meaning of collections. Jack Lohman (2006: 12), Director of the Museum of London, pointed out that 'dialogue and spaces to speak are particularly important in countries that have repressed the stories of others', and museums were appropriate institutions to create such spaces. In the US, museum consultant Kathleen McLean argued that 'an exhibition designed to encourage face-to-face interaction and dialogue among visitors' was 'one of the most vital contributions museums can make to the social dynamics of our times' (McLean 1999). In Australia, Margo Neale (at the time a fellow at the Centre for Cross-Cultural Research at the Australian National University) asserted that museums should become 'sites of negotiation. . . (p)laces where multiple histories are told by diverse voices. . . where contradictions are allowed to exist, hard questions are posed without qualification, answers are debated and conclusions are forever rubbery. . . "encounters" and "people" will hopefully remain the keystone of all future museums' (Neale 2001).

Other researchers focused on inclusion and diversity in the context of disability, migration, indigenous, race and gender issues. Such is the case with Richard Sandell's (2002) edited volume *Museums, Society, Inequality*. This volume provided an account of museums and their social responsibility in addressing inequality for a wider range of minorities, including the disabled, sexual minorities, children, indigenous people and migrants, as well as themes that might be censored, such as traumatic events and political conflicts. Sandell (2002: 8) was cautious in stating that 'it is problematic to establish a direct, causal relationship between museum practices and contemporary manifestations of social inequality or their amelioration', yet 'museums . . . cannot be conceived as discretely cultural, or asocial – they are undeniably implicated in the dynamics of (in)equality and the power relations between different groups through their role in constructing and disseminating dominant social narratives'. He pointed out that the main argument was not that museums alone must tackle disadvantage and discrimination, nor that they should become tools for social engineering, but that these institutions must be aware of their social responsibility and be committed to social equality (Sandell 2002: 21).

Also in the 1990s, Ivan Karp and co-editors published a series of books whose approach grew out of the debates previously raised by 'The New Museology' (McCarthy 2007: 182). The first book of the series, *Exhibiting Cultures* (1991), was the product of a conference entitled *The Poetics and Politics of Representation* organized at the Smithsonian Institution in 1988, which focused on cultural diversity in museums (Karp and Lavine 1991: ix). Karp presented the initial argument that '[w]hen cultural others are implicated, exhibitions tell us who we are and, perhaps most significant, who we are not. Exhibitions are privileged arenas for presenting images of self and "other"' (Karp and Lavine 1991: 15). Other authors in the volume analysed the challenges of incorporating alternative perspectives in and about museums. These included the problems of translation when presenting another culture's aesthetic standards, the way in which cross-cultural exhibitions could prompt the questioning and reorganization of knowledge, and the differences between experiencing an object in a museum setting and in its original setting (Karp and Lavine 1991: 16–24). All of these issues pointed to relations of power and control initially over objects but ultimately over articulations of identity, which in this volume were especially related to 'the other' and, to an extent, to postcolonial critiques of Western museums.

The second book in the *Exhibiting Cultures* series, *Museums and Communities* (1992), focused on 'the politics of public culture' (McCarthy 2007: 182). In it, Karp asserted that 'art, history and ethnography displays, even natural history exhibitions, are all involved in defining the identities of communities – or in denying them identity' (quoted in Sandell 2002: 12).

A Tipping Point: 2000 to 2010

These ideas resonated around the globe, both within and beyond museums. In Australia, Andrea Witcomb, a museum studies academic then working at Curtin University, called for museums to become 'contact zones', spaces focused on dialogue and exchange for diverse stakeholders (Witcomb 2003a). Helen Light, then director of the Jewish Museum of Australia, contrasted previous ideas of museums as 'the keepers of things' and society's 'providers of links with the past', with contemporary conceptions in which museums were now 'negotiating experience about culture' and becoming 'places where knowledge can be contested' (Light 2005). In Norway, Katherine Goodnow, also a museum studies scholar, argued that the changing nature of dialogue in museums affected the non-experts to the extent that they needed to move toward a '"full" or "legitimate" participation', and affected experts in that they were now required to 'yield various aspects of responsibility to those initially classed as less expert' (Goodnow 2006). This was the beginning of a critique of the museum's authority over 'the true message' of collections.

The third book by Karp et al., *Museum Frictions* (2006), was also published during this period. This volume addressed museums in a global context, looking at 'museological processes that can be multi-sited and ramify far beyond museum settings' (Karp et al. 2006: 2). In this volume, Fred Myers (2006: 506) advocated a focus on the political economy and the social relationships of producing culture, rather on the analysis of exhibitions, as this would highlight 'the complex intersections and reorganizations of interest that are inevitably involved in any production of culture'.

Amidst all these changes, the dot-com bubble exploded in 2000 and left a large number of websites out of business (including museum websites and some of the early social media sites). Around the same time, in 2001, Wikipedia was launched. Wikipedia used wikis – a content management environment that permitted the transparent tracking of changes made to a document – to create a massive, collaboratively built online encyclopaedia. The project became one of the most debated experiments in the democratization of culture. In contrast to well-established encyclopaedias such as Britannica and Encarta, Wikipedia offered free access for users and content producers. It also did not seek 'expert-only' content and expert peer-review, but rather relied upon crowdsourcing and good will as its quality assurance mechanisms. Although not regarded as viable at first, Wikipedia would in time become a major competitor – and perhaps also an example to follow – for more established sources, including museums.

Parallel to this, a service called Friendster rekindled SixDegree's idea of using social data as core service, and began to enable the listing of 'friendships'. Quickly following suit, MySpace launched in 2003, followed by Facebook in 2004. Tim O'Reilly synthesized the business principles of these companies through the term 'Web 2.0'. Used interchangeably with 'social media', the term 'Web 2.0' was coined at the 2004 'Web 2.0 Conference' organized by O'Reilly Media. Tim O'Reilly described Web 2.0 as 'an implicit "architecture of participation", a built-in ethic of cooperation, in which the service acts primarily as an intelligent broker, connecting the edges to each other and harnessing the power of the users themselves' (O'Reilly 2005).

For Munster and Murphie (2009), O'Reilly's vision was limited in that it did not foreshadow how the Web 2.0 could also be seen as an activity somewhere between a) doing, as in 'apping, blogging, mapping, mashing, geocaching, tagging, searching, shopping, sharing, socialising and wikking', b) being, as in 'Gov 2.0, Identity 2.0, XHTML™ 2.0', and c) qualifying, as in 'dynamic, participatory, engaged, interoperable, user-centred, open, collectively intelligent'. They went further to state that

> In light of the strange space and odd temporal dimension it inhabits, it seems appropriate to call web 2.0 an 'event'. Something has certainly happened to the web as we knew it circa 2001 and that something is both a new technical infrastructure

> for online ICTs – what is now referred to as 'an architecture of participation' (O'Reilly, 2004) – and a change in attitude, a change in the ways we think about doing, communicating and inhabiting networks. The web 2.0 event moves the technical infrastructure of networks even closer to the transitive, to the nature of event itself. (Munster and Murphie 2009)

By 2005, throughout the period when Web 2.0 was emerging and gaining strength, most museums in the UK had websites, and were also entering into partnerships to establish external online projects to expand the network of museum related sites (Rellie 2006). Yet adopting social media was still seen as 'going too far'. Talking at the 2006 Museums and the Web Conference, Rellie (2006) discussed phenomena such as Wikipedia, and wondered whether museums were reluctant to adopt formats such as wikis and social tagging because they would imply 'that the public might be capable of contributing, in an interesting and meaningful way, to collection related content'. She was hopeful, however, that in the future museums would see social media as a tool to fill gaps in their information and to enhance participation (Rellie 2006).

Outside the realm of museums, theorists and commentators were convinced that social media represented a prime opportunity to build a utopian society where selfless volunteerism and radical trust would prevail. For them, social media heralded a new era of expanded participation and democracy (Benkler 2006; Bruns 2008).

It is important here to remember that the shift from mass media to new media as a journey towards increased democracy is a predominant interpretation of the technological changes that the web has brought about. According to Martin Lister and his colleagues, the concept of new media has been said to call upon the modernist belief in social progress as delivered by technology (Lister et al. 2003). It points to the apparent break with the mass media system. This apparent break, in turn, has become synonymous with a break with a restrictive technological order, a move from passive audiences to active (or rather inter-active) publics, and as Manuel Castells points out, the inclusion of a multiplicity of messages and sources (Castells 1996). Lister et al., however, note how these technologies may not represent a break but can be seen rather as a continuation of a principle already in place, that of transforming a physical artefact to a signal, but that the scale and nature of their extension make us experience them as a break (Lister et al. 2003).

For Lister et al., new media invokes new textual experiences (computer games, hypertext, special effects cinema), new ways of representing the world (immersive virtual environments, screen-based interactive multimedia), new relationships between subjects and media technologies (users as producers), new experiences of the relationship between embodiment, identity and community (changes in how we experience ourselves and the world), new conceptions of the relationship between biological body and technological media (prostheses, virtuality), and new patterns of organization and production (Lister et al. 2003). For Terranova, the concept of new media also opens up the discussion to the ideological aspects of the uses of technology in relation to issues such as historicity and temporality, specifically by drawing attention to the question of what is new (Terranova 2008).

A different narrative of the impact of new technologies is found in the concept of cyberculture. This is a concept that calls for a study of technology that takes into account its relationship to nature. Terranova has written that cyberculture 'can be used to refer to the larger cultural experience of being immersed in a world that is increasingly saturated by cybernetic technologies . . . by technologies that operate through a very intimate and tactile interface with the human body', and also that cyberculture points to the problems of dividing user and tool, nature and culture, and biology and technology (Terranova 2008: 589). A main preoccupation in studies of cyberculture is whether we can still maintain that technology and nature are separate or even opposites, since our bodies, our food, and our environment make it increasingly difficult to distinguish between the two.

Lister et al. argue that studies of cyberculture attempt to address a blind spot in media studies, which is the materiality of technology, and the way in which it produces highly tangible changes in our everyday life (Lister et al. 2003). They also attempt to highlight the need to understand the internal qualities of the technology itself. With cyberculture, we come back to the fact that it is not only the relationship to culture that matters: the internal characteristics of the technology have also to be taken seriously into account.

In this debate about visions of cultural or technological determinism, Lister et al. also emphasize the importance of the notion of the technological imaginary. The technological imaginary refers to the way in which dissatisfactions with social reality are projected onto technology as capable of alleviating them or producing the desired change. This imaginary, this set of desires, influences the development of a given technology. This imaginary also has a cycle, in which the technology is first seen as conductive to progress and is later criticized and disfavoured in light of the promises held by newer technologies.

For example, Benkler (2006) claimed the demise of the market as the main driving force of the evolution of the web, saying that 'the network information economy [is characterized] by decentralized individual action. . . Action carried out through nonmarket mechanisms that does not depend on proprietary strategies plays a much greater role'. For Benkler, there was an emerging networked information economy 'centred on information and cultural production, and the manipulation of symbols' which was inclusive of 'a communications environment interconnected in a pervasive network. . . the phenomenon we associate with the Internet'. In essence, Benkler argued that the social web was giving everyone the opportunity to be more sophisticated and engaged makers of culture (Benkler 2006). The heightened opportunities for individual action were at the core of these changes: 'The core technologically contingent fact that enables social relations to become a salient modality of production in the networked information economy is that all the inputs necessary to effective productive activity are under the control of individual users' (Benkler 2006).

Benkler suggested that the consequence would be the rise of a new folk culture, a 'commons' or set of shared resources that had more and more active participants who were more self-reflective and critical 'readers' of their own culture and who were freer to participate in 'tugging and pulling at the cultural creations of others' (Benkler 2006). Yet Benkler also worried about how this new environment of increased freedom would be regulated. His two main concerns lay with the competing forces that fought to make of the web either (a) a commons accessible and available to all, or (b) a market of primarily proprietary resources (Benkler 2006).

For Bruns (2008), the large-scale ad hoc communities emerging on the Internet signalled the demise of traditional modes of production, and the demise of barriers to participation based on geography, language, or even class. He also predicted the rise of collective intelligence phenomena and collaborative behaviours that would help to surpass limitations imposed by the mass media system on individuals wishing to produce and distribute culture on a larger scale. Bruns (2008) claimed that all the changes brought about by the social web meant that people's community building capacity was now expanded: 'users can now communicate with each other at a global scale, bypassing the traditional producers and distributors of information' and the network 'poses a significant challenge to traditional hierarchies'.

Hinton and Hjorth (2013) also note how the narrative of empowerment associated with social media has its roots in the techno-utopian movements of the 1960s in the US, where ideas such as 'virtual frontier' were used to denote new open spaces free of restrictive controls. They highlight how this influence from the US shaped notions of what the web would become, with early authors such as John Perry Barlow (A Cyberspace Independence Declaration, 1996) and Douglas Rushkoff (Cyberia 1994), who proposed a web beyond industrial and government control. Yet Hinton and Hjorth (2013) also remind us of how social media can be seen as increasing the control afforded by information technologies, where business colonizes the narratives of personal identity, since a person's entire online activity can be recorded in the browser, and thus stored, sorted and analysed (unless the person intentionally turns on private browsing and prevents this logging of activity). The result is a commodification of online personal identity, and of the search engine user as the real product to be sold to markets. As seen in their argument about this commodification, Hinton and Hjorth (2013) describe Google's advertising model as follows: upon typing a search term, Google will try to profile keyword combinations that have been purchased by advertisers, so the user will get both commercial pre-purchased results, and results coming from Google's index of the web. In this scenario, the ability to maintain a separation between commercial and non-commercial results is vital to Google, since overcommercialization could result in the perception of a less effective service. Also, the constant analysis of search terms against any information available about the person who performed the search allows the creation of increasingly accurate mappings of what makes an online service or product popular to large audiences. Services such as Google Trends and Google Analytics are examples of such data collation: Google Trends provides snapshots of keyword popularity, and may thus help to shape the text used to offer a service to a particular audience; Google Analytics gives access to location data and to any data that can be mined about the gender, age and product preferences of the person accessing a particular site. Thus, while the explicit assumption is that what Google offers are search results, the fact is that with Web 2.0, Google's real products have become user profiles. Following these arguments, one may conclude that Web 2.0 is a pivotal event in the saga of the conquest of private space by market forces.

Challenges and Hope: 2010 Onwards

As Drotner and Schrøder (2013) point out, social media have crossed all gender, political, economic and age borders and become a pervasive means of communication around the world. They are either viewed as an expression of the rise of individuals and the demise of corporate power, or as yet another way to dilute and trivialize knowledge online (Drotner and Schrøder 2013). Throughout these changes, museums have tried to engage more actively with these new online tools. In 2009, Mosoddik explained the boost that social media represented at that time for the MOL:

> It became obvious from my research that the Museum of London (MOL) was not losing visitors by having content sitting on other sites but was in fact, gaining more visits to MOL websites as a by product of its existence on Facebook and the existence of MOL's blog (MyMoL). In addition, as a result of its presence on Facebook, Facebook members were making some actual visits to the Museums that they previously may not have made. (Mosoddik 2009a)

Yet social media have had an unforeseen consequence: they have fuelled debate about the place of museums as gatekeepers of heritage. Seb Chan, former head of web services at the Powerhouse Museum in Sydney, puts it this way:

> Once a visitor carries a fully searchable encyclopaedia in their pocket (not to mention access to all our collection including the objects not on display), the whole idea of a 'museum' and how it could and should be designed changes. . . In my view these are long-term tectonic shifts and the libraries sector has had a 20+ year start on that journey in the move from 'collections to services'. Museums can learn from that in some ways but not in others. . . Like any future gazing, these shifts are not ones that come with clearly visible outcomes or even a sense of predictability. There is a wide gap between the techno-utopianism that underpins the Californian tech start-up culture and political pragmatism – not to mention public acceptance. (Chan 2011)

As Chan suggests, for museums that view themselves as bearers of encyclopaedic knowledge represented by their collections, the challenge posed by social media can seem enormous. They need to transcend the narrow focus on researching the best knowledge available about a given artefact to also include a concern with their relationship with the public. And the need for this may come from wider political, economic and social changes. Chan further comments:

> I think is important that we don't just see tech as impacting on museums and culture. Political climate, economic climate, work/life balance, recreation time, community ideas about 'good education', media and entertainment – all these and more have at least as much effect on the future of museums as technology. (Chan 2011)

Cathy Ross, curator of the twenty-first-century galleries at the Museum of London (MOL), suggests that this frees the museum to take on more abstract topics:

> I also think that actually in this day and age of the Internet, museums don't have to do the basic things because people can go into Wikipedia and they can get every single thing about transport etc. So to do something a bit more abstract about the feel and character of London is good – and I hope it comes out as big chaotic city

> a lot going on with rich and poor and people coming in and out and I am happier with that than people knowing the story of transport in London. More information they can get elsewhere. (Ross 2009)

The hope is that social media will help visitors engage with collections in more meaningful ways than as mere spectators, help museum staff access a new pool of knowledge from the public, and foster networks that result in broader local and global stewardship for heritage. This relates to ideas about the social responsibility of museums, as David Fleming, the Director of National Museums Liverpool, discusses: 'museums are increasingly involved in contemporary social issues. They are changing from institutions that were preoccupied with the past, and obsessed with collections, into institutions where the public can find opinions about the present day, and where human stories predominate' (Fleming 2011).

Meaningful Engagement

The 2011 Museum Edition of the Horizon Report (a study of technology absorption and trends in museums around the world) dealt with some of the above hopes and concerns. The report described the task of understanding digital technology management as a critical one for museums (Johnson et al. 2011). In views that echoed those of Benkler and Bruns, the report stated that:

> There is a growing chorus of voices advocating a more active role for visitors in shaping what museums do. As people become accustomed to tools that allow them to do things that previously required a great deal of expertise (i.e., video editing, or publishing to the web), they begin to appreciate the creative skills involved in actually producing science or art or the like. 'Makers' are an emerging category of museum visitors, especially for science museums, who want to not only appreciate what they see in technical, historical or other contexts, but to also understand how it was created. 'Maker' experiences, which engage visitors of all ages in individual and collective experiences of tinkering, making, and discovery are a growing trend, and there is a role for all categories of museums in supporting and encouraging such experiences. (Johnson et al. 2011)

However, and as we shall see in the following chapters, exactly how the museum will scaffold this 'maker' role is the subject of much debate, research and experimentation. For example, although mostly optimistic, commentators in the report highlight the uncertainty of how the effect or usefulness of social media can be assessed (Johnson et al. 2011).

Yet many practitioners are convinced of the benefits for museums in making the leap to social media. Ragni Zlotos, web manager from the Hordaland Municipality in Norway, comments:

> Publishing and communication activities like these can help make a rich and prolonged learning experience. Libraries, archives and museums would not work without people making them available and putting the materials into context, and social media are a better-connected way to do that. It is not only a question of good marketing, although it is good marketing nowadays to open up content in social media. It is also a question of participation possibilities for people with disabilities, or simply little time, to still find an entrance to a world of knowledge in context. (Zlotos 2010)

Better Curatorial Practices

Kelly (2009) has addressed how the analysis of audiences can help to explain how these new technologies may enhance architectures of participation in museums. In a study conducted at the Australian Museum, Kelly used social media to assess how audiences would approach a controversial topic (in this case, 'evil'). The resulting data informed exhibition design (Kelly 2009). Through Facebook and a blog, Kelly and her colleagues were able to compare a previous focus group study to what they encountered in social media, and found similarities in the types of responses from the public. This then helped to shape exhibition content. In addition, the museum used social media that allowed contributions from the public, such as photographs and annotations of museum material, thereby creating an enriched digital layer for the exhibition (Kelly 2009). From this experience, Kelly concluded that the use of social media was an effective, low cost tool to enable a dialogue between the museum and its community. What was missing, however, was a discussion of how more diverse interaction between staff and visitors could also add complexity to managing the institution's 'voice' in these media.

When museums enter into such an expanded dialogue with the public, the conundrums are well known: should they allow the individual staff member to have a voice in the social media service, or should they use an institutional voice? And how much should the museum try to moderate not only the voices of their staff, but also the voices of visitors? As Richardson (2009) points out:

> Each website has a different set of unwritten rules and spending time looking and listening helps you get your head around them, and starts to change the way you think. You start to realise that now any and everybody gets to create content, distribute content and control his or her own user experiences and to start to consider

how a museum can fit in to this. . . For me the organisations that have succeeded most across a diverse range of social media platforms are the ones who have taken time to understand how things work. . . It is a difficult line for a museum to walk – you want to be active in social media spaces and to do that you must reconcile the human-to-human informal conversational style of these networks with the fact that you are large institutions who can't just let everyone say what they want. (Richardson 2009)

Broader Networks of Support

Social media require new technical skills among staff, and make additional demands on the institution's budget and time. Zlotos refers to this issue, and to a certain lack of support at management and government levels for social media activities in archives, museums and libraries in Norway: 'Museum boards and politicians should acknowledge that it is important to think about participation in society's discourse in social media. So, museum employees should be enabled to learn and use this (social media) without it hurting the time budget of traditional museum work' (Zlotos 2010).

The question of which members of staff get to participate in the institution's social media spaces has management implications. Michael Hughill, from the Australian Museum, talks about the measures the museum took in 2011 to address this:

You might say, broadly speaking, that there are two approaches to social media: 'open' and 'closed'. . . With an open approach, all (or many) employees in an organisation are given access to Facebook and Twitter and encouraged to post whenever they want. With a closed approach, an organisation has a dedicated social media employee who generates all posts and tweets. . . Our new action plan involves a small, co-ordinated *team* of employees from across the Museum that take turns monitoring and posting on our main social media accounts (Facebook and Twitter). It's not completely open, but it's not closed either (we have a social media group on our intranet where all staff can share ideas and in fact, we make a point of following other museum accounts, sharing and retweeting content). (Hughill 2011)

Hughill points out that while staff may be experts in their field, they are not necessarily experts in social media. This creates a new subdivision amongst museum employees based on their technological skills. The reference to a small team from across the museum points to individuals assuming a new role on top of their traditional one, for example, curators becoming 'blogging curators'. The small team also takes on the role of moderator of social media within the organization, although it is assumed that the whole organization can at any point be involved with the museum's social media. Defining a small team of museum employees as the core of social media in this museum makes the system more sustainable and easier to manage. However, this can become a problem if social media management is too dependent on specific individuals. The solution at the Australian Museum is to maintain channels of consultation with all museum staff, thus ensuring that a pool of potential collaborators is available.

As these foregoing issues show, social media present a challenge for many museums. However, a number of institutions have successfully managed the change and are actively trying to find ways to benefit the community through it, as we shall see in case studies discussed in this volume.

An even broader range of stakeholders have made their voices heard about the future of online (and offline) museum communication. In the US, Nina Simon, then museum consultant and creator of Museum 2.0 (a blog focusing on participation in museums and the role of new technologies), proposed conceptualizing participation and communication in museums as a series of progressively better 'levels' that an institution could aspire to. Simon (2007) defined five different 'levels' that museums could reach. Employing the more vernacular style characteristic of social media, she named her levels as follows: 1) 'Museum to me', where visitors are passive receivers of content (reminiscent of Shannon and Weaver); 2) 'Museum with Me', where users have some degree of interaction with the content but no significant input; 3) 'Me & Me & Me & Museum', where individual interpretation and interaction with the museum are the focus (similar to polysemy, but with the user able to see how others have interacted); 4) 'Me to We with Museum', where data from individual interactions is gathered in a system that provides a sort of 'collective intelligence' to enhance the museum as a social place; and 5) 'We in Museum', where the scope of conversations generated by the museum experience goes beyond the subject of the exhibition, making the museum into a forum for larger social issues (Simon 2007).

The following table summarizes the above chronology. I have also added a column where I state what is the focus of each communication model.

In this chronology, what becomes evident is the continuity in efforts to expand and enhance the mission of the museum through the incorporation of new technologies. Commenting on the coining of the term Web 2.0, Timpson (2010) notes that 'rather than a fundamental change or version (of the web) in 2004, there has been incremental and progressive evolution of technology and methodology over time that has facilitated

Table 1.1. A chronology of communication theories used in museums

	Model	Focus
1960s–1970s		
Shannon and Weaver	Sender-message-receiver In museums, adapted as museum-objects-visitor	Institution
McLuhan	Interactive visits and co-creation	User
Cameron	Subject-verbs-nouns: Museum-relations between-objects	Collection
1980s		
Morley	The hypodermic needle: museums injecting ideas into visitors	Institution
Miles	Audience research	User
New Museology	Inclusivity, dialogue, participation	User
1990s		
Hooper-Greenhill	Holistic approach: socio-economic contexts, history, architecture, location, discourses	Institution
2000s		
Practitioners and researchers from around the globe	The social mission of museums, dialogue, negotiation, power struggles	User
Simon	User-centric architectures of participation (social media)	

what people were already doing' (2010: 299). Indeed, the overview above shows that many of the concerns that are emerging in discussions about museum social media predate the emergence of the technology by several decades. It is likely that the same issues and challenges will continue to inform future uses of technology by museums.

The various models presented in the preceding overview are useful for an understanding of the thinking behind some of the choices we see in museums online. The above table shows that three foci of communication can be distinguished: the institution, the collection and the user. Below is a summary of how these foci relate to various types of websites.

Institution-oriented Websites

Institution-oriented websites mirror the one-way sender-receiver model of communication in that they often lack any means of engaging in a dialogue with the museum.

Institution-oriented websites are brochure-like websites (or sections of a website) where the goal is to communicate to the public general information about the museum (opening hours, mission and vision, contact details or static maps). General presentation pages are the usual starting points for these websites. Typical institution-oriented sections of websites are 'history of the museum', 'mission statement' or the 'about' section with information about curatorial and administrative departments, details about the building, etc.

The characteristic of institution-oriented websites and social media is that collections and visitors will be placed in function of the institution. Control over the channels of communication with the public will remain in the hands of the museum. The museum's presence will be more predominant than the presence of any particular artefact it holds.

Collection-oriented Websites

Efforts behind the creation of collection-oriented websites often have as a goal to improve the semantic navigation of the web. These websites remind us of Cameron's linguistic model where the principal role of the museum is to create meaningful relations between objects.

Collection-oriented websites feature artefacts prominently in their start pages, and the museum works mainly as a transparent cabinet. 'Highlights' or pieces of the month are the main focus of the website's landing page. Throughout the website, multiple pages and sections describes objects in more detail. Many of these websites act as specialized search engines geared to guide users through the collection. Collection-oriented websites also often act as 'journeys' that take visitors through the collections in a well-defined path.

Some collection-oriented websites attempt to establish a relationship between visitors and objects, while others just focus on presenting accurate factual information.

User-oriented Websites

User-oriented websites and social media aim at highlighting the interconnections between people. Artefacts express these interconnections, and the museum works as a forum where a diverse array of stakeholders meets. These websites centre on issues of dialogue and participation that have gained traction in museums in the last few decades.

Although provisions for user participation may be a feature of both institution and collection-oriented websites, it is more likely that user-oriented websites will be based on social media technologies. In these websites, the presentation of the museum's public image and even of the collection will be open to input from the public.

These websites incorporate user-generated content, and will also attempt to personalize their sections (for example, sections for kids, adults, families and seniors, or going further, with sections generated from harvesting individual visitor's declared interests).

One example is 'I Like Museums', a website which was the product of a collaboration between museums in the North East of England, developed as a campaign to change public perceptions of museums and galleries in the region (see Richardson 2008). In a blog post by Sumo lead designer Jim Richardson (Sumo is the design company in charge of developing media for the 'I like. . . museums' campaign), Sheryl McGregor, Communications Manager at Tyne & Wear Museums, stated that 'the most important part of the campaign for us was to actually get people engaged with "I like Museums" and we wanted them to tell us what it was they actually did like about museums' (see Richardson 2008).

Another case, though much less adventurous and mainly in the form of provision, is the MOMA's Online Communities section. The museum has integrated into its pages a feed of photographs taken by visitors and uploaded via Flickr (a photo sharing site).

In Conclusion

As we have seen throughout this chapter, there has been a paradigm shift in museums' views of the World Wide Web, from a storage space to a place for encounter. For museums, this shift has opened a Pandora's box of opportunities and challenges, where the key issue is the redefinition of their relationship to their communities.

As the digital and physical realms continue to merge, there is an increased need for museums to speak the language of technology and to add their voices to the collaborative project of building a better digital environment. Many changes have been positive: a more diverse range of people can engage with the museum's treasures; former physical barriers are overcome, allowing heritage to be more easily shared; and communities have more access to the officials who care for their heritage. As we have seen, however, these changes have also brought about many challenges for museums. Furthermore, in this process of renewal, it is still uncertain whether social media will benefit museums in their mission of supporting open and democratic societies, or whether it will render them (and other institutions) obsolete.

Using a communication perspective, critiques have been made of the various positions and methods adopted by museums in the process of communicating knowledge about their collections. Starting with New Museology and continuing with discussions about social media, museums have moved to a focus on users. Recently, Drotner and Schrøder (2013) have discussed how social media have altered the communication models available for museums, with a shift from the 'transmission model', which is primarily concerned with what the museum itself wants to communicate, to the 'user perspective', where the focus is on what visitors may want to discover. This shift implies a change from unilateral to interactive communication (Drotner and Schrøder 2013). According to these authors, social media push the museum to ask itself why it wants to communicate in the first place. As highlighted by these authors, and as discussed throughout this chapter, all these changes provide an opportunity to reconsider even more deeply the goals and mission of the museum.

As we will see in the coming chapters, there are still many cases in which the institution or the collections will be given priority in online communication. This is not necessarily undesirable and may help the museum to fulfil the multiple aspects of its mission. One aspect, however, seems to be missing in this transition from focusing on the institution to focusing on the user. The emphasis on users, or rather, the apparent frenzy to use social media to attract ever-larger numbers of users (sometimes because government or financial pressures may push museums to do so), can make museums lose sight of a key issue: the sustainability of their online ecosystems. As will be discussed in the following chapter, the opportunities for audience growth and broader participation that social media and the shift to users enables need to be part of a framework that considers the longer term impact of these activities for museums as institutions at the service of this and future generations, for their collections, and for users themselves.

Chapter 2

Digital Heritage and Sustainability

The digital culture sustainability framework presented in this chapter[1] serves to highlight areas of importance in considerations of the long-term viability of museum social media. The areas of analysis in this framework discussed below are 'stakeholders', 'contexts' and 'digital practices'. Analysing these areas should help build a holistic picture of sustainability issues related to the preservation, dissemination and study of digital culture by museums and other heritage institutions. Analysing stakeholders allows us to ask 'who is included', and thus helps us identify public engagement challenges related to the management of the digital culture resource. Asking about contexts helps one to understand governmental, economic or other pressures upon the museum, in terms of how these will affect viability; for example, assumptions about the desirability of eternal growth and pressures to 'attract audiences' may not correspond to or aid in fulfilling the mission of museums. Finally, a look at digital practices sheds further light on preconceptions about the management of culture that may clash with, complement or build upon the demands of the digital domain. This questioning of the technology used by museums is a necessary step towards developing systems that are more resilient, flexible and adaptable, and that offer pathways into the future.

Even in the fast paced environment of current technological changes, museums cannot lose sight of the very important role they play in keeping digital culture available for present and future generations. An understanding of what lies at the centre of interest (whether it is the museum, the collection or the visitor, or a combination of these) and an awareness of issues of digital culture sustainability are both essential ingredients of an analysis of ways forward. Focusing on digital culture sustainability as the goal of the analysis leads to more pinpointed questions about authority and ownership. It helps to problematize underlying assumptions that more participation is always better, and to highlight concerns about diversity and the negotiations of rules between museums, their communities and technology stakeholders concerning the shared responsibility for museum social media spaces.

To understand current shifts, a number of analyses of museum digital media use audience studies approaches (Kelly 2009; Russo et al. 2006a); other analyses explore changes in discourses about the purpose of online museums (Marstine 2011); and practice-oriented approaches describe how digital media-based participation can aid community building in museums (Simon 2010). Yet analytical approaches which tackle questions of sustainability are still lacking, even though the growth of digital media as the prime material of contemporary culture should bring sustainability concerns to the fore.

The Digital Heritage Sustainability (DHS) Framework is a step in this direction. It approaches analysis of the benefits and drawbacks of the use of digital media in museums from the point of view of their sustainable management, as well as from the point of view of digital heritage in sustainable development.

This chapter is structured as follows: the first section presents definitions and a theoretical background of digital heritage sustainability, as well as tracing a short history of the growth of concerns with sustainability in digital heritage; the second section presents the DHS Framework.

Digital Heritage and Sustainability

A first step in understanding the sustainability challenges presented by digital heritage is to define 'digital heritage'. UNESCO defines digital heritage as:

> Resources of human knowledge or expression . . . are increasingly created digitally, or converted into digital form from existing analogue resources. Where resources are 'born-digital', there is no other format but the digital original. Digital materials include texts, databases, still and moving images, audio, graphics, software, and web pages, among a wide and growing range of formats. They are frequently ephemeral, and require purposeful production, maintenance and management to be retained. Many of these resources have lasting value and significance, and therefore constitute a heritage that should be protected and preserved for current and future generations. This heritage may exist in any language, in any part of the world, and in any area of human knowledge or expression. (Webb 2003)

However, several issues arise with this definition. While digital heritage can be defined by provenance (as UNESCO does when including analogue to digital conversion or 'born-digital' as potential origins), the fact is that digital heritage can be stored in digital and analogue formats (3D printing is a good example). The blend of digital and analogue (the 'internet of things') makes this distinction increasingly irrelevant. Another problem with the definition provided by UNESCO is that while it acknowledges the fact that the material can be produced anywhere in the world, it omits to state that 'any part of the world' has to have the digital technology available.

I offer an alternative definition of digital heritage:

> Digital heritage is material primarily stored and retrieved in binary format. It may be the product of an analogue to digital conversion or it may be 'born-digital' (originate and remain exclusively within the digital domain), and it can include both analogue and digital components. The key difference between digital heritage and other forms of heritage lies in its binary format, which demands distinctive approaches to the conservation of its significance and value.

The definition above, however, leaves out a number of important concerns better covered in previous volumes about digital heritage. A few edited collections have engaged with the more philosophical questions about defining digital heritage (Cameron and Kenderdine 2007, Giaccardi 2012, and Kalay et al. 2007). Of the discussions in these volumes, a few are worth noting.

One is Andrea Witcomb's resistance to a neat separation between materiality and virtuality (Cameron and Kenderdine 2007). The argued loss of aura of objects when they enter the digital domain is contrasted to the new associations that can be formed through this process. Importantly, Witcomb points out how the act of labelling can make virtual material into 'an object', and can make it worthy of attention not as an added layer to a more 'real' physical object but as an artefact in and of itself.

Another discussion to note is Cameron's take on the object-centredness of material culture, and the pitting of digital heritage against its 'superior' physical counterparts (Cameron 2007). Cameron examines the original-material/copy-immaterial divide, where the immaterial is inferior, unauthentic and lacking an aura. The underlying reason for these characterizations seems to stem from a disgust with mass production and the attributes of disposability that it entails (stemming from the writings of Walter Benjamin in the 1930s). Yet another reason is the need to assign value to heritage, for which 'Digital historical objects and their definition therefore are difficult in a context where reified concepts of representation, interpretation, perception, aura, affect, authority, authenticity, material, provenance, and aesthetics are used to inscribe value and meaning from the traditional conventions of an object-centred museum culture' (Cameron 2007).

For Cameron, the divide – where the material is preferred to the digital – is deeply rooted in the evolutionist empiricist way of thinking of the nineteenth century, where objects carried an unequivocal meaning just by their own being.

However, the literature on museums from the past century has sought to dispel this assumption and show how the meaning of objects can be manipulated for specific economic and political goals. Thus, both digital and material objects have the same capacity to elicit meaning and invoke emotions. However, there may be a necessary interplay between material and digital, where they both serve to support the network of meaning and affect that heritage represents.

Both Witcomb and Cameron's remarks show that these concerns with ideas of aura and authenticity have been in the minds of museum researchers and professionals since the advent of digital media. Already in 1997 Anderson was wondering whether the Mona Lisa was better studied and appreciated over the Internet than in the Louvre. In a more pragmatic answer to the question, Anderson commented that in the museum, the bulletproof glass, the crowds and the cacophony of interpreters presenting the work out loud to audiences in three different languages would make it almost impossible to have a close encounter with Leonardo, and that perhaps the image of the Mona Lisa enlarged at will on a screen during a quiet night at home or in the office would be a more fruitful meeting with the master painter (Anderson 1997). Yet he also argued that the reproduction could never produce the 'visceral thrill' of being face to face with the original, and predicted that the question would be argued over in the museum profession 'until our dying breaths' (Anderson 1997: 22).

In her edited volume, Giaccardi points out that heritage today is much more about identity and about being able to interact with 'lived traces of a common past', and thus the social constructed nature of heritage means that it is not constrained by material artefacts or physical locations (Giaccardi 2012). She points out that these ideas underlie changes in the definition of heritage such as those proposed at the 2005 Council of Europe Convention on the Value of Cultural Heritage to Society, where certain barriers to what heritage can be are removed, and where participation and engagement become central (Giaccardi 2012). The Convention opens up the definition of heritage to multiple formats when it states that 'cultural heritage is a group of resources inherited from the past which people identify, independently of ownership, as a reflection and expression of their constantly evolving values, beliefs, knowledge and traditions.

It includes all aspects of the environment resulting from the interaction between people and places through time' (Europe 2005).

For Giaccardi, this definition avoids the tangible/intangible divide and also includes a desire to consider heritage that may be preserved in the future (Giaccardi 2012). This is not to say that addressing the specifics of digital heritage is irrelevant, but rather that it is equally important for our understanding of the role of heritage in contemporary society, and should not be placed second to the concerns related to material heritage.

For his part, Kalay is worried about the sheer amount of data and the increased precision with which digital technologies can capture cultural artefacts, and asks if that process is going to alter our perception of culture. The act of taking away the process of contextualization that occurs when visiting a physical site, and replacing it with the most minute and accurate details available of an artefact through 3D technologies is not to be taken lightly by cultural institutions (Kalay et al. 2007). Yet Cameron and Robinson embrace the excess and variety, and highlight the way in which it can help to empower curators and visitors as it is possible to create and contest the narratives that give objects meaning, and expand them with multimedia and information such as semantic maps etc. (Cameron and Kenderdine 2007).

These and other discussions complement and nuance the above operational definition, which in itself only attempts to capture an important feature of the digital, namely binary encoding.

The next step is then to define digital heritage sustainability. The well-known definition of sustainability presented in the Brundtland Report 'Our Common Future' can serve as a base: 'Humanity has the ability to make development sustainable to ensure that it meets the needs of the present without compromising the ability of future generations to meet their own needs' (Brundtland, Environment and Development 1987).

I thus propose the following definition of digital heritage sustainability:

> Digital heritage sustainability involves the collaborative maintenance, enrichment and enjoyment of digital heritage resources over periods of time that span across generations. It involves the maintenance of the integrity of data and metadata in binary format, and the maintenance of the digital technologies that make these data and metadata accessible to the broadest range of stakeholders.

This definition highlights the importance of a shared approach to the stewardship of digital heritage. The assumption is that only with the combined effort of institutions and communities will it be possible to harness and maintain humanity's digital heritage. Also, the idea of caring for resources that mediate generational connections is at the core of the above definition of digital heritage sustainability.

The next step is to review discussions about sustainability in the context of heritage. Broadly, these discussions can be divided into two foci: one is the role of museums in sustainable development, and the other is the sustainable management of digital resources.

Museums and Sustainable Development

Although the term sustainability is linked most prominently to environmental issues, efforts to broaden its scope to include culture and heritage date from at least the 1990s (Duxbury and Jeannotte 2010), with precedents as far back as the 1970s.

In 1972, a conversation about heritage and sustainable development began in Latin America at the Roundtable in Santiago de Chile. In this international meeting, museum scholars and practitioners discussed the role of heritage institutions such as museums in communicating environmental issues and in 'setting forth alternative solutions to social and ecological environment problems' (UNESCO 1972).

In 1995, digital heritage was addressed in conversations about the role of heritage in sustainable development, when ICOM began pressing museums to engage in the online world (Parry 2007).

Although it did not specifically target the heritage sector, a conference was organized in 1999 in Florence by UNESCO and the World Bank, entitled 'Culture Counts – Financing, Resources and the Economics of Culture in Sustainable Development'. Here, both culture and heritage were emphasized as fundamental components of a holistic view of development (Wolfensohn 2000).

Clark (2008) traces the embedding of ideas of sustainable development into social and political frameworks from the mid-2000s onwards. With the Rio Earth Summit of 1992, a number of governments across the globe set to the task of redefining how social behaviour might address the problem of the destruction of environmental resources. In the UK, after a review of the state of affairs in terms of sustainable development, in 2005 the government addressed the link between economy, society and environment (Clark 2008). Amongst the actions proposed was the reuse, rather than the demolition, of historical buildings, for the purposes of reducing waste and conserving energy, and the creation of policies that acknowledged how heritage could contribute to economic development through new jobs and through tourism activities (Clark 2008). In terms of the role of heritage in the development of sustainable communities, Clark also highlighted favourable benefits related to personal identity, social cohesion, and even health in the form of public spaces for recreation and engagement, which were being taken into account in heritage policies.

Sustainable Management of Digital Heritage

In 1998, documents such as UNESCO's 'Memory of the World – Safeguarding Documentary Heritage' showed growing concerns with the heritage sector, with particular regard to the challenges of keeping electronic media resources available for future generations. Throughout the late 1990s and early 2000s, museums started to invest more resources in online media: they began offering the public access to specialized collection databases, and began investing in web-based learning activities (Marty and Jones 2012; Parry 2007). In 2003, UNESCO released their 'Guidelines for the preservation of digital heritage' (Webb 2003), where the focus was on preserving the material integrity of digital heritage.

Since the mid-2000s, however, discussions about digital media in museums have shifted towards an understanding of the potential growth of participatory culture thanks to technologies such as social media.

The 'Knowledge Commons'

Beyond the realm of heritage, other scholars have addressed digitality and sustainability. One example is the discussion on the 'Knowledge Commons' (Hess and Ostrom 2007), which applies the Institutional Analysis and Development (IAD) framework (Ostrom 2005) to the Internet and digital information. The central idea is that while normally knowledge possessed by one person does not subtract from its use by others, digitization and the Internet make possible the emergence of 'knowledge commons': knowledge captured via digital means turns into a resource that can be shared in an exclusive fashion, thus requiring sustainable management (Hess and Ostrom 2007).

To understand the challenges posed by the shared use of the 'knowledge commons', a three-pronged approach is used. The first avenue to explore is the nature of the resource itself. This is done by looking at the biophysical characteristics, attributes of communities and rules in use (Hess and Ostrom 2007; Ostrom 2005). Studying the nature of a resource is vital in order to highlight material constraints that cannot be avoided and that shape all subsequent interaction around the resource. If one is more interested in understanding institutional change, a second avenue to look at is 'action arenas'. These are the specific action situations (for example, a given institution in a given place at a given time) and specific actors (Hess and Ostrom 2007; Ostrom 2005). Finally, a third avenue is patterns of interaction, ways of evaluating these patterns, and their outcomes. Outcomes have an effect upon the nature of a resource, as they help to reshape the biophysical characteristics, the rules in use and the attributes of the community. Outcomes also have an effect on action arenas, as they influence the situations and therefore condition the patterns of interaction that may emerge. These three broad areas of analysis are deeply interconnected.

One of the goals of the IAD framework is to help to make predictions and recommendations about ways of enhancing sustainability. A number of general 'rules' have been extracted from successful and unsuccessful situations. Natural common pool resources exhibit the following rules (Ostrom 2005):

1. Clearly-defined boundaries (effective exclusion of external unentitled parties)
2. The governance of the resource is congruent with its environment
3. Decisions are collective and provide appropriate participation
4. Effective enforcement/monitoring
5. Graduated sanctions against violators
6. Low-cost and easy-to-access conflict resolution mechanisms
7. Recognition of right to self-govern
8. Rules are organized and enforced through multiple layers of nested enterprises.

The above perspectives form the background for questions about how contexts and patterns of interaction between museums, their communities and technology stakeholders generate or hinder sustainability. Sustainability highlights shared responsibility. Analysing these patterns of interaction reveals underlying assumptions, for example that more participation is always better, regardless of the quality or kind of participation. They also help to assess the impact of placing visitors at the centre of the museum's digital endeavours. The idea is to break with the fictitious divide between caring for the collections and caring for the public. Collections, institutions and their publics are all part of the equation, not as ends in themselves, but in a system in which all components are interdependent.

A Digital Heritage Sustainability Framework for Museums

The framework presented here builds from IAD but seeks to be more than a mere translation: the areas of study proposed below place digital heritage at the centre. Using the museum as an axis, the framework involves analyses of contexts, stakeholders and digital practices. It is also useful to look at Parry's five aspects of the work of museums online (Parry 2007):

1. Direction of contact – does the museum make the visit online, or does the user go to visit the museum website? How does this affect responsibility and ownership?
2. Space of interaction – is it within the walled garden of the museum, or in other online spaces? How does this affect protocol of behaviour, and where does accountability reside?
3. Duration of interaction – is it fleeting, project bound, or representative of long-term commitment?
4. Content of interaction – in technical terms, in terms of language, culturally?
5. Motivations for interaction – systematic, spontaneous?

The DHS framework addresses these aspects: the direction and duration of the interaction are embedded in the analysis of digital practices, while content and motivation are embedded in the analysis of stakeholders. Parry's 'space' is viewed through an analysis of contexts.

It is also useful to discuss Drotner and Schrøder's (2013) reflections on how social media impact on the five aspects (acquisition, conservation, research, exhibition and communication) of the ICOM definition of museums. They point out that in terms of 'acquisition', social media may lead to an expansion of a museum's ability to obtain objects; in terms of 'conservation', social media may enhance community input through new practices such as 'folksonomies' (folk-taxonomies); for 'research', ordinary people may not only be the subjects but also the collaborators in a curatorial investigation (and this is not necessarily new, since outside the digital realm, museums sometimes engage members of the community as co-investigators); in terms of 'exhibition', inclusive practices where visitors are invited to comment and rank can be supported by social media, and furthermore, exhibits may be re-contextualized through sharing in social networks; and in terms of 'communication', social media invite a broadening of the spectrum of communication approaches used by museums, which may include both specialist and public communication approaches.

The DHS framework takes into account and can help identify such impacts. For example, a context such as an exhibition may involve novel digital practices in terms of research, acquisition and conservation, and broader ranges of stakeholders resulting from these new digital practices will need to be considered. The DHS pays special attention to these new stakeholders, the broader community in and around the museum, which is a focus that may be lacking or may need to be more explicitly stated in ICOM's five aspects of museums. To an extent, this is precisely the focus that Drotner and Schrøder seem to suggest in their analysis of social media in the museum.

A set of questions and concerns for each area follows below.

Contexts

This area includes relevant social, political and economic heritage contexts at local, national and global levels. An understanding of contexts is useful if it leads to an investigation of rules and norms in topics such as trust, privacy and security. In this way, the goal of the analysis is to identify restrictions and openings in policies and legislation that enable or impede sustainability. In addition, the analysis seeks to contrast official positions with those practices emerging from the communities of stakeholders themselves. Service providers and technology companies form part of these contexts, as they indirectly condition the network of sustainability and preservation in which museums and their communities interact.

From a sustainability perspective, some of the topics of interest are as follows:

- How do the various economic, political and social drivers impact the way in which stakeholders interact around a digital heritage resource?
- Do these contexts promote or deter sustainability?

Stakeholders

A look at stakeholders points to the challenges of expanding participation through digital media. Relevant questions may include:

- Who are the presumed, actual and expected stakeholders? Who is included, who is excluded?
- What are their roles (technical, curatorial, non-expert, collaborator)?
- How have these roles changed with the use of digital media?

After identifying these stakeholders and their roles, the next step is to analyse the potential homogeneity of goals. Measures of homogeneity of goals are important for considerations of sustainability: for traditional common-pool resources, the homogeneity of the community of stakeholders has been one of the key aspects of successful management (Hess and Ostrom 2007). When trying to identify this homogeneity in the profiles, however, measures such as the geographical location or demographic data gathered through analytics software are poor, since 'the shared space is virtual and/or intellectual rather than physical' as well as 'polycentric' (Hess and Ostrom 2007).

This means that the analyst must be able to recognize various levels of decision-making: from individual to institutional, and with disperse and volatile forms of agency amongst stakeholders. By the same token, a look at the 'roles' or 'ties' of the various users has to be multilayered, and has to abandon the museum as the central point of interest. Instead, the focus is on how accountability towards the resource is spread throughout a network.

From a sustainability perspective then, three main topics of interest emerge:

- To what extent do stakeholders share the same goals around the digital heritage resource?
- What roles do stakeholders have in the decision-making process?
- And how does this translate into sustainable or unsustainable management of the digital heritage resource?

Digital Practices

Analysing digital practices points to biases programmed into the services. Questions asked could be:

- How is digital heritage modelled by the language and technologies a digital media service uses?
- What are the assumptions in the software analytics packages that sit at the backend of these services, and how do they shape museums' digital heritage practices?

The analysis includes tracking changes in service features, formats, standards, analysing features of the software such as the type of profile metaphor ('friend', 'follower', 'community member', 'user'), and type of

Computer Mediated Communication (CMC) supported (synchronous, asynchronous, CMC combined with other activity). It also involves understanding the institutional characteristics of technologies, such as policies on ownership, terms and conditions of use, liability provisions, intellectual property claims, and security measures that in turn affect technical decisions. This area is also about analysing digital practices such as types of communication (monologue, dialogue or multilogue), categorizations of the digital heritage resources being disseminated, and patterns of dissemination of the digital heritage resources. Questions asked can include:

- How do the types of communication enabled in a given digital media platform contribute to establishing common goals around a digital heritage resource?
- Which curatorial practices are applicable to digital media? Which ones are not?
- Which digital media practices enrich digital heritage, which ones pollute it?

Analysing digital practices is useful for an understanding of issues of sustainability such as overuse, underuse, enclosure and free-riding (Hess and Ostrom 2007). Enclosure points to problems with the expanded restriction of access to the resource (the debates about copyright are an example), while free-riding points to barriers which prevent access to the resource to those who threaten its maintenance and enrichment (for example, via misinformation inserted in a co-created collection database).

Monitoring digital practices would be useful in enabling us to understand issues of control and quality of participation. By measuring 'types of communication' (monologue, dialogue, multilogue), number of nodes, and patterns of dissemination, the aim would be to monitor instances when stakeholders create rules of accountability, and to track how goals are agreed upon.

Figure 2.1 displays the DHS framework as analytical modules.

In Conclusion

The DHS framework highlights areas of importance in considerations of the long-term viability of museum digital media. Stakeholders, contexts and digital practices are overlapping components of the holistic picture of the future of digital heritage in museums.

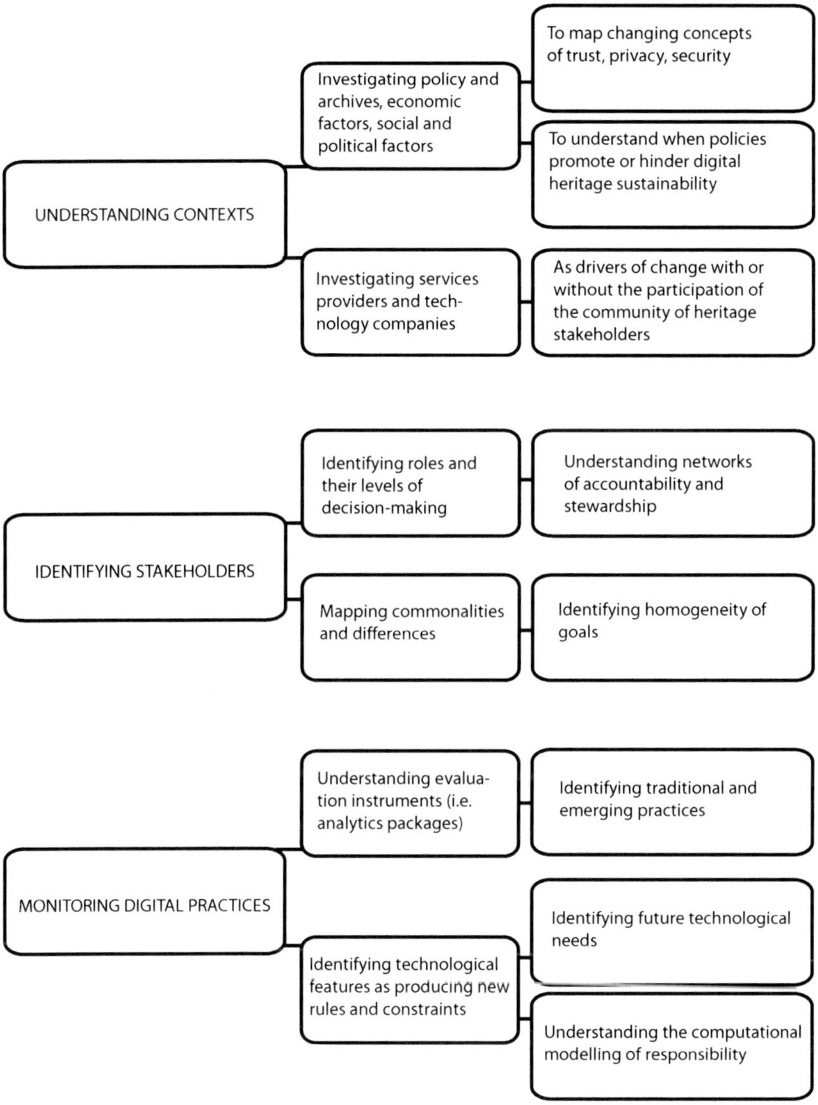

Figure 2.1. DHS Framework module overview

While digital media are not new to museums, the newest technologies have prompted a rethink in museums about concepts of heritage and relationships with stakeholders. Social media in particular push museums to negotiate novel ways of collecting, curating and interpreting their collections. The direct, decentralized and broader access to cultural resources that social and mobile media afford allows museums to expand their outreach and thus enhance their social mission. However, these media may also threaten the museum's gatekeeping role.

The pressure is on to change online museums from storage spaces into places for encounter. In the same way that museum scholars asked in the twentieth century for a transformation of the physical museum into a forum (Cameron 1971), so digital media come to further support the project of moving museums away from a role of 'authority' towards one of 'facilitation', towards a more participatory view of heritage. But for this transformation to take place, a further element also needs consideration, and this is the issue of trust. The next chapter delves deeply into the challenges of trusting the online museum.

Endnote

1. A different version of this chapter was published in 2014 in the journal *Museum Worlds* (Berghahn), edited by Kylie Message and Sandra Dudley.

Chapter 3

Trusting the Online Museum

Parry has described how in the UK, the language of conferences such as Museums and the Web has begun to shift from 'usability' and 'standards' to 'care', 'trust' and 'responsibility' (Parry 2011: 219). He defines this as the emergence of 'compassionate computing', which involves the realization that at the heart of the web are people and communities. This chapter deals with the way in which social media effect the trust the community has in the museum, the assumption that museums are places that the public trusts, and the argument that, with virtuality, this trust may be shattered (Müller 2002).

As seen in the previous chapters, social media reinforce the web as a place to make connections between people, who in turn have started to connect their collections of valuable possessions in many creative webs of knowledge. Enthusiastic amateur curators and collectors are eagerly participating in the online preservation, conservation and dissemination of heritage. In this landscape, museums are re-evaluating their work as hubs for community and identity building online, especially the way in which they can become places for collaboration and for relations based on mutual trust and understanding.

The idea of the museum as an institution of trust is not new but the role of the museum in shoring up trust is. Museums can influence public opinion, but they do not have the legal power to limit it. They are weaker kinds of organizations, yet they can be very pervasive forces in identity building. Museums have the potential to promote positive relations in a community. In sum, museums are weak organizations yet are influential enough to be of interest in an exploration of trust in government and trust in community cooperation. With the use of social media, however, museums enter an unclear space where their reputation (and trustworthiness) is intertwined with that of the services they choose to participate in. As Trant points out:

> Trust is built on identity; identity requires identification. . . Trust is also built upon assumptions that behaviour will be appropriate. Assessments of trust require a history of an individual's actions – linking their trace with a distinct identity. . . Personalization could be a great way for libraries, archives and museums to build connections between collections and individuals, and between people and collecting institutions. . . Once again, though, we need to realise that we're creating an on-line space that doesn't share all the characteristics of our past space, on-line or on-site. (Trant 2006)

However, before entering further into the discussion of trust in the context of social media, a brief background on the theoretical understandings of trust is necessary.

A Theoretical Background to Trust

The tripartite definition of trust proposed by Baier (1986) is well known: A trusts B to take care of C, and this means that A gives some discretionary power to B over C. C has to be very important for A (Baier 1986). C has to be valuable enough for the trustor (A) to experience the trustee's (B) power as a risk (Gambetta 1987).

However, trust is not a zero-sum game (i.e. A trusts B to take care of C). Nootebom (2008: 259) highlights the importance of context, and sees trust as a 'four-place predicative: a trustor (1) trusts a trustee (2) in some respects (3), under some conditions (4)'. As Baier (1986), Jones (1999) and Gambetta (1987) also point out, trust can be affected by power asymmetries in the relationship, by context, by the 'agenda' of each party and the parties involved. Trust involves risk (Gambetta 1987), vulnerability (Rousseau et al. 1998), and opportunities for the trustee to take advantage (Nootebom 2008: 249–52). But ultimately, it involves the expectation of members of a community or group for cooperative behaviour, upon which social capital can be built (Fukuyama 1995).

Even though museums are part of a collaborative process for which trust is key, it is important to make distinctions between individuals, organizations and institutions. These can be considered as different levels of society, which are in turn interrelated (Currall and Inkpen 2008). Some authors emphasize the institutional level as a fundamental pillar for trust at all other levels of society (arguably, this position is implied in current writing about the social role of museums). Grimen (2009: 110) affirms that without good institutions, it is harder to trust at the community or individual level (for example, in strangers or in neighbours). In a lawless state, fear and distrust of other people is the norm.

Yet Nootebom (2008: 261) argues that trust takes place simultaneously and interdependently at multiple levels: one's trust in people is linked to trust in the organizations they work in and the institutions that surround them. This point is important for the way in which we may understand the impact of phenomena such as curators' blogs in the trustworthiness of the museum.

There are then several 'levels of trust' (Currall and Inkpen 2008) that are of fundamental structural importance for the work of museums offline and online. The first three levels involve the museum as trustee. These are 1) the person's trust in the museum, 2) other organizations' (i.e. the community) trust in the museum, and 3) other institutions' trust in the museum. The next three levels involve museums as trustors. These are 4) the museum's trust in the person, 5) the museum's trust in the various communities of stakeholders, and 6) the museum's trust in the institutions that surround it. These levels are interrelated and dynamic, which means that they co-evolve in time (Currall and Inkpen 2008). The following table provides a brief summary:

Table 3.1. Trust at the Museum

	Museum as trustee	**Museum as trustor**
Personal level	Individuals donate objects and information to the museum (they entrust it with artefacts)	The museum trusts that individuals donate artefacts of credible origin, and that they provide accurate information about these artefacts
Organizational level	The community supports economically the work of the museum (via visits and donations) and trusts that the museum will not misrepresent or take advantage of them	The museum trusts that the community will continue to support their work and will stand by their side when needed (for policy, as volunteers) The museum trusts that professional communities will provide their expertise
Institutional level	International bodies and national institutions trust that the museum will perform its duties with professionalism and good will	The museum trusts that the institutions around it will provide the conditions for it to conduct its mission and functions (legislation, funding)

In the first three levels (museum as trustee), an individual or a community gives a museum power over its memories by endowing it with the artefacts that attest to these. The person or community trust that the museum will tell its story in a truthful and respectful manner, and that because of the good work of the museum, future generations will have access to the knowledge these artefacts embody. Museums as trustees make implicit vows to never betray this community by misrepresenting its history and identity. State, regional, national or international bodies trust that the museum will abide by their codes of conduct and guarantee the safety of the heritage housed within. These institutions also trust that the museum has the expertise to do so.

In the next three levels (museum as trustor), the museum trusts the individuals and the community to believe in its goodwill and capacity to safeguard the artefacts it collects and displays. The museum entrusts them with its reputation, and furthermore, the museum puts in the hands of the community its most important means for survival (revenues from visits, access to funding, favourable legislation). The museum also trusts that the institutions surrounding it will make the provisions necessary to enforce fair play and to guarantee its ability to perform its duties, and it also trusts that by complying with their norms and regulations, it will continue to receive their support.

One example of this kind of trust expressed in museum social media is found on references to 'radical trust' in Jim Spadaccini's Ideum blog for museum technology. In a post in 2006, Spadaccini commented on takes on the idea from the library sector by Darlene Fitcher, who stated that:

> We can only build emergent systems if we have radical trust. With an emergent system, we build something without setting in stone what it will be or trying to control all that it will be. We allow and encourage participants to shape and sculpt, and be co-creators of the system. We don't have a million customers/users/patrons . . . we have a million participants and co-creators. Radical trust is about trusting the community. We know that abuse can happen, but we trust (radically) that the community and participation will work. In the real world, we know that vandalism happens but we still put art and sculpture up in our parks. As an online community we come up with safeguards or mechanisms that help keep open contribution and participation working. (Spadaccini 2006)

For Spadaccini (2006), this statement reflected many of the discussions about the development of social media for museums experienced by his team. Museum social media were seen as spaces that required risk-taking from museums, in the sense that the museum would have to let go of a great degree of control over content or over online interactions. Furthermore, this was a risk that could be minimized but never completely avoided.

Museums, Trust and Power

As was mentioned above, Baier (1986) has pointed out that in the statement A trusts B to take care of C it is easy to miss the underlying assumption that the trustor (A) and the trustee (B) are equal. This is what Baier calls the contractual view of trust (1986). The contractual view of trust does not account for relations where someone follows regulations because of fear. It also fails to account for situations where a trustee is given discretionary power without being fit to accept it. These observations immediately bring to the forefront the question of the power equilibrium in a trust relationship.

Museums, for instance, have been under scrutiny for the kind of power they hold over collections once the artefacts leave their communities of origin. For a long time, they have been criticized for what some perceive as their authoritarian (rather than authoritative) position about the knowledge they safeguard. As discussed in Chapter 1, since the late 1970s theorists have pointed out these imbalances in the relationship between inner and outer spheres of museum practice, and have raised awareness in museum practitioners about the social and cultural role of museums in opening up their spaces to more diverse audiences (Vergo 1989; Neale 2001; Goodnow 2006). As part of this, the neutrality and the de facto exercise of power by museums (as the sole voice in determining what should be on display) have been questioned. Selecting objects and labelling them as valuable derives from an agenda. It has been discussed previously how Lidchi (1997) points to the fallacy of objectivity in the 'logical assemblages' provided at exhibitions: those assemblages come from a perspective or classificatory schema that is specific to the curator and to the historical context in which he or she is embedded. As a product of these critiques, a modification of the concept of museum that allows for more flexibility and room for discussion has thus taken place since the last quarter of the twentieth century.

The debate about power and openness in the museum is nevertheless far from resolved. Online, a community drowning in over-information yearns for an authoritative voice to light the path to trustworthy knowledge. This community may feel betrayed when the museum does not 'say how it really was'. Also, with increased participation, and increased appropriation of the space of the museum by various and at times conflicting voices via social media, there is greater potential for some of the more polarized sectors to feel betrayed when museums do not tell 'the truth' as they see it. By opening up to negotiation, the museum becomes vulnerable to hidden agendas. New problems with maintaining the aura of neutrality and professionalism threaten the museum's trustworthiness. This is especially apparent in social media.

The Value and Sources of Trust

For museums, trust is invaluable, and is implicit in all its relations even if it is not explicitly stated. Consider the act of collecting: collection items are precious and unique objects that once belonged to a community or an individual. Without trust, how could anyone endow the museum with such objects? Nevertheless, museum officials have at times taken objects without respecting the desired of originating communities. In this case, trust in the organization has no doubt suffered.

Consider also learning in museum online (and offline) visits. As McLeod (2011) points out, trust is an essential element of knowledge acquisition. The student needs to trust that the teacher is not maliciously imparting wrong facts. Without trust, the public would not even go to exhibitions, for how could they accept the knowledge presented? More than ever, museum visitors seek to be assured that they are engaged with trustworthy knowledge.

Undoubtedly, an important source of trust in the museum is its perceived competence, and this of course includes that of its staff. Museums depend on the professionalism of curators, conservators and exhibition designers, who are in turn 'certified' by universities. The museum's trustworthiness also grows in strength through membership in organizations such as the International Council of Museums (ICOM). Even when they are not members of staff, the reputation of other individuals participating in the museum adds to its trustworthiness. For example, a high profile human rights activist on the museum board can bring credibility to the organization. Yet this also depends on the position of these stakeholders within the organization, as will be discussed below when dealing with the parties involved. The first source of trust for a museum project is probably the reputation of the stakeholders involved. From the beginning, a museum social media project will rely mostly upon the reputation of individuals on the board to build trust in the organization.

The Object of Trust

As has been pointed out above, C, or the object of trust, has to be something vulnerable, valuable and unique. It can be something material, but it can also be something intangible (feelings, emotions, memories, secrets). The obvious objects of trust in museums are artefacts. These are items of archaeological importance; they constitute material historical evidence. In the ethical frameworks available for museums, provisions for such kinds of artefacts are extensively developed (from issues of conservation to issues of repatriation and so on). Current changes in the materials that support evidence, however, such as the turn to polymeric materials as major containers of cultural products in the form of audio-visual recordings or digital documents, mean that the concept of heritage and its safeguarding are in need of revision. This has been the concern of scholars, practitioners and organizations such as ICOM for a number of years, as is evidenced by programmes such as Memory of the World. Concepts such as documentary heritage have emerged in new frameworks geared at preserving contemporary forms of heritage.

In addition, with digitization and broader participation through the rise of phenomena such as social media, a second object of trust – the information about artefacts – becomes the object of distrust. Experts and non-experts struggle to find trustworthy ways to share their knowledge so that it enriches, rather than tarnishes, museum collections.

In Conclusion

Digital heritage has first to be recognized as valuable, unique and important by both parties for it to become the object of the trust relationship. While the community may already recognize the importance of preserving online material and even social media dialogues, the lack of an official recognition at an institutional level means that it may not be so easily entrusted to organizations such as museums. Adopting appropriate institutional frameworks that validate documentary heritage may be one way for the museum to establish that relationship of trust with the community which is needed to transfer such materials to the museum, the first step to safeguarding them.

Museums use a very large palette to legitimize their version of history or culture. Images, texts, sounds all coexist in a museum display and work to materialize culture and history, giving bodily form to a way of seeing the world. Yet an important concern is whether museums should make clear the inconsistencies and debates that surround many of their curatorial interpretations – in an even greater degree than what has so far been done, and furthermore, whether they should open up for the inclusion of alternative interpretations coming from users. The choices made by museums with regard to each of these questions will affect their trustworthiness and the relationships they can establish with their communities.

This chapter concludes the theoretical section of the book. The following two chapters present an overview of the more practical and technical aspects of museum websites and social media, supported by selected examples of current practice.

Part II: Practice

Chapter 4

A Practical Social Media Primer for Museum Staff

This chapter explores the practical aspects of museum website and social media design. One essential consideration when defining and implementing a museum website and its social media services is the need to understand the current production skills (both conceptual and technical) of museum staff. In many cases, social media and the process of website design will be foreign to museum staff, who have been trained in curatorship but who increasingly find themselves having to deal with multiple other aspects of the communication of their expertise. Increasingly, museum staff will be required to engage with these technologies not only as providers of raw material, but also as technology practitioners, so it is vital to address how museums may incorporate the web in their practices and institutional structure.

Some organizations, such as the Museums and Galleries Service in Queensland, offer free social media courses tailored to the needs of the libraries, archives and museums in their region (Queensland 2014). This has been done in Norway too, for example, with the Hordaland course, 'A taste of social media', also tailored for archives, museums and libraries (Fylkeskommune 2010). In this case, the course was part of a much broader offering by the then Norwegian Office for the Development of Archives, Libraries and Museums (ABM Utvikling), which funded similar courses in other municipalities.

Cultural institutions around the world have tackled the need to increase staff expertise in website design and social media through programmes based on the principle of self-discovery. The goal of such programmes is to motivate non-technical staff to explore social media by themselves and to generate a peer-based network of assistance for more advanced technical challenges. Often, an institution will have developed a policy for engagement with social media, but will not necessarily provide training for staff.

Knowledge is scattered amongst staff who have the social media technical expertise but no curatorial background, and staff who have trained themselves due to their own interest or to increasing pressure from their organizations. In addition, a few museum studies programmes directly engage with training in social media or in web design more generally. One example is the course on Museum Technology as part of the Museum Studies programme at University of Delaware (Delaware 2014), and other courses are organized within the discipline of Information Sciences. However, the bulk of training lies in conferences such as Museums and the Web, and through general marketing and web design degrees, where the special considerations required for museums may not be covered adequately.

The next section discusses how staff can start building up their technological expertise by themselves through the use of various social media. It includes an overview of basic social media technologies, as well as a glance at more advanced software that would require the assistance of IT staff to set up (but which could be managed by non-technical staff). The nature of the topic requires a certain degree of technical jargon (and unfortunately a few sections of dry code discussion), but it has been the author's intention to clarify as much as possible each technical term so that a general audience can understand it.

First Step: Understanding the Difference between Static and Dynamic Web Design

A common distinction made in web design is the difference between static and dynamic web pages. When used to describe the web, 'static' usually refers to pages that seldom change and technologies that are (at first sight) unresponsive to changing contextual conditions (such as user preferences etc.). Static also has, to a certain extent, connotations of 'old technology', and is 'viewed as undesirable or uninteresting'. This is a connotation, however, that we need to examine more carefully.

Along with URLs (uniform resource locators) and HTTP (hypertext transfer protocol), HTML (hypertext markup language) was one of the building blocks of the 'World Wide Web' that Tim Berners-Lee put in motion in 1989. To an extent, HTML has become synonymous with static in the negative sense.

Static websites are usually based in HTML, a language that encodes a document, or 'marks it up', in a way that is understandable by a computer, so that it can display and interpret its content appropriately. In HTML, a heading will be enclosed by tags that define it as such for the computer; for example <h1> is the tag that tells the computer that this is the most important heading of a page, <img> will tell it that this element is an image, <p> will tell it that a piece of text is a paragraph, and so on (note that in most instances, the tags will need to be opened and closed, e.g. <h1>This is a title</h1> has the opening <h1> tag and the closing </h1> tag). These tags will only be seen by the browser software rendering the document, and will remain invisible for the user.

The technical understanding of 'static', as the above definition states, means variables that do not change while programs are executed. As it was meant to be descriptive language, HTML did not execute changes while a page was being viewed. Once a tag and its content were defined in the original document, these items would not change. There were no variables in the language (in computer science, variables are identifiable storage locations to which a value can be assigned).

The common understanding of 'static' as opposed to 'dynamic' pages then is those pages that are not structured for regular change, regular here meaning every day, or even every click. This tells us a bit about the changing pace of the web; while it used to be enough to update a page every month (one would hope that employees would remain that long in their job), now users expect updates every second (thanks to Twitter and Facebook).

One example of a 'static museum website' is the website of The Museum of the Kuna Nation in Kuna Yala, an indigenous *comarca* (region) in Panama. This website provides an overview of the institution's history, its location, exhibitions and collections. The information presented has not changed since the page was created, probably around 2005. Although the information on this page has not changed for quite some time, it would be very easy for the manager of the website to update the content without having to recreate the entire page. HTML is forward compatible, meaning that new browsers can interpret older versions of the language. This page can potentially change at any time. Therefore, regardless of how 'static' a page on the web seems to be, the use of this adjective in the context of the Internet is quite different to what it would be in the context of other media.

In contrast to the negative connotations that 'static' has come to possess, 'dynamic' is the quintessential adjective for the web today. It is all about instant gratification: the website knows who we are, where we are, what we like and dislike. . . or in any case, a clever algorithm is trying to convince us that it knows our desires better than we do. Before social media, dynamic was the beloved word of marketers and technophiles for the new web: positive, progressive and full of energy. The 'dynamic' web started to emerge with the creation of CGI (Common Gateway Interface) in 1993, executable files (small programs) stored in the server that could generate web pages (server-side scripting), and with the implementation of scripting languages such as PHP (Hypertext Pre-processor) in 1994, which had the advantages of being able to generate HTML pages 'on the fly', modifying them according to context, and JavaScript in 1995, where the browser would help to modify the pages (client-side scripting). CGI, PHP and JavaScript focused on changes according to contexts of use. These contexts were environmental variables such as language, time of day, geographical location, user preferences, type of browser and so on. At first, this meant pop-up windows and web forms, as these technological developments coincided with the 1995 Dot.com boom where companies, with the motto 'get large or get lost', were using scripts and forms to expand their networks (and in addition to gamble on the stock market, which led to the bubble and subsequent burst in 2000).

Today, dynamic technologies are used for websites designed to cope with regular updates. Dynamic websites also allow multiple administrators and web editors to change content and manage the site's various components simultaneously or asynchronously. Web developers have used scripting languages to create highly customizable 'Content Management Systems' (CMS), packages that can be either bought or downloaded at no cost (I will examine open source later on) to be used by technical and non-technical staff in order to create websites. The advantage of dynamic websites created using CMS is that they provide non-technical staff with a web forms-based infrastructure, allowing them to add new content to the website. From the first versions of the web, where users were learning HTML to write their pages, the introduction of scripting languages produced a new, indirect way of participating on the web, through the mediated structures provided by developers.

One example of a dynamic museum website is the Museum of Modern Art (MOMA) website. Content on its Calendar and Exhibition pages is updated in relation to time or can be filtered by type of event. The website will always land on the current date, and events can be regrouped by users depending on their interest in a particular type of art.

It is the dynamic web that has made Web 2.0 possible. As a new cohort of middlemen took on the role of creating easier to use interfaces to the web through the use of scripting, more people became able to participate in the creation of web content. During the 1990s any user of the web needed to understand at least a minimum of HTML and the way in which servers worked to be able to produce and publish their own pages. Otherwise, they would need to hire web designers. Now, any user can sign into a blogging service (basically, a system built with scripting technologies and designed to be modified through web forms), and create an online presence. This technological change has marked a shift in the conception of the web, and is what underlies the creation of social media services.

Starting out with Social Media: Blogs

One of the first, and easiest, ways to approach social media is by creating a blog. Blogs are useful tools to teach users how to write for the web and to connect with other museum staff, designers, curators and museumgoers from around the globe.

Blogs are an easy starting point because they require minimal attention to technical aspects. There are many free services where one can start a blog, amongst them Wordpress.com and Blogger.com. There are also paid services such as Typepad.com. All of these are set up so that new users only have to sign into the service to have immediate access to a publishing system that looks very similar to a text editor, with customizations and additions that can be discovered progressively.

Most of the time, services will allow users to create a private blog, which means it will not be listed on search engines. This is useful if the purpose of the blog is for staff just to get a quick overview of how the technology works, and for discovering whether one wants to blog at all. In the case of publicly visible blogs, however, provisions should be taken to ensure their continuity upon signing up for a service. Users should preferably create a generic blogging account so that new staff can pick up or even delete the blog if the original creator is no longer taking care of it.

Staff should take some time to familiarize themselves with the interface, maybe post some test texts and try to upload photos or embed audio and video. This process should be relatively straightforward, as most blogging services strive to make their interfaces as easy and as user-friendly as possible. Blogging services also have support pages and tutorials about how things are done, and any technical questions can also be posted on their forums.

Choice of Topic

After signing in, the first hurdle when starting the blog will most likely be the choice of topic. As a first approach, staff can search around the web for examples of blogs in their areas of interest. Joining a social bookmarking/

social cataloguing service (Delicious, CiteUlike, Digg, StumbleUpon) can also be a way of finding interesting content to blog about or to aggregate. A number of examples of possible topics will be given in forthcoming chapters, such as blogs about objects, about museum technology, or about working for an exhibition or in a given department.

A second approach might be to think about blogs as avenues for building a community, and therefore to focus on whom one wants to reach. In software development, it is increasingly common to develop 'user stories', short cases that should fit into an index card (see Keith 2010). User stories follow the pattern 'As a <type of user>, I want <some goal> so that <some reason>' (see Kumar 2011). Museum staff could borrow from this idea and create a pool of possible user stories for the blog from which the most appropriate are selected as points of departure for the blog's focus.

For example, a user story for a museum blog might be 'As a young student, I want to find someone at the museum who works with dinosaurs, so that I can ask questions for my natural science essay'. Another user story could be 'As a tourist, I want to find out more about how an exhibition that ran at the museum at the time I visited was created, and I want to send the link to a friend'. Yet another example might be 'As a museum curator and blogger, I want to keep in touch with other museum bloggers in order to share news and events that might be of interest'.

User stories are mainly exercises in thinking about what voice and content will be most appropriate for the blog in relation to its potential audience. Even though user stories are written at the beginning of the blogging project, it can be useful to keep these at hand and revisit them after a while to see to what extent the blog corresponds to its original intent, or if it does not, to discover why this is the case. In Chapter 9, the 'augmentation' of the Garden of Australian Dreams at the National Museum of Australia provides an example of the use of these design techniques.

As we can see, one might find the focus for a blog by thinking about one's own personal interests, about the possible audience, or about the larger role of the museum in its community. In all these cases, the important aspect is that the blog's topic must be something that the blogger is deeply involved with and cares about, so that the author's interest can be maintained, thus ensuring regular updates. In addition, Kathryn Box, marketing officer for the Manchester Museum, points to the personal benefits that blogging as an activity can bring to curators and researchers:

> From my experience at Manchester Museum, the blogging curators get to 'diary' their day-to-day practice. Ultimately building up a record of activity and events, as well as thinking (and typing) about findings, research and theories. They get to join

> in debates and show off about the fantastic collection they get to explore. As most academics spend years writing their thesis, blogging is an instantaneous e-journal, which breaks down the barrier between the learner and academic. Students and peers get an amazing insight into a world which goes on behind the scenes at a museum, gaining a better understanding about how curators tick and how these big cultural institutions work. (Box 2014)

Advertisements and 'Monetization'

One issue in trying to maintain a professional – yet not corporate – voice in the blog is unwanted commercialization. The difference between many of the blogging services often lies in how much advertisement one has to allow. This is a crucial consideration that can affect how the public perceives the blog. If there are too many unrelated commercials, the public will feel as if they are wandering through a shopping mall rather than a museum! Also, staff should follow up with the changes in terms and conditions of use, as it might be the case that a previously free service becomes a paid one at some point, or progressively increases the amount of advertisement, etc. The museum will not want to drive its users towards highly commercial spaces, and will not want to be associated with vendors that have nothing to do with the museum, as advertisement on blogging services is the product of algorithms that match keywords in the content with keywords from vendors buying marketing services. As a rule of thumb, services with a large amount of ads should be used for training and not for publishing as part of the museum website, or at least a balance should be sought between advertisement and information content. As of the time of writing, users can buy themselves out of advertisement for a yearly fee in some of the free services, and when installed on the museum's own servers, systems have no advertisement at all, although this is at the cost of having to hire IT staff to maintain them. However, advertising revenue is an option that some museums should consider, as it can indeed be a considerable and helpful source of funding. One of the schemes involved in assessing revenue is counting 'impressions', or how many times an ad is seen, which does not take into account clicking on the ad. The concept of a page being 'seen' is the product of a calculation of the web server's responses for a particular page request, excluding robots and errors. Another scheme is 'pay per click', where publishers are paid when an ad on their website is clicked. In some cases, an advertiser directly contacts the blogger to establish a marketing contract. In other cases a blog may have a number of keywords that a group of advertisers are interested in. A search engine provides a 'bidding' platform, where advertisers bid for the keyword and get a slot in the blog. The internal aspects of the bidding process can get quite complex, so it is always necessary for the bloggers and the advertisers to understand the impact of keyword selection in such revenue schemes.

Branding and Networking

When the blogger is ready to go beyond practicing, the blog can be linked to the museum's website through a menu on the homepage. There should be consistency in terms of graphical elements between the blog and the main website, so that visitors know that they are still within the museum's site. When the connection has been made to the museum and the blog is open to the public, bloggers should go on to create a list of related blogs and insert this list on their service. This will help to spread the word about the blog, as a number of the blogs listed will also link back. Links should also be made within the text of posts to the museum's official website. As Mosoddik points out, linking back in every post to the museum's website is a way of ensuring that the blog is effectively helping to drive people to the institutions main entry gate (Mosoddik 2009b). Similarly, linking from the main website to the blog can add depth to collections and exhibitions by providing the kind of backstage access that we have discussed in previous chapters.

In addition, when the blog is well on its way with content development, one might want to link it to one's social networking accounts (Facebook or equivalent). This is a useful point of departure to understand the challenges that arise with regard to limits between personal and public personas when blogging and social networking on behalf of an institution.

Some users might find it challenging to decide whether to link their work-related blog to their personal Facebook account, while for others this will not represent a problem. It is a question of whether one wants to use social network sites as promotional tools or as places to keep in touch primarily with family and friends. In any case, going through the experience of maintaining a blog and linking it to one's social media networks is a good way of confronting the many questions of privacy and trust that arise when the boundaries between private, public, commercial and not-for-profit are blurred, as is increasingly the case in social media spaces.

For example, Bilkis Mosoddik points out that she is always conscious of the fact that she is a member of staff at the MOL and will in one way or another always be representing the museum when posting something online. This is something she keeps in mind even when using her personal accounts of Facebook or Twitter (Mosoddik 2009b). For her, it is important to maintain a professional tone both on the MOL's blog and on any other social media sites she might be participating in. Shelley Bernstein, Manager of Information Systems at Brooklyn Museum, explains the policies that the museum has put in place for its blogging services:

> Authors, following a set of institutionally approved guidelines, write posts focusing on behind-the-scenes information not readily accessible to the public. Diverse in terms of content, posts are written personally by staff members and retain each author's unique voice and perspective; they also identify each author with a small picture and short biography and use tags to integrate posts with appropriate exhibition pages on the site. (Bernstein 2008)

Scheduling

Finally, new bloggers should keep in mind that blogging can be a very time consuming activity. A key to keeping the blog updated is to tie it to current research or daily work. It is a good idea to make a schedule for updates, for instance daily, once a week or twice a month, and incorporate these updates as part of the normal work routine. It is also possible to invite other staff to do a 'guest post' on the blog when one cannot post because of travel, etc.

Next Step: Embedding and Producing Media

After a period of blogging, staff can progress to trying to produce and embed other types of media such as audio and video, and/or joining communities around these media. Staff can set up accounts in Blip.tv, YouTube or Vimeo (video sharing), and use these to post audio or video to the blog. Flickr can be used for photo sharing and embedding in the blog, and free software such as Gimp or Picasa can be used for image editing. VoiceThread can be used to create rich conversations that include video, audio, photos and text. Services such as Vimeo have started to launch mobile editing applications, all of this geared towards making it easy for users to produce and share media.

While blogging can be a very time consuming activity, as we have mentioned, this is nothing in comparison to the amount of resources required to actively participate in media sharing sites. Writing a post can be daunting, but producing a video can be overwhelming, especially for staff that have never done anything like it before.

A good place to start is with audio, by recording staff conversations (with everyone's approval, of course), or by interviewing a fellow curator. These recordings can be used to create short podcasts. One conversation could centre, for instance, on a couple of questions related to a museum artefact. Another could be about the process of curating an upcoming exhibition. Conversations or interviews can be recorded and edited with free software such as Audacity. In Garage Band (software for the Mac), it is easy to add sound effects to the recording later. Background music can be added from websites such as ccMixter or Jamendo to avoid any copyright issues. These can later be uploaded to the museum's servers and linked to the blog.

As for video, it requires a considerably larger amount of effort. Staff could start by making a slideshow and adding music. Other material could consist of talks and seminars, posted with permission from speakers. It is also possible to obtain raw, copyright-free video material from media sharing sites such as Spin Xpress (http://www.spinxpress.com), or sites such as The Internet Archive (http://www.archive.org).

Yet another alternative is to seek collaboration with tertiary or vocational education institutions. For example, media students may be enrolled on professional media production courses where they are required to work with clients to develop a video. Students from the Department of Information Science and Media Studies at University of Bergen collaborated in 2009 and 2010 with various museums in Bergen to produce videos that would be distributed via social media. Bergen University Museum displayed the student produced video on the front page of their website throughout the year, and the students also distributed it through their networks. So far, Vimeo statistics indicate that the video has been seen 4,000 times. In comparison, two other institutionally produced videos, also available on Vimeo, have gathered 65 and 3,000 views respectively.

The museum can also ask followers to add media content, for example through a Flickr group, thereby benefiting from user-generated content. Provisions need to be made, however, to ensure that appropriate filtering is conducted in order to prevent the intrusion of inappropriate content.

For example, in 2008 the Brooklyn Museum discovered that their video sharing strategy in YouTube was not attracting audiences as much as they wished. As in the case of Bergen Museum mentioned above, the Brooklyn Museum partnered with students from a Brooklyn design college (Pratt Institute), and created a Public Service Announcement which seemed to be much more engaging (Bernstein 2008). The museum then came up with the idea of a YouTube contest asking for Public Service Announcements created by the community. Shelley Bernstein comments on the results of this effort:

> The power of this exercise lies in the spontaneity and diversity of the participants and what their fresh, unbound perspectives can bring to our daily working environment. We happily discovered that PSAs created by our visitors are quite different from what the institution would typically produce. . . As a testament to the power of user-generated content, we were excited to discover that the videos submitted for the competition were viewed four to five times more than anything else we had previously posted on YouTube. And when YouTube decided to feature our contest in its 'Groups' area, the view counts increased exponentially. (Bernstein 2008)

Finally, the more elaborate strategy is to hire a professional agency to produce videos, for example promotional videos for upcoming exhibitions or documentaries, and to collaborate with staff to spread these through social media.

Going Further: Wikis and Collaborative Project Management

Producing media material is a collaborative activity, but there are other forms of online collaboration through social media that may be more feasible for a number of staff. Amongst them are wikis, webpages where users can write collaboratively in a single document, without the need for programming or technical expertise, and without needing special software, as the system is entirely web based (Challborn 2005). Of these, Wikipedia is perhaps the best example of the challenges of administering social media collaboration. Staff can search for the museum's entries in Wikipedia, and, once they have accessed the article, begin to edit it or join the discussion section to propose changes. The complexity of collaboration in Wikipedia is most apparent in these discussion pages. It has prompted the creation of a fascinating set of guidelines or codes of conduct, which are worth taking a look at if one is planning on implementing a wiki on the museum's website.

Setting up the wiki has to be done by technical staff, and setting the rules of use of the wiki can also be a collaborative process. For instance, Forte, Larco and Bruckman (2009), upon investigating the self-governing mechanisms of Wikipedia, conclude that this can produce an 'organization with highly refined policies, norms, and a technological architecture that supports organizational ideals of consensus building and discussion'. However, and as is also the case with other types of websites that allow participation, the community must also have mechanisms to monitor and contain the activities of trolls, persons who hide behind fake online identities to engage in various forms of vandalism and destructive behaviour on the website in an attempt to harm the community (Shachaf and Hara 2010).

The managerial process around an exhibition or a museum project can be recorded and enhanced through the use of social media, for instance by using 'cloud' services (applications hosted in remote services and administered by a commercial company) such as Google Docs (a word processing application), or by using commercial project management software such as Basecamp or other open source alternatives (for example, Open Atrium, explained in more detail below).

For EduTangible, a research project about multitouch technologies in museums that I conducted at the Panama Viejo Monumental Complex, the team used Basecamp. In the Basecamp interface, team members can write messages, create tasks and milestones and assign which members of the team will participate in each message thread or have responsibilities for tasks, etc. This software greatly facilitated collaboration, as it was possible for all team members to have the most up-to-date information and quickly access any needed material or follow up on important tasks.

An open source alternative to Basecamp is the Open Atrium suite, a Content Management System solution that can be installed in the museum's own servers. The functionality of Open Atrium is similar to that of Basecamp, as it allows for messages between team members, the storing of shared documents and calendars. With solutions such as Open Atrium, however, the museum already needs to have dedicated staff or an IT Department in place, as it requires some degree of technical knowledge in order to install it in the server and customize it.

If readers have taken the time to experiment with each one of the technologies summarized in this chapter and discussed throughout this volume, they should by now have a good understanding of the many possibilities and challenges that can arise with the use of social media. This is of course dependent on how much time is invested in self-study.

For small museums, the less time consuming and perhaps most effective technology will be social network sites (SNS) such as Facebook, Badoo or Renren. Museum pages on SNS take little time to create, do not require lengthy posts, and can be kept alive by posting information, for example about upcoming events. Blogs might be more demanding, and small museums will have to take into consideration the fact that blogging staff will need a certain amount of time to dedicate to the writing of posts. Larger museums will perhaps have more issues with keeping the image of the museum consistent across all social media, whether it is the blog of a particular staff member, a Facebook page, or a YouTube account. There should also be room for the web team to experiment with new social media, or discard outlets that are no longer relevant or whose profile does not fit in with the image the museum wants to give.

Other Technical Aspects

In relation to the technical aspects of web design, readers might want to keep track of the work of the W3C, available at http://www.w3c.org. Web standards and accessibility issues should be a major concern both for project managers and designers, as should usability issues.

A valuable technical resource for these issues is the 'A List Apart' magazine's website, available at http://www.alistapart.com. This magazine, founded by web standards advocate Jeffrey Zeldman, is dedicated to presenting the latest developments in website design practice.

It is important to bear in mind that web technology is constantly changing. A website that is perfectly serviceable today might be unusable or heavily crippled in the future, just because browser vendors have changed their technology and discontinued support for older versions, or because the web has moved to other platforms such as mobiles. Thus, institutions should plan on doing regular updates to their pages if possible, or at least consider that a redesign will be needed around three years after the initial launch.

Website Testing

As noted previously, according to usability gurus such as Nielsen (2012), asking five people how they feel about a website can render enough information to assess whether the website is usable or not. For Steve Krug (2006), on the other hand, user testing should be done often and for short periods, instead of doing one big test when a project is almost done. The general trend is to approach website design as an incremental process composed of small, yet meaningful steps, which should be tested along the way.

A user test does not need to be a complicated affair. Although there is sophisticated eye tracking equipment, and tests can also be videotaped, a user test can be done very effectively and inexpensively with just pen and paper. An observer will stand by the test participant writing down how she or he performs a given task (for example, to find an item in the museum's collection). The observer should not help the participant accomplish the task, but rather encourage them to speak their minds while they are making a trial. This is referred to as the think-aloud protocol (Lewis and Rieman 1993).

In each design iteration short tests can be programmed as intermediate stages. The knowledge gained from the tests then feeds back into the design, and the team can meet to discuss the appropriateness of the user stories that are up for development, and make the required changes.

Search Engine Optimization

The most common way to find information on the web is to use a search engine. Google, Bing and other such services have become the de facto entry point for most websites. In basic terms, the process of indexing the contents of the Internet depends on four aspects: a database to store a given state of the web, agents to crawl (browse) and retrieve webpages, a dispatcher to coordinate the agent's activities, and an indexer to update the database (Pinkerton 1994). Given the predominance of search engines as the access mode to the web, one of the key issues of the effective delivery of online content is Search Engine Optimization (SEO). SEO is about making a website findable by optimizing how search engines such as Google and Bing crawl it. A web crawler has the ability to both identify new documents (through their URLs) and to decide whether these documents are worth retrieving. SEO thus involves using structured HTML (such as microformats and microdata) to tag specific types of content (addresses, people, type of business); preventing robots from following links that are not related to the website; using appropriate metadata (keywords, authors, description) to mark content and make it more understandable for crawlers; and other related techniques. The goal of SEO is to help to produce better and more relevant search results for web users, thus adding value to the Internet as a repository for information.

Search engines use links in other documents to discover new documents, so the inbound links are an important component of optimization. This fact, and the way in which it affects search engine placement (how high in the list of hits the URL to a search result is placed), has led to abusive practices such as link farms and link spam, which mislead the algorithms of search engines that give weighting to a page based on numbers of links (Gyöngyi and Garcia-Molina 2005). For this reason, search engines have started to implement methods to assess the quality of a link. Also, the terms natural and paid placement are used to distinguish different types of search engine results, and Google and other reputable search engines make an effort to distinguish sponsored search results from unpaid, organic search results (Davis 2006).

Search engines are interested in constantly improving the quality of their service, and for that reason they make huge efforts to provide information to webmasters about the kind of web content they prefer. In its latest guidelines, Google states that an information-rich site is preferred, in addition to websites that are optimized for loading speed (Google 2014).

According to Davis (2006), a website has to provide breadth, meaning that an array of pages have to constitute a cohesive whole and deliver expansive information about a subject. In addition, there is no substitute for good content, so no SEO campaign will be able by itself to provide for poorly developed websites. Amongst the various categories of content that Davis (2006) highlights as effective are pages that are humorous, that provide a free service, that provide distinctive opinion or news, practical information, or that provide a service for the community. So in thinking about developing a SEO strategy, the first consideration is what will be useful to the visitors of the page, what is the value of this website in the heterogeneous constellation of the World Wide Web? A good strategy to increase value will ultimately result in a better natural placement of the website in any search engine result.

Literature

An invaluable resource is Nina Simon's blog Museum2.0, available at http://museumtwo.blogspot.com/. This blog has been online since 2006, and it has become a hub for discussions on all aspects of participation in museums. In this and other blogs dedicated to web 2.0 technologies in museums, one can also find regularly updated lists of bloggers and reviews of upcoming technologies, and one can even ask for advice about the implementation of a given social media service.

One important issue to take into account is the durability of social media services. Users might desert a given service in droves to move to a newer offering, which might lead to the closing of the service. This is an essential consideration when the plan is to make a collection available through social media, as this requires many hours of work in choosing and uploading files, sorting out copyright, etc.

There are numerous philosophical and ethical questions surrounding the use of social media by museums. Many of these issues have not yet been explored, hence this volume seeking to act as an introduction. However, readers who want to start familiarizing themselves with these discussions might consult publications such as Axel Bruns' *Blogs, Wikipedia, Second Life and Beyond*, Jill Walker Rettberg's *Blogging*, Yoshai Benkler's *The Wealth of Networks* or Lawrence Lessig's *Remix*.

Practicalities

In the last section of this chapter, I briefly address practical concerns. This section is predominantly technical, but it introduces concepts that should be considered by managers and technical staff jointly, such as the use of web standards and issues of accessibility.

For museum officials who are more used to coordinating projects for print than for the web, it is important to bear in mind that it may be difficult for the web designer to translate a concept created for print. In fact, attempts at direct translations from print or other media may result in a poor web experience. Unlike print, and also in contrast to time-based media like television or radio, the web seems like an endless space where information can accumulate infinitely in conveniently transferable packets. Many of the restrictions other media have for the type of material that can be used are invalid on the web, as (almost) everything can be digitized: museum databases storing millions of records from collections from around the globe will attest to that.

At the moment, there are limitations for web typography, and the designer will often have to decide whether to use fonts which are most likely to be available in a general user's computer, or to find workarounds to be able to display less common fonts (in this area, a number of developments are under way, such as the CSS3 font tag). Likewise, the heavy use of photographic material, such as that covering the background of a website, can lead to an increase in downloading times and therefore to a less satisfying experience for users.

Static pages generally have institutional 'branding', the creation of a distinctive image for the museum, as their main function. Usual branding elements include graphics, slogans, logo and typography. These elements may be already available from a previously existing style guide that is adapted to meet the website's goals and reach its online target audience. Such graphic elements and slogans are likely to be the product of collaboration between the institution and a professional marketing or design agency that attempts to create a consistent image across print, on-site and on-line experiences.

The MOL maintains a consistent image across print, web and mobile media, yet profits from the strengths of each. In print, the museum can make use of full size and full colour images to show the venue. Online services and more detailed information can be offered, while for mobiles, the MOL has launched applications that help people to locate the museum and navigate the area.

If, however, the main purpose of the website is become a hub where the community can find out about upcoming events and temporary exhibitions, or visit the museum's collection, or there is a need to have a system that is easy to update frequently, a dynamic website is needed.

It has been historically difficult for designers and programmers to achieve a consistent functionality and display of pages across all browsers and operating systems. This chaotic situation emerged from each browser vendor implementing its own way of interpreting the various scripting languages, HTML and CSS markup, and changing these interpretations with every new version of their browsers. It was often the case that developers had to create copies of pages, each one catering for the needs of a particular browser, and then find ways in which to identify the client's browser and thus present the correct page. It was also likely that a website that worked well in current versions of browsers would not be compatible with future versions.

To improve this situation, the World Wide Web Consortium (W3C), an international organization with members from academia, government and business led by Tim Berners-Lee, the creator of the World Wide Web, has a mission to develop standards for the web.

Currently, the W3C recommends that the various elements of a website be divided into separate documents to deal with structure, form and functionality. For static pages, the structure would be written in HTML and/or XML (extensible markup language); the form would be handled through CSS (cascading style sheets); and finally the functionality would be written in languages such as JavaScript. These can be separate documents linked together in the HTML document, or they can be snippets of code inserted in a single HTML document.

A similar division into separate documents for structure, form and functionality applies to dynamic pages, although here the hierarchies of documents can get very complex. In a CMS it is common to find a large number of folders with files separated by type of function (for instance, a folder for files dealing with language localization, and another for files dealing with user profiles and so on).

Another important aspect that the W3C is interested in is accessibility and how to make browsing the web an effective and enjoyable experience for anyone. The W3C has therefore established the Web Accessibility Initiative (WAI) to create more inclusive standards for people with disabilities.

Through the WAI, the W3C has developed Web Content Accessibility Guidelines (WCAG) in which it recommends that web content be designed to be 'perceivable, operable, understandable and robust' (W3C 2008). 'Perceivable' means that the content cannot be invisible to the user's senses; 'operable' means that the website should not require the user to do an operation she cannot perform; 'understandable' means that developers should ensure that the information cannot be beyond the user's understanding (language, wording, level of complexity); and 'robust' refers to forward-compatibility, that is, that the webpage should be usable even with upcoming technologies (see W3C 2008).

The next chapter presents a series of examples where discussions about the technologies covered in this overview are expanded, with more philosophical aspects being covered.

Chapter 5

A Survey of Museum Social Media

This chapter provides a broad overview of the various ways in which museums are harnessing social media to engage audiences. The focus is on approaches to blogging, user-generated content and social network sites where visitors are invited to participate in information processing. In the next two chapters, we will discuss in detail two cases, the Museum of London and the Museum of World Culture, where the theoretical framework provided in the previous chapters will be applied in full. The purpose of this chapter is to provide the reader with a taste of the many possibilities offered by social media for museum work, without attempting to present an exhaustive account.

Blogs: Backstage Access and Dialogue with Curators

Museum blogs often show museum curators and their preferred objects, thus allowing access to specialized museum staff. One of the most important aspects of blogs is that they may provide opportunities for user participation through commenting as a form of asynchronous dialogue. For some authors, the commenting feature allows blogs to become spaces for debate, in this way helping 'democratize public debate, even reinvigorate the public sphere' (Garden 2012).

Blogs (or weblogs) are websites with dated content arranged in reverse chronological order, often written in a personal and informal manner, which have as antecedents the diary and the nautical log (Drotner and Schrøder 2013; Walker Rettberg 2003, 2008). Walker Rettberg groups blogs into three general categories: personal blogs, filter blogs and topic-driven blogs.

The personal blog is a diary, a form of ongoing autobiography and repository of thoughts and intimate events. In relation to the personal voice blog categorization, blogs started as personal diaries, and it is still expected that the blog will feature not an anonymous corporate voice but the personal voice and opinions of the blogger. However, museum bloggers are obliged to constantly remind themselves that what they write will inevitably be associated with the museum (Mosoddik 2009b). The Museum of London blog we will discuss in upcoming chapters shows the challenges that museums face in how to keep the personal touch while also providing access to expert insight into the workings of the institution or a specific field.

Nick Moyes from the Derby Museum and Art Gallery discusses the voice that museums may adopt in their blogs as 'Informed but Informal; Human and sometimes Humorous; Friendly but not Flippant; Engaging but not Erudite; neither Corporate nor Trivial; Questioning but not Querulous; Respectful and Realistic' (Moyes 2011). For him, it is key to acknowledge that this friendly tone might lead to mistakes or misunderstanding, and that staff have to 'know that content posted online is impossible to remove entirely, so we must be willing and able to respond quickly to criticism' (Moyes 2011).

There are other ways to group blogs, such as the one offered by Nina Simon (2007) in her Museum 2.0 blog. Simon uses the categories of 'Institutional Info Blog', 'Aggregate Content Blog' and 'Community Content Blog'.

In the 'Institutional Info Blog', the focus is on providing information about events, so the whole blog works more like a calendar than like a diary.

Simon defines 'Aggregate Content Blog' as one that gathers together bits of content from the main site as well as from elsewhere on the web in order to lead visitors to full stories at the main website or just present them with interesting information, like a navigational aid with promos of the 'best of'. For example, the Science Museum's blog 'Stories from the stores' works as an aggregator blog in that it presents objects from the collection, accompanied with more information about their history as well as about their location in the museum.

Finally, the 'Community Content Blog' has as its goal to encourage the community to post on the blog. Simon points out that these types of initiatives require a lot of effort to build a real community around the blog. They also demand a lot of time in setting up the appropriate permissions structure to keep the content safe from spammers and abuse. The Brooklyn Museum maintains a community blog, in which museum staff and guest bloggers provide content. Visitors are also encouraged to participate by leaving comments.

Other categories identified by Simon include the 'Specialized Content Blog' and the 'Personal Voice Blog', very much like Walker Rettberg's personal and topic-driven categories.

Below are some concrete examples of museum blogs.

Topic-Driven Blogs: Palaeo Manchester and Fresh + New(er)

The topic-driven blog is centred on current issues or specific areas of interest, such as the political blogs, environmental, hobby blogs, etc. (Rettberg 2008). One common approach is to create a periodically updated 'special object' blog. An object might be displayed because of its broad popularity, because it is too fragile to have on display, or because it is not well known. The MOL Docklands' 'Object of the month' and the Powerhouse Museum's 'Object of the week' are such types of page. At the Powerhouse Museum, the curators who blog choose their favourite objects, while at the MOL Docklands objects are related to an ongoing temporary exhibition. The use of blogs gives density to what goes on behind the scenes in an unobtrusive fashion. In both the expert insight and special object approaches, comments allow for a two-way model of communication.

A second approach is to combine collections with backstage access to the workings of the museum. An example of a topic-driven museum blog is David Gelsthorpe's 'Palaeo Manchester', a blog for the Manchester Museum. The blog has been running since 2008, and it was set up to provide visitors with backstage access to Gelsthorpe's work as curator of the Earth Collections of the museum. A typical post in this blog will discuss the latest additions to the museum's natural history collection, or will explain the history of some of the collections the author is working on. In addition, Gelsthorpe allows volunteers to contribute with guest posts, where they will for instance explain what is involved in conservation work. Dialogue via comments show visitors wanting to know details about specimen identification procedures, and also staff from other institutions asking Gelsthorpe for expert advice on literature and on technical issues.

The following example shows the type of dialogue taking place with the general public:

> Hallmark Hotel Derby, on June 27, 2012 at 4:20 pm said:
>
> It always fascinates me how you know its a Cochroach can you DNA test it because as it looks it could be anything. It looks more like a bird to me
>
> David Gelsthorpe, on July 2, 2012 at 7:20 am said:
>
> Hi, Good question, but unfortunately DNA doesn't get preserved when the fossil is this old. The main reason we know it's a cockroach is that we can closely compare the features of the wings and head to modern cockroaches and they are extremely similar. David (Gelsthorpe 2012b)

Gelsthorpe replies in this post with a thorough answer that is nevertheless easy to understand for any level of expertise. In an example of a live dialogue (an arranged Q & A session) with museum staff from other institutions, his reply is more technical:

> enlightenmentderbyshire, on May 22, 2012 at 1:37 pm said:
> Some of our Geology volunteers last week were keen to acid test some specimens in our collection. Obviously there will be health & safety implications for the volunteers but with regards to the collections, do you recommend acid texting (testing) museum specimens? . . .
> David Gelsthorpe, on May 22, 2012 at 1:49 pm said:
> Hello, my advice would be to avoid damaging specimens unless absolutely necessary. First check the shape of the crystals (calcite rhombohedral and quartz diamond shaped) and other properties like lustre. There is some more information here http://www.mindat.org/min-859.html and http://www.mindat.org/min-3337.html, but Wikipedia is a good place to start. You should be able to be get a confident identification without acid. Hope this helps, David (Gelsthorpe 2012a)

Another topic-driven blog is Seb Chan's 'Fresh + New(er)', which presents discussions and thoughts about technology and digital media in museums. The focus is on the details of deploying all kinds of technology-based physical exhibitions and web services. An example of a dialogue about the idea of '8-bit versions of history' in digital collection records (posted in March 2013) illustrates how Chan, while answering comments, also invites further dialogue:

> Ellice Engdahl • 3 months ago
> Thanks for the great post – this discussion is similar to one our institution has been having recently as well. I'm very curious to know more about the new fields you're considering adding and why you think those might be the key toward higher 'narrative potential'.
> sebchan Ellice Engdahl • 3 months ago
> we're not settled on it yet but we're looking at fields that more explicitly explore use/user and intent – perhaps more akin to the narratives of significance in other institutions (e.g. http://www.environment.gov.au/. . . – but reduced to set of thesauri. A lot of this has to do with institutional positioning – how is a design museum different from an art museum, and a history museum? what is the specific lens used to interpret and describe? how does cataloguing and the systems used for it bring an inherent framing? (Chan 2013)

Unlike Gelsthorpe, who gives clear and definitive answers to questions, Chan is much more speculative and inviting in order to encourage long(er) conversations with his readers. In this sense, however, Chan seems to be talking mostly to the specialized museum blogging staff audience, while Gelsthorpe seeks to address a much broader set of stakeholders.

Providing opportunities for dialogue through blogs helps the museum to gain an insight into audiences. For example, Chan described in his Fresh +

New(er) blog a visit that Wikimedia Australia made to the Powerhouse. The post described not only how Wikipedians have been granted access to the museum, but also how Powerhouse museum officials benefited from the opportunity to see 'behind the scenes' how Wikipedians worked together. Chan summarized: 'As we learnt about how Wikipedia editors think about how to document and improve articles in Wikipedia, our Museum staff spoke of how we document, classify and research. Unsurprisingly between the Wikipedians and the Museum staff we found a lot of common ground' (Chan 2009).

An important aspect of this kind of backstage or behind the scenes blog is that it helps to make the museum more personal, giving a face and a voice to staff. Thus, a second goal of blogs is to strengthen trust between museum and community. By letting audiences look at the issues that make up museum practice, such as the hurdles that have to be overcome when planning an exhibition or the concerns museums have in relation to their collections or their work in the community, the museum can garner support from the community for its activities, for example through donations, visits, voluntary work, etc. However, this trust building means that museums have to be even more careful with the tone used and the information released through the blog. In all, a key problem is how to avoid making blogs merely a public relations tool. Using the blog primarily for marketing can potentially degrade its credibility. If the museum predominantly 'pushes' information to users, or is late in responding to comments or acknowledging the contributions of online visitors, the public may feel as if the implementation of social media services is no more than a marketing gimmick void of any genuine wish to engage.

Filter Blogs: The Brooklyn Museum's Posse Tagging Service

The filter blog has as its function to point visitors to other useful resources, like a human aggregation service. Examples of aggregator websites include services such as Delicious, Digg, StumbleUpon and the academia oriented CiteULike, which allow users to organize and rank their bookmarks and preferred sites while also making it possible to share these with others, producing what has been called a 'user-generated filtering' of the Internet.

Another way of approaching filtering and aggregation is by using tags (free labels created by the public) and folksonomies (taxonomies created by users). For example, Delicious users can share a bookmark and tag it. The service shows at the side of each bookmark how many people have shared it, producing in this way a ranking of user-recommended online resources. Other 'aggregators' and filtering tools can collect lists of RSS feeds. RSS (which stands for Rich Site Summary for version 1.0 and Really Simple Syndication for version 2.0 of the technical specification) are updated regularly files that contain a summary of content and its metadata. Users can subscribe to feeds that automatically update when new content is available on a website. Some of the tools used to read RSS feeds include Bloglines and Google Reader.

The Brooklyn Museum allows users to tag their collections through their Posse Tagging Service. The tags are checked by the public, which can recommend a particular tag to be removed because of its irrelevance.

The development of mechanisms for Posse is ongoing. For example, after seven months of running, the service had provided almost 59,000 tags contributed by registered users and over 7,000 tags contributed by anonymous users, together with the almost 4,000 created automatically by the system. Bernstein describes how registered users in the Posse service provided the best tags in terms of quantity and quality, but she also talks about how they ran into some issues with anonymous tagging. While 94 per cent of the anonymous tags were valuable, at least 6 per cent were pranks, including tags such as 'how long will it take you to delete this tag' and 'are you going to block me' (Bernstein 2009). As a solution to the problem, the museum deployed a second tagging game, 'Freeze Tag!', which allowed registered users to veto anonymous tags (this had previously only been done by system administrators). The idea is to harness the 'Wisdom of Crowds', where a collective decision resulting from the aggregation of independent decisions is deemed to be more accurate than the decisions of a single individual, even if this individual is officially part of the organization. The example is interesting in that it is more permissible to classify information online through the structural involvement of audiences, in a more democratic process. It would be hard to imagine a curator allowing two random volunteers at the museum to veto the label of an object! In any case, interesting possibilities emerge on how or whether the democratizing practices taking place online (which in many ways are driven by the sheer amount of information having to be managed) will make it into the management of physical collections.

Social Network Sites and the Creative Reworking of Collections

On the topic of the democratizing potential of new technologies and phenomena such as social network sites, Yochai Benkler talks about how the web is changing our sense of personal advocacy (Benkler 2006), about how people now understand that they can do things in the world together and in loose association, and in fact have an effect on their surroundings, in contrast to the previous sense that people were fighting against a world that would not move. Benkler argues, however, that there is a tension between social actors that push for the rationalization and generalization of systems of control throughout society (technical, bureaucratic, economic, etc.) and social actors that defend an ideal of individual freedom. These systems of control are ways of improving material welfare and the effectiveness of large collectives. This happens through the muting of human agency and the structuring and harnessing of human action into well-designed and predictably effective outcomes. In opposition to this is the idea that personal freedom is valuable and conductive to innovation, and that these systems of control might in fact block the innovative process. Benkler asks, however, whether there are some relationships of authority that should be maintained, as for example the teacher–student relationship.

David Reed has also dealt with the social web and the expansion of communication technologies, touching in particular on the issue of value and social capital (Reed 2002). For Reed,

> what's important in a network changes as the network scale shifts. In a network dominated by linear connectivity value growth, the content is what holds value because there are a small number of sources (publishers or makers) of content that every user selects from. The sources compete for users based on the value of their content (published stories, published images, standardized consumer goods). As the network scales up, transactions become central. The things that are traded in transactions (email, money, securities, contracted services) are what hold value. With an even larger network, a group forming network law dominates, and the central role is filled by jointly constructed value (such as specialized newsgroups, joint responses to requests, gossip, etc.). (Reed 2002)

These ideas of social capital lie at the very heart of Social Network Sites (SNS). These are web-based services that allow their users to create public or semi-public profiles and use these to create lists of other users with whom they share a connection, with the possibility of making their networks visible to themselves and also, with various degrees of access, to the public. These technologies also allow for communication between members of a network, with various degrees of control and privacy (boyd 2004; Ellison 2007). Hinton and Hjorth note that in SNS, 'relationships are geographically and socially oriented towards the local' (2013: 44). They refer to the results found by Parks (2011) when investigating SNS as virtual communities, when he discovered that the majority of users were using SNS to reinforce existing online relations. Hinton and Hjorth build upon this research to argue that SNS reveal how intimate connections may be the most important to users, so that instead of looking at the size of a network, it may be more interesting to look at the quality of the connections in the network.

The various SNS use different metaphors for the ways in which they model relations (and also their perceived strength). For example, Facebook concentrates on friendship and family, while LinkedIn is about careers, and Academia.edu is built to support scholarly networks. Each social network platform will attract users (and uses) that fit with these metaphors, and it is important for museums to understand the differences.

One example of an SNS in a museum context is the Brooklyn Museum's Facebook page. This page displays updates about museum activities, including the latest exhibitions, artists and upcoming events. The page helps to distribute posts from the museum's blog to networks on Facebook that do not necessarily subscribe directly to the blog itself, thus serving as an invitation to visit the museum's website.

Another example is the now closed Brooklyn Museum's ArtShare Facebook application. ArtShare was the product of collaboration between the Brooklyn Museum, other cultural institutions and the general public who came together to create a database of works hosted at the Brooklyn Museum's server. This database was disseminated through a Facebook application.

With the ArtShare application, users could display selected artwork in their Facebook profiles, thereby 'sharing' the works with their Facebook friends. Instead of focusing on the single user's experience, as the silence surrounding a visit to an art museum could sometimes suggest, the application tried to model art collections online as something to be talked about and shared.

The application raised some interesting issues in relation to copyright. Some users contributed Van Gogh's 'Sunflowers' through the 'upload yourself' function of the application. Although this upload did not break copyright in the US – as the artist has been dead for more than seventy years, the artist, and not the museum, is the copyright holder, and photographs of two-dimensional artwork cannot have copyright themselves in the US because they do not meet the criterion of originality – the question remains as to whether users could be uploading material that would be breaking copyright.

This was an important question for the Brooklyn Museum with regard to liability. A comment related to copyright was posted at the Brooklyn Museum's website: the user asked whether there were copyright issues emerging from the fact that all the photographs of artwork belonging to other institutions were being hosted on the Brooklyn Museum's server. The response from Shelley Bernstein, in charge of the application and of the Brooklyn Museum's web services, was that the museum had 'specifically asked permission from the copyright holder if we didn't have an existing agreement that allowed for such use' (when the artwork was part of the Brooklyn Museum's collection) and that 'Each participating institution has the responsibility to deal with this issue for any images it shares, per the app's Terms of Service' (see Bernstein 2008).

These examples bring us to the issue of creative reworking of collections. Creative reworking goes beyond access, provision or consultation, and focuses on promoting structural involvement. Using social media, museums allow users to create their own exhibitions through open databases that can be personalized by users to create their own collections, input interpretations or combine various sources, and publicly share their results, either independently or through the museum's own website.

Creative reworkings often take the form of 'mashups', which refers to the process of putting together various social media tools and services to produce new applications. For instance, a museum might mix Google Maps with Flickr to produce a guided tour for its users. To achieve this, the service provider must have released an API (application programming interface), which describes how the information on the service database can be accessed. A number of museums (MOL, Powerhouse Museum, Brooklyn Museum) have started to make their databases available for mashup creators through the release of APIs.

For example, the Powerhouse Museum offers users a Flickr and Google mashup to navigate photographs in their collection. Two different service providers (Flickr and Google) are combined to create a rich map, where users can find more information about historical buildings in Sydney. A mashup gives archival material new life due to its direct placing in a contemporary context.

With mashups, museums attempt to support users as producers, and to tap into the knowledge of audiences. Bringing such knowledge into the museum is key to connecting the past that collections often represent with the present and future of which they are also part.

Mashups often rely heavily on media sharing sites, which are a more specialized type of social networking site. Media sharing sites offer users both the space and tools to share different types of visual and audio file formats. They also allow users to rate and comment their media (Drotner and Schrøder 2013). They are usually distinguished by the type of format that is shared, such as for instance video sharing sites (YouTube, Vimeo, Blip.tv), photo sharing sites (Flickr, Picasa, Kodak EasyShare Gallery), and audio sharing sites (ccMixter). Media sharing sites are the epitome of 'produsage', a term coined by Axel Bruns (2008) to denote the changes in the creation of media that meant that users continued to consume, but, most importantly, increasingly began to make, audio-visual media.

Podcasting, a form of media sharing that allows users to subscribe to content and receive updates in applications such as iTunes, has been used by museums to feature artists, curators, or other experts. Podcasts can be thought of as weekly radio programmes that people can subscribe to. One example is Radio Web MACBA, the Barcelona Contemporary Art Museum's repository of podcasts of interviews with artists and audio features about exhibitions. As well as presenting a collection of all events held at the museum in the form of audio files, it also provides PDF versions, and even includes additional material not featured in the original event.

The Museum of London also offers podcasts in iTunes, such as the series 'Podcasts from the past'. One of the goals of providing the podcasts is to make the museum accessible for visually impaired audiences. The podcasts themselves were the product of one of the museum's social inclusion initiatives, where a group of unemployed adults was given the opportunity to receive training in audio production and scriptwriting.

Through social media, museums can encourage users to contribute with content that adds a new layer of interpretation to a collection. For instance, the Auckland Museum launched an initiative for children entitled 'I am making movies 2'. The projects included the 'Museum Remix Challenge', where students were invited to take images from the collection selected by the museum, and bring them to life through digital motion effects.

The Torrance Art Museum is one of a number of art museums and galleries that host online exhibitions with user input. In 2007, artist Ryan Gallagher exhibited 'Camera Tossing Live' at the Command-Z show. The project consisted of a Flickr account that allowed users to upload their own images, which were simultaneously displayed at the museum's galleries. The audience submitted more than 11,000 photos to a Flickr feed (Gallagher 2007). This process ran during the whole two-month period in which the exhibition was active in the museum space.

This example is interesting, not necessarily because the artwork is very good, but because of the choice the museum made to use an existing site or software (Flickr) rather than develop its own software. For those who have not experienced Flickr before, it is a site or server where anyone, free of charge or for a modest sum, can gain access to editing and presentation tools, and can create a gallery that friends or the general public may add images to related to the topic or event specified.

One of the projects through which Flickr has made itself known in the museum world is the 'Commons'. This is a service provided by Flickr to participating institutions that allows them to post their photographs and let the public tag or comment on them freely. The idea is to encourage users to contribute their knowledge so as to enhance understanding about the various photographs on display. As of January 2011, there are forty-six participating institutions in the Commons, including major museums, libraries and archives. Images posted in this service are either in the public domain or have the copyright status of 'No known copyright restrictions'.

An example of the kind of participation that Flickr has encouraged through the creation of the Commons and the release of an API is the 'Flickr Commons Explorer' created by Hinton and Whitelaw (2010), which provides a different way of navigating museum and library collections by creating visual maps between various keywords and associated images. It was developed in response to Mashup Australia, a competition run by the Australian government in the context of its Federal Government Gov2.0 Task Force (Hinton and Whitelaw 2010). The Flickr Commons Explorer, created without the support or involvement of either Flickr or any of the cultural institutions providing images, was meant as a research project into better interfaces for cultural material, and was released for free download online.

Some of these sites combine sharing with social networking tools, where users can rank content, comment, and add friends and links to lists of related content. 'Voicethreading' (from the company Voicethread, providing software for networked conversations), or commenting on others' content through audio, was one of the recent ways in which media sharing sites experimented with expanding the way in which people interacted around the files they uploaded. In 'coLAB', Nina Simon used the Voicethread service to explore new ways to incite people to engage in conversations about museums. The system let logged-in users leave comments in a variety of media, and worked as an enhanced collaborative space. In 2007 Simon launched an experiment in collaboration with Eric Siegel, director of NY Science. The aim was to open up for comments and suggestions the development of an exhibition on human enhancement technology (Human +).

In coLAB, asynchronous conversations took place around a node (the artefact). Each user photograph led to an audio file, written text or video about the object, or about what the other users were saying. In assessing the experiment, Simon found it very successful in terms of attracting participation from all over the world (131 cities, mostly in North America but also in South America, Europe, Australia, New Zealand and South Africa). The site had peak participation after a few days of launch, after which some problems with coherence started to emerge. As Simon discusses:

> The content was interesting, but not always what was asked for. Some (including the creators of the technology) found it varied and fascinating. But there was no easy way to spin off individual 'threads' of conversation on a single slide, so a divergent (interesting) point brought up by a couple people became hard to follow. The content stayed fairly surface-level, though many interesting comments, both personal and professional, were contributed. The purpose wasn't totally clear. While Eric and I actively responded to other contributors, I think we could have done better to give people explicit challenges or goals so they could apply themselves concretely to solving a problem. The problem given, related to collaboration, was somewhat open-ended and proved less appealing than the Human + controversies themselves. (Simon 2007)

In addition, users commented on the need for clearer user identification. Some visitors wanted to be able to check the background (professional interest in the topics and level of expertise) of the persons making comments. For Simon, a core aspect of the whole process became the balance between letting visitors contribute in their own way and with their own objectives or constraining them so as to get the results the promoters of the collaboration wanted. Another issue was how to create online spaces that could help to humanize remote collaboration, rather than dehumanizing the experience of talking together in groups (Simon 2007).

These types of services exploit the fact that there is the opportunity to have many-to-many asynchronous conversations online – conversations that might continue for as long as the topic is interesting to someone. This is very different to the types of experiences we had before the Internet, such as radio, where even when the show opened for comments from the public, the interaction could only take place synchronously. The fact is, however, that the same problems occur regardless of whether the conversation is synchronous or asynchronous. For instance, some users will want to dominate, too many voices will become noise, errors in fact-checking will creep in (e.g. blindly trusting an authority or expert voice), the creators of the interfaces may prefer certain types of outcomes over others, etc. These problems, however, are not restricted to online interaction, but are in effect challenges for any kind of collaborative process.

A final example of work that uses social media to include user-generated content in museum displays is the 'Væggen' project, originally Absalon.nu. When it started as Absalon.nu, the aim of the project was, on the one hand, to show city inhabitants the history of Copenhagen, and on the other, to let the public share their knowledge about the city. Upon its completion as

'Væggen', the project had evolved into a massive multitouch wall placed in the city centre, effectively bringing the museum to the streets.

In 'Væggen', users can explore Copenhagen's history by touching particular buildings on the interactive wall and map. They can then choose between personal stories, historical images and written documents about the city. The database is organized such that the public can add comments and stories. Væggen can also work as a navigation tool similar to 'what's on' (Copenhagen Museum Website 2012). Through the inclusion of social media as part of the interface, users are invited to upload their own images, which will later be on public display at the 12 x 2 metre public interactive wall.

'Væggen' is an example of blending virtual spaces seamlessly with the physical world. This is something that museums have fully embraced with the introduction of large multitouch displays in exhibitions.

Involving Users as Curators

The Digital New Zealand project is an interesting example of approaches to the distribution of curatorial responsibility to the public. The website allows users to create their own exhibitions or 'memory spaces' from material in a number of collections. The Digital New Zealand website attempts to act as a hub between institutions who hold collections or archives about New Zealand. It is as a searchable database that also provides an API to access the metadata for collections and archives, making it easy for others to build search tools, make remixes with the database and create mashups. Anyone from the general public or other institutions who wishes to explore how to make those collections more visible is welcome to use digitalnz.org. The project emerged as a response to the difficulties many New Zealand public and community organizations faced in making their content visible to New Zealanders amid the mass of international content available on the Internet. In 2007 it received four years' government funding as a flagship action of the New Zealand Digital Content Strategy, Creating a Digital New Zealand.

As in the case of ArtShare, however, Digital New Zealand brings up issues of copyright. It responds to the challenges in this way:

> We've also set up a DigitalNZ Kete for organisations to upload any content that doesn't have a home elsewhere on the web. Kete (basket in Māori) is an open source community repository system. . . One of the great things about Kete is the built-in Creative Commons licensing structure – our 'technology' (in the sense of tools) for dealing with the issue of uncertainty around what people can and can't do with content. We extended this by adding in the 'No known copyright restrictions'

> statement as well – taking a leaf out of the wonderful Flickr Commons book. A number of Aotearoa People's Network Libraries are using Kete to gather community treasures and we are including that content in DigitalNZ as it comes online. (Digital New Zealand website)

Amongst the examples of possible applications that can be made by using the Digital New Zealand API is a website which demonstrates new ways of searching through the images available. This particular example is used to illustrate the possibilities of the Digital New Zealand API. Clicking on an image leads to a new window where users can either see or suggest a location in New Zealand for the image. By inviting the general public to collaborate in this way, the site helps to harvest information (such as knowledge about geographical location) that would probably be harder for curators to gather. The website also makes use of services such as Google Maps to provide means for geotagging the images.

These types of mashups in museum websites can be taken a step further by inviting the public to take part in an exhibition's creation process, therefore effectively providing them with access to the role of curators. Such was the case with the Brooklyn Museum's more adventurous 'Click! A Crowd-Curated Exhibition', an experiment in audience participation through the use of social media.

In this 2008 exhibition, Shelley Bernstein, in charge of the museum's web technologies, invited artists to submit images electronically under the topic of 'The Changing Faces of Brooklyn', together with an artist statement. The public was then asked to vote for the best images using a custom evaluation tool, which included a tool to declare one's own level of expertise, from 'none' to 'expert'. The public was asked to take into consideration aesthetics, the photographic techniques used, and relevance to the theme. Each anonymous evaluator rated his or her own knowledge of art on a scale from none to some, more than a little, above average, and expert. Respondents were divided approximately equally between these categories. 3,344 people made 410,089 evaluations, viewing each image approximately 1,054 times. Each person looked at an average of 135 works (this rose to 289 if they had submitted a work themselves), and of the 575 who evaluated every photo, 163 were participating artists. The top 20 per cent of the images curated by the crowd were installed in the physical gallery. Five of the top ten photographs selected by experts were also selected by those who rated themselves at the opposite end of the scale as having no knowledge of art at all. An interactive visualization of the top ten for each level of knowledge showed considerable overlap across all levels (Brooklyn Museum 2008). A heated discussion took place at a public seminar about the exhibition, where curators, organizers and the public debated the hypothesis that non-expert crowds can evaluate artistic quality at a level comparable to that of individual experts (Brooklyn Museum 2008). The works amongst the top 20 per cent were later displayed at a temporary exhibition, and were also displayed online. Users visiting the online version of the exhibition could look at the statistics of evaluations, with an option to look according to the self-rating of evaluators.

The idea behind the exhibition was to harness the power of 'collective intelligence'. The exhibition borrowed from 'The Wisdom of Crowds', a book written by James Surowiecki, who also acted as one of the exhibition consultants. 'Click!' was a daring exercise in 'democratizing curatorship'. The exhibition received some criticism because it seemed to abandon the trained eye of the curator in favour of the popular vote. Surowiecki responded by saying that

> when you look at the top ten favourites of voters as a whole, and at the favourites of the different subgroups, what you find is that they're actually not that different. Many photographs show up on all or most of the lists. To me, this is really the most striking result of the show, because it suggests (though it doesn't prove) that at least in some mediums, the gap between popular and elite taste may be smaller than we think. (Surowiecki 2008)

It could be further argued that the evaluation tool was not designed to be concerned with voting for a favourite, but rather about showing the process of curatorship and exploring the similarities and differences in the taste and evaluation of different groups. For Kevin Stayton, Chief Curator at the Brooklyn Museum, this exhibition was thought provoking for the following reasons:

> an exhibition that was only about the changing faces of Brooklyn in photography might be interesting, but an exhibition that is also about the nature of selection, and all the questions it raises about taste, background, interpretation – and a myriad of other issues – creates a richer discourse. In Click! the theme of the work and the selection and installation process complement and mutually reinforce one another, forming a compelling snapshot of who we are and how we chose. (Stayton)

In any case, the exhibition was a helpful way to measure how far to go in the process of opening the Brooklyn Museum to broader public participation, and to assess where the limits might stand in the future.

Virtual Visits

An important keyword for the web is 'virtual'. Often linked to gaming, virtual spaces offer 3D renderings of worlds both real and imagined. Virtuality is attractive to museums as it allows them to explore ways of conveying the real physical space of the museum to remote users. At the same time, it can be a way of giving some sense of 'physical reality' to museums that in fact only exist online.

SecondLife is amongst the most well-known services used to create virtual museums. Educational and cultural institutions have created spaces to hold conferences and exhibitions with the tools offered at the site. The International Spaceflight Museum, for example, is a volunteer created virtual museum about space aeronautics, hosted in SecondLife. The museum also has a website that links to the SecondLife site, blogs, and further information about the museum.

Another museum which exists only in the Internet is the Museu da Pessoa, dedicated to collecting life histories. Established in 1992 in Sao Paulo, Brazil, the museum has a very long history of using digital media to communicate life histories (Matos et al. 1999). The philosophical goal of the museum when it was launched was 'to create the possibility of preserving, and turning it into an information source, the life history of each and every person' (Matos et al., 1999), where no narrative has more 'historic value' or 'truthfulness' than another. Choosing digital as the medium for this museum came from the versatility of digital records, which could easily be used to register audio, video, photography and texts in a unified database. Interestingly, and long before the emergence of Facebook and the more rampant commercialization of personal information, the creators of Museu da Pessoa were juggling with ideas about how to turn a profit from their effort, so as to be able to maintain the project. For this, they created a series of products emerging from their collection, from products for company anniversary celebrations to team training products for Human Resources departments (Matos et al. 1999). In 1996, the museum went online, and after a reassessment of its mission and methods, a decision was made to turn the museum into an entirely online offering, as well as to make the best use of the World Wide Web to attract new stories. By 1998, the museum was collecting 15 histories per week and receiving 430 visits per day (Matos et al. 1999). The Museu da Pessoa was also innovative in that it created a platform for people to post their own stories online, a kind of curated blogging platform (as many of the stories took the form of diaries), and in this sense it pointed towards the direction the web would take later on with social media. Today, the museum continues to make use of the concept of digital storytelling, aiming at empowering people by allowing them to use digital media to share with others their memories. When reflecting upon the value of the museum in a more traditional sense, the creators argue that they collect histories of the quotidian, which have multiple benefits for those who read them (e.g. very detailed personal narratives intertwined with the history of a city or a country) and especially for those who write them: 'At last, for short, that was a little of my life. I hope that those who are patient enough to read it, like it. I liked, a great deal, of having lived all that, and the fact of having written it made me remember many things, and this is wonderful' (Leandro Francisco Ferreira, student, born in 1977; Matos et al. 1999).

The Adobe Museum of Digital Media, partly PR campaign and partly museum, is another virtual 'museum', backed by Adobe, makers of media production software. Working as a marketing tool, this virtual museum presents the company's latest technology in a series of rich audio-visual experiences. In this virtual museum, the emphasis is on an emotional immersive experience, based on cinematic sequences of blended live action with digital artwork. Upon entering, the visitor is presented with a menu of exhibits to browse, together with a statement from the museum's curator, Tom Eccles. The museum presents selected digital artists and digital media pioneers such as John Maeda, who offers an audio-visual history of the craft of digital media. Interestingly, while the museum in itself is all about a mix of the physical and the virtual that only occurs on the screen, interventions such as Maeda's serve to remind visitors of the importance of the material world outside of digitality.

One of the most recent examples of attempts to recreate the museum visit virtually is Google Art Project, a collaboration between Google and seventeen international museums. Participating institutions include the Metropolitan Museum in New York, the Hermitage in St Petersburg, the Uffizi in Florence, the Museum of Modern Art in New York and the National Gallery in London. The idea is to make online visitors feel as if they were walking through the galleries of these museums, using Google Street View technology. The virtual visit allows access to high-resolution images of more than 1,060 works of art, with selected artworks in Gigapixel format that allow visitors to see even the cracks in oil paints.

Critics of the project point out that the meagre amount of images available means an excessive cherry-picking by Google, which is contrary to the actual freedom visitors experience when they go to the real gallery and are able to choose amongst hundreds of artworks which one they want to contemplate.

In an article in the *Telegraph*, Alastair Sooke expresses his concerns about Google's project:

> The worrying implication of [Google] Art Project is that in the future there will no longer be any need to visit a museum. According to Google's own press release, an image containing around 7 billion pixels allows the viewer 'to study details of the brushwork and patina beyond that possible with the naked eye [sic]'. If Google's technology trumps the powers of the naked eye, then why bother with reality at all? What can be gleaned from looking at Holbein's Ambassadors on a trip to the National Gallery that cannot be enhanced by looking at a simulacrum of it on Google Art Project?
>
> This is a profound philosophical problem, but my instinct is that I would much prefer to visit the National Gallery to see Holbein's Ambassadors with my own eyes than to examine it through Google's 'super-high-resolution' prism. Every time. Google Art Project is a wonderful resource, but it is no substitute for the experiencing of looking at art for real. (Sooke 2011)

According to Google's press release as quoted by this commentator, Google Art Project acts as a microscope to the artworks, opening new avenues of exploration via digital means. The digital resource enhances the experiencing by providing means through which a visitor (modelled as a potential expert) can dive even deeper. For an expert needing to access the artwork remotely, the potential benefits are clear. However, for a non-expert, 7 billion pixels may not necessarily enhance their understanding of the cultural resource.

For Sooke, representative of mass media's take on museums, when the digital resource becomes a replacement of the original (Google's claims of providing more detail than the naked eye), the resource itself is at risk. What is lost is the 'experience of the museum', to which the commentator attaches high value. A view of museums as places of contemplation is apparent in this comment. However, digital access to the galleries may permit other types of experiences of the museum (for instance, the classroom). As long as it does not in fact replace museums (as the commentator fears), Google Art Project in no way prevents people who have access to the physical museum from going. In any case, the contention that it will deter visitors from travelling to the museum (or for that matter, encourage them) has to be addressed through a study of the audience responses before anything can be concluded about it. However, the project can serve as support for new practices around collections, as many other virtual museum projects have set out to do before.

A more immediate concern would be how long and under what limitations the images will remain in Google Art Project, in comparison to virtual museum projects that have been led by museums themselves. A final question for the museum sector that Google's intervention brings to the fore is whether outsourcing the technical expertise to companies such as this is a good arrangement in the long-term strategy of the museum sector, or whether the sector should invest in attracting (and educating) professionals that have both curatorial and technical skills.

Using Social Media for Heritage Activism

The impact of social media on political movements around the world is well known. While the Arab Spring is certainly the best-known example of social media's use for empowerment and activism, social media is supporting less publicized yet equally important initiatives in heritage.

One example is the 2010 'Memorias Disruptivas' (Disruptive Memories) encounter, organized by the Red Conceptualismos del Sur (Concepts from the South Network) and Museo Reina Sofia in Spain. The encounter harnessed the power of blogging to initiate debates around the expropriation of Latin American art collections and the patrimonialization of visual culture associated with the social movements in Latin America during the nineteenth century. More than 100 researchers and artists met at these encounters and participated in the off- and online discussions (Ministerio de Cultura de España 2011). The goal was to discuss processes of national identity that privileged certain narratives while using silence to remove other unwanted parts of history (for instance, Indigenous or Black history).

During the encounter, street interventions also took place, such as the one organized in Madrid by the Peruvian Transvestite Museum. The museum's representatives took their message to Madrid's streets through the distribution of leaflets and the strategic placement of graffiti 'keywords' related to sexual discrimination. Other events involved Caribbean issues, for instance the political and social situation in Haiti. The series of events encouraged a critical look at colonial history and post-colonial relationships between Spain, Latin America and the Caribbean.

Overall, the project attempted to use social media and the Internet for political protest against the background of heritage conceived as an expression of the State's power. Such approaches to heritage are a hallmark of the sector in Latin America – one only has to be reminded of the 1972 Round Table in Santiago de Chile (ICOM 2010), where the role of heritage in sustainable development, identity and in politics more widely was a central topic.

In Conclusion

As seen in the examples above, social media enables museums to explore new ways in which to engage the public with artefacts. Some of these ways are passive, as when the user is guided through a tightly structured narrative, while some are more active, inviting visitors to provide their own content. Going a step further, museums can even use a public, open data approach and let the more technically savvy contributors propose alternative architectures of participation using the museum collection as the point of departure.

A number of issues related to ownership and copyright emerge, but, as shown, it is possible for museums to find ways to provide broader access within current frameworks and practices. In some cases, the push for growth in audience numbers is the sole motivation for the uptake of digital technologies, and can result in expensive efforts that do not necessarily add to the long-term challenges of preserving and enriching digital cultures. Once again museums are confronted with the need to redefine heritage, this time so that it can accommodate the digital. Social media services are blank canvases; much can be achieved, but it is important to bear in mind that these media can also be time consuming and not necessarily the best way to communicate the museum's message, or to establish solid links with the community.

The key challenge is for museums to attract new audiences but to do so because this contributes to the sustainability of their digital culture, and of the institutions created to preserve it, as well as the museum's mission, aims and programmes. In addition to contributing to the sustainability of heritage in the digital domain, social media and new technologies can be fruitfully used for the museum's social work in the community.

This chapter concludes the theoretical section of the book. The following case chapters will draw on the above discussions to present a closer look at combining possible foci of communication, issues of sustainability and questions of trust in analyses of specific cases. The next chapter focuses on social media as used in the website of a large museum, the Museum of London. Other cases include the Museum of World Culture, museums and galleries in Sydney and Panama City, The National Museum of Australia, and the Questacon National Science Centre.

Part III: Cases

Chapter 6

The Museum of London (MOL)

In this chapter, the DHS Framework is applied to the Museum of London (MOL). In recent years, the MOL has made important investments in institutional renewal that have included a restructuring and expansion of digital media activities. This analysis reveals the strategies used by the MOL for its goals of serving the community, maintaining the cultural resources (digital and physical) and enhancing the role of the institution. As will be seen, the MOL moves within a spectrum of open and closed approaches to online public engagement. Closed approaches serve to prevent various forms of data loss or corruption, and open approaches at times lack deep structural involvement from the public. Therefore, the analysis identifies a distinct threat to the sustainability of MOL's digital activities, due to a current failure in harnessing public engagement to aid in the enormous task of managing the MOL's rapidly growing digital resources.

Contexts: A Push for Learning, and Contemporary Culture

In the last decade, the MOL has gone through two major changes that have conditioned its use of online resources. The first is a shift to a deeper focus on education, prompted by a government push in this direction; the second is the redesign of the physical space, which involved the creation of twentieth-century galleries.

In 1997, Labour won the general election in the UK, following eighteen years of Conservative rule. According to Frazer Swift, in charge of the MOL's Clore Learning Centre, the new government's priority was education, which included reassessing the role of museums in supporting learning (Wu 2009). In 1997, David Anderson conducted research that looked at education provisioning in museums across the country. This resulted in a report entitled 'A Common Wealth: Museums in the Learning

Age'. Amongst the key points of the report was the idea that the concept of the museum needed to be expanded so that it would go beyond collections. Museums should also encompass their natural and cultural environments (Anderson and Britain 1997). In order to accomplish this, the report highlighted the need to strengthen the museum as an educational institution that engaged actively with its communities in lifelong learning partnerships (Anderson and Britain 1997).

In 2001, the 'Renaissance in the Regions' programme introduced a government initiative where key regional museums received additional funding to improve the quality of their exhibitions and educational programmes. A report on the programme stated that museums in England had 'an important part to play in education, learning, access, social inclusion, the regions, and the modernization of public services', yet in order to fulfil this role, their spaces need to be 'opened up for all to use in a creative way for learning, inspiration and enjoyment' (Evans et al. 2001).

The MOL was lead partner in the London region's 'London Museums Hub', therefore the Renaissance in the Regions programme heavily funded a rebuild of the museum's learning department. Swift explains the impact of these changes:

> The learning department duplicated in size in five years. . . Also Jack [Lohman, at the time the director of MOL] has been a strong advocate for learning in the organization, so with that kind of support and Jack's involvement, Renaissance in regions, government, all these things have come together and put us (the Clore Learning Centre) in a strong position in the organization. (Wu 2009)

The MOL also needed to respond to the Renaissance in the Region's call for more openness and dialogue in museum spaces. Swift commented:

> There's a much greater emphasis now on engaging learners interactively so rather than the museum being a teacher and just transmitting information, it's a two way process and we think much more about the learning needs of visitors and tailor what we do to their needs we tend to talk more about learning than education, education has connotations of instructions, whereas what we want to do is have a dialogue with people as opposed to being a formal didactic approach so we use lots of actors and storytellers and visitors doing things as opposed to people passively receiving. (Wu 2009)

A second important change at the MOL sprang from large investments in redesigning the museum's space. For a long time, the MOL had a gap in its galleries, as the history of the twentieth century was missing.

When Jack Lohman became director in 2001, he began work to include the twentieth century in the exhibition. Between 2002 and 2010, the

MOL went through a period of complete institutional renewal. For Cathy Ross, curator of the twentieth-century galleries, one of the keywords of the MOL's redesign was 'reinvention': beyond the physical structural work, the redesign also involved deep changes in institutional practices and in the culture of the organization (Wu 2009). The reinvention of organizational culture included the drafting of a new strategic plan, the Museum of London Strategic Objectives 2010–2013, which described a mission based on engagement, sharing, creating opportunities for learning, and extending the network of the museum.

To summarize, two contexts drive the MOL's current digital media activities: firstly, the government push for learning and the funding provided for the museum in this area; and secondly, the desire to connect with contemporary Londoners and global audiences, expressed via the inclusion of twentieth-century materials in both physical and online exhibitions. The first context requires the MOL to carefully monitor potential changes in government policy and legislation, and to make provisions so that if current funding diminishes, the museum will still be able to provide the now well-developed learning online services to the community. The sustainability of the digital investment in learning is therefore compromised by the dependence on government policies and funding. In the second context, given that it is the MOL's internal objective to present the twentieth century, it has a great deal of leeway in choosing how it will deliver those resources to its local and global audiences.

Stakeholders: Looking Inward and Outward

Beyond the educational mission, geared primarily at the local community, Ross explains that the resource that the museum tries to enhance online is the city of London itself (Wu 2009). There are two potential audiences for whom this resource is valuable: Londoners (the local, inward function of the museum) and the rest of the world (outward, London being a global and highly diverse capital). Ross states:

> Our whole story of London needed refreshment. The old galleries tell the story of London in quite an inward looking way: it was the story of the city, of the infrastructure, the roads, the search, the transport, very much looking inward. These galleries were done in the 1970s 80s and 90s so there were some stories that we are interested in today, like migration and identity, that were just not in there. We wanted to tell a new story of London with new emphasis on it, new points of interest . . . we have these two big narratives: London and the world and the other one is London and people, people coming to London from the world. In both

> of these we wanted very much to underline change, so we have got how London changes the world how the world changes London and how people change London and London changes people. (Wu 2009)

This interest in the inward and outward function of the physical galleries is mirrored online. Mosoddik explains how the MOL balances an array of potential uses and visitor profiles:

> Our site is not tailored for just one general visitor. There is the visitor, tourists, the researchers, academics, students who want to research and then we have other museums who want to find out what we are doing. It is four audiences rather than one. . . so each part is tailored towards different audiences. Our learning section would be very different from exhibition section, but our collection section is quite different, because that is for researchers. . . The whole site is not one audience: each part of the site has different voice for different audiences and needs. (Wu 2009)

Furthermore, the inward type of collections that the museum holds (artefacts from London) mean that it must actively seek out other channels to strengthen the desire to reach outward. This helps to clarify the choice made by the museum in using its website to showcase primarily its human expertise (which is composed of experts from all around the world): '(The blog helps) reach out to people as MOL employees and showcase the expertise within the MOL. We are not just about artefacts and gallery exhibition events, we are actually more than that: we are expertise. Every curator has an expertise that is valuable, and is showcasing that' (Wu 2009).

Artefacts in the collection are used primarily to bring experts and communities together. Collections exist for audiences and work as mediating experiences between curators and visitors as well as between generations across barriers of time and space. Cathy Ross states: 'We are not typical of London museums, we are not about collections of objects but about stories and every object has to be eloquent about the story of London. We have never been about collections of objects but about engagement and you may say that is the corporate culture' (Wu 2009).

As a social history museum, the MOL, looking beyond the individual aesthetic or historical value of an artefact, wishes to create an arrangement in which those artefacts help to communicate stories, as well as help to problematize these stories and the assumed meaning of objects. The MOL's website aims to bring people to the museum, to showcase its collections, exhibitions and events, and to break the boundaries both geographically and in terms of cultural diversity.

Beyond these overarching goals, however, each section of the MOL website is geared to a particular audience, and decisions about the main stakeholders for each section guide the website's design. For example, the 'Collections and Research' section is designed for academics; texts in the 'Schools' section must be comprehensible to an array of different age groups (Special Needs Students, K-12, Adults and Teachers) and so on.

From this discussion, the following groups are identified as participating in the network of stewardship towards the digital heritage MOL safeguards: curators, web managers, teachers, learners, researchers, Londoners, and global audiences. However, and as will be discussed in more detail below, it is mainly curators and teachers who collaborate (with web managers standing in the background to support their activities); Londoners and global audiences do not directly influence the digital media resources – the relationship is modelled so that it flows from the MOL to its audiences.

Digital Practices: Combining Open and Closed Approaches

The MOL began to have an online presence from the mid-1990s. The latest redesign took place in 2010, with changes include a rebranding, an increase in server capacity to expand the collections database, and the introduction of social media. The website has become the first place to display updates about events and exhibitions, and to report any news about the MOL. The MOL is in fact a large institution encompassing two museums and one research centre (Museum of London, the Museum of London Docklands and London Archaeological Archive and Research Centre). The website needs to cater for all three institutions.

Inside the Museum of London's own page, the visit starts with the institution-oriented sections 'What's on' and 'Visiting Us'. The collection-oriented section follows ('Collections & Research'), and finally, the website moves on to user-oriented sections ('Schools', 'Explore Online' and 'Get Involved'). In-depth analysis focuses on these last three sections.

'Schools' Section

The 'Schools' section of the MOL website is the fourth link in the top navigation. It contains a vast array of resources, several of which are geared to special groups and have been thought of as a way of making the collection as accessible as possible. The section also has a searchable calendar of events for visits conducted by museum officials for schools organized as a 'What's on' page. In addition, the MOL offers 'At your school' workshops and combined 'School and Museum' visits. More technologically prepared schools can make use of the videoconferencing offerings of the MOL.

The 'Schools' section initiates a more structurally participatory engagement with the website. Its focus is on catering for the needs of teachers and students, and also on providing ways of contacting the museum in case of even more specialized needs. This is visible through the main links in the section, which include 'Contact the Schools Team', and 'Teachers Network'. In the 'Teachers Network' link, the MOL promises that subscribers will have the opportunity to get involved in the development of sessions and resources. The MOL has a formal process of getting involved with the museum when the collaboration goes further than contributing temporary content. This procedure is well explained in this section, with a clear description of what it entails, how long the whole process would take (from six weeks to several months), and the kind of documentation that people wishing to contribute or start a collaborative project would need to provide.

'Explore Online' Section

From the 'Explore Online' section onwards, the MOL website starts incorporating more heavily the use of social media. The 'Explore Online' section connects the museum website to social network pages (Facebook and Twitter), and to mobile applications such as the London Streetmuseum app for Android and IPhone where users can select spots through their mobile's GPS and map, and superimpose archival photos upon the live street view through the mobile's camera.

In relation to the blogs, Bilkis Mosoddik, in charge of web services at the MOL, explains that it is still relatively hard for museum staff at the MOL to understand social media, the concept of blogging and the Internet, as staff are much more concerned with curating and showcasing the object in the physical space (Wu 2009). Mosoddik invested a large amount of her time explaining to curatorial staff that the Internet would not take away people from the museum, but would rather help bring them in and enhance their understanding of the value of the institution. The blog is a door through which people can see the 'behind the scenes' expertise that is required to run an exhibition.

Mosoddik points out that the blog is not meant to be the MOL corporate voice, but rather the individual voice of MOL employees. Certainly, employees represent the institution, but each blogger is allowed to have a different tone or voice. So far, the MOL has not had any problems with this policy (Wu 2009). In terms of the staff 'voice', there is a tacit agreement that staff should not publish information that can harm the museum. Some staff will input information themselves into a MOL blog, and the web team will act as moderator, alerting authors when they have to respond to comments from the public. The policy is to respond to everything, even if it is a negative comment, by thanking users for taking the time to say something about the MOL. A concern with transparency lies behind the decision not to delete any comment.

'Getting Involved' Section

The last link of the top navigation is the 'Getting Involved' section. The kinds of involvement offered vary from invitations to physical visits to the museum, to organizing competitions in which users can send in their own content and have it displayed on the museum's walls. The informational flow is mainly a one-way flow from museum to public.

However, the section also includes experiments with participation. One of the MOL's experiments showcased here is the London Street Photography exhibition, held in September 2011. This exhibition is a good case study to show the limits the MOL imposes on the general public's participation online: the ways of contributing to this exhibition were through a photographic competition open to the public, an invitation through Facebook and Twitter to choose or recommend music for the same exhibition's Spotify Playlist, or invitations to specific groups such as the *Big Issue* vendors to contribute photographs to the exhibition (the *Big Issue* is a magazine distributed by homeless and vulnerably housed people). Through the selection of these channels, the MOL kept tight control over the process of rejecting or accepting the public's contributions.

The above discussion of the MOL website makes it clear that the institution retains full control of user participation except for the 'Getting Involved' section. This section, however, is mainly about temporary interventions in the museum. The MOL solves any potential issues of overuse or pollution of its cultural resources (the collections) by maintaining a tightly controlled gatekeeping role.

From the analysis, the following rules can be extracted:

1. Tightly controlled access and participation: for sensitive sections such as Collections, Learning and Institutional information, all technology is tightly controlled by the museum. This closed approach disallows direct input from the public, unless they have become members of the museum's community (for example, by being part of teachers' networks). In sections where temporary material is presented, open approaches are in place,

and the public can engage in dialogue and negotiation. However, when participation is more structural, such as during the setting up of a community curated exhibition, rules for participation are clear, and there are set boundaries and mechanisms to take into account. These mechanisms, however, are appropriate for work with local communities, where face-to-face contact complements what happens online. For the global audience, participation is restricted to commenting on blogs or following on social network sites. The MOL is yet to experiment with global crowdsourcing of curatorial work. The current strategy of the MOL may be suitable for protecting the institution from potential threats to the integrity of its digital collections; however, when thinking about the outward mission of the MOL, in order to be relevant to global audiences other mechanisms to boost global public engagement should probably be explored. The MOL's recent participation in Google Art Project may be one way to achieve this, since through Google Art Project, the public is invited to virtually wander around the museum, and to contribute to other visitor experiences through the creation and sharing of their personal collections. Offering a virtual walk and a space to create one's online gallery of famous artworks is, however, still lagging behind the much more involved participation activities that MOL provides in the physical museum.

2. In-house control of technology: from the analysis it is also clear that MOL has adopted a tight control of all its web technology, using a cautious approach to the deployment of new digital experiences. All the sections that deal with the core activities of the museum (its branding on the landing page, the What's On, Visiting Us, Collections and Research and School sections) are produced with in-house technologies. Only the more ephemeral content of Explore Online and Getting Involved is deployed using a combination of in-house and external technologies.

3. Congruence between museum's mission and online activities: the MOL has responded to the mandate to become a highly relevant institution for learning in the London and Regions hub by creating a responsive online and offline environment for learning. This learning community has clear boundaries; it is governed in a manner that is congruent with the policy context in which it operates, as well as with the requirements of educators, students and the museum; and mechanisms for access and participation are clearly established. In terms of sustainability, the MOL manages core resources such as the learning sections in a collaborative manner that requires a high level of commitment from the parties involved.

With the 'global community' (outward function), however, the museum might need to do more work in the future to enhance its relevance and reach out to alternative communities that may wish to collaborate (for example, artists and developers, communities that do not necessarily have readily available digital technologies; as an aside: the MOL released an API to the LAARC collection catalogue in 2009, but since this is not explicitly advertised in the current website I have omitted it from the analysis).

Finally, going back to the definition of digital heritage, at the moment the MOL is focusing on digitized heritage, rather than on born-digital heritage. The ephemeral character of materials (content and software) used in the 'Explore Online' section shows that the MOL still has to implement policies to start classifying and storing this material as digital heritage.

In Conclusion

As was seen in the case of the MOL, the DHS framework helped to pose questions in three main areas:

Political, economic and social drivers: Contexts have a direct effect on the decisions made concerning digital resources. Understanding these contexts (in the case of MOL, for instance, this means understanding government requirements of an emphasis on learning and work with local communities) is vital for the strategic decisions to be made about priority areas online.

Diversity and Inclusion: Considerations about online stakeholders are similar to those regarding communities who physically interact with heritage. More important than the numbers of online visitors may be the question of what communities they come from, and in turn, how the museum caters for these communities. Analytics packages or audience research are currently the main tool to assess this question, yet they are insufficient. IP numbers and page hit counts reveal little about the composition of audiences. Museums also need to question how they are expanding their outreach: are they going beyond the access structures provided by technology companies?

Valtysson et al. (2010) make a similar point in the case of Scandinavian museums. They argue that the trend towards encouraging user participation through digital technologies in museums has often been accompanied by a wave of 'quantification', where metrics and performance goals related to audience numbers are increasingly imposed upon museum directors as prerequisites for continued funding. However, 'little attempt is made to conceptualize what kind of user is preferable, why increased involvement is positive, and in the museum context, what kind of use is considered appropriate' (2010: 108). This focus on metrics and visitor numbers can in turn lead to some technologies being adopted purely because they represent a makeover for the museum, a way to become contemporary and trendy, instead of reinforcing the social mission of the museum (Valtysson et al. 2010).

Authority, ownership and stewardship: Questions about digital practices highlight the need to understand who is in control of the digital heritage resource, who can contribute to its enrichment and who is involved in its safeguarding. In fact, questions about copyright, digitization, participation in social networks and other such 'hot topics' in discussions of digital heritage point to the growing need for collaborative platforms in digital heritage conservation, dissemination and interpretation.

As we have seen throughout this chapter, current policy in the UK has had a direct impact on the choices the MOL has made with regard to web and social media use. The MOL has focused on creating teaching assets online, and enhancing partnerships with schools. This helps the museum connect with its local and regional audiences. Social media in turn are used for overseas audiences and also for the local general public, and function as tools for casual, unstructured learning activities.

In terms of sustainability, the MOL manages core resources, such as the teaching sections, in a collaborative manner that requires a high level of commitment from the parties involved (the teachers who request features or book programmes). Other non-core resources are managed in a more open fashion, but are never completely released to the public. Curatorship remains firmly in the hands of the MOL, although the institution has created channels for consultation via its blogs.

From the example of a learning-oriented museum website, the next chapter moves to a museum that seeks to portray 'world culture', on and offline, for both local and global audiences.

Chapter 7

The Museum of World Culture (Världskulturmuseet) and the Carlotta Portal

This chapter deals with the website of the Museum of World Culture. This museum takes a range of approaches to the use of social media for disseminating collections, including catalogues, journeys, highlights, and creative reworking of collections. Each approach harnesses participation in various forms: provision of digital objects, classification, interpretation and even curatorship by audiences.

Contexts: A Museum for Sweden and the World

The project of a National Museum of World Culture first came to the agenda of the Swedish government in 1996, but it was initiated in January 1999, with the museum finally opening its doors in 2004 (Klein 2008: 155, Lagerkvist 2008: 89). This institution absorbed the then Ethnographic Museum in Gothenburg, which arose from collections built through Swedish 'ethnographic' fieldwork carried out in Latin America, Africa and Asia in the nineteenth and twentieth centuries (Lagerkvist 2008: 90). The Världskulturmuseet (Museum of World Culture) in Gothenburg is part of a network of state museums of world culture that also include the Etnografiska museet (the Ethnographic Museum), the Medelhavsmuseet (the Mediterranean Museum), Östasiatiska museet (the East Asian Museum), and Bergrummet (the Cavern) in Stockholm.

The original Ethnographic Museum had inherited collections associated with the exotcization of 'other' cultures, and, as was the case with many other ethnographic museums, was vulnerable to the critiques emerging in the 1960s and onwards about the role of these forms of collecting and exhibiting in excluding some groups from full participation in society. The answer at the Ethnographic Museum was to transform it into a place to represent a 'World Culture' (see Lagerkvist 2008).

This transformation also reflected broad political changes in Sweden's cultural sector. Barbro Klein (2008: 153) argues that in the mid-1990s in Sweden, cultural heritage became wrapped in ideas of sustainable development and human rights. The idea of museums as places for the discussion of issues of multiculturalism came in around 1995, when all museums in Sweden were given a mandate to take on this topic (Klein 2008: 154). For Klein (2008: 155), the ideas of museums as enmeshed in processes of sustainable development and human rights and the issue of diversity are inextricably linked, and it is only natural that they would be joined, and furthermore, expanded so as to include, in addition to ethnic diversity, issues of gender, sexuality and social class, amongst others (Klein 2008: 155). However, Klein argues that this fusion has come at the expense of dealing with the question of ethnicity, which in Sweden seems to be much more controversial than gender, sexuality or class (Klein 2008: 156).

Lagerkvist (2008: 92) argues the Museum of World Culture tries to bridge two different policies of multiculturalism, namely the politics of universalism and the politics of identity, which on the one hand demand that all views are mainstreamed into society, and on the other ask for the respect of everyone's individuality. For Lagerkvist (2008: 93), the Museum of World Culture combines singularity via special exhibitions and targets universalism through the articulation of all these specific efforts into a more general narrative of multiculturalism. The context of Världskulturmuseet lies then between the local (Gothenburg, Sweden) and the global (Western, World) contexts, a 'glocality' (see Lagerkvist 2008). Expanding on the meaning of the 'glocal', Giulianotti and Robertson (2004) argue that it points to the fact that globalization confronts the particular with the universal, and in so doing, reveals their deep interconnections, what Robertson (1992, in Giulianotti and Robertson 2004: 547) has called a 'globewide nexus'. A two-way process takes place, in which the particular becomes universal by way of demanding that all individuals are able to belong to a specific group, and the universal becomes particular through the appropriation of global trends by local groups (Giulianotti and Robertson 2004: 547).

Several features of glocalization are present in Världskulturmuseet's declared aims (as found on the Världskulturmuseet website, 2012) of serving local and global audiences: its mission is to display and bring to life the cultures of the world, in particular those whose origins are outside of Sweden (bringing the global into the local); to make of the world's cultural heritage an active force in the shaping of a sustainable global development (making of those localities forces into the global); and to express and interpret cultural variation, and to do so within historical and contemporary perspectives (what Giulianotti and Robertson refer to as the universalization of the need for particularity). As a moderator of globalization, the museum sees its role as one of 'a meeting place that can help build trust and shared responsibility for a global future in a world of constant change' (Lagerkvist 2010: 91). As further expressed in the museum's website: 'Vår ambition är att vara en kunskapskälla som i dialog får besökarna att uppleva världens mångfald och att museerna och webben blir mötesplatser för kunskap och dialog där man upplever världens mångfald – historiskt och i samtiden' (Världskulturmuseet website, 2012) ['Our ambition is to be a source of knowledge which through dialogue makes visitors experience the world's diversity, and that the museum and its website become the meeting point for knowledge and dialogue where people can experience the world's diversity – both historically and in the present'] (translation by the author).

The collections are therefore vehicles into the concept of 'world culture', which the museum defines as follows:

> Vi använder en definition av begreppet världskultur som tar sin utgångspunkt i global, samhällelig och individuell föränderlighet och ömsesidighet. Det beskriver en global rörelse mot att existensen på vår planet i ökande grad blir sammanhängande och får gemensamma former, men att detta också möter motreaktioner, exempelvis ökad nationalism och isolationism. Metodologiskt använder vi begreppet som ett förhållningssätt där vi utgår från att kultur hela tiden skapas och att vi kan ge relationell kunskap och perspektiv på lokala och globala kulturyttringar – historiskt och i samtiden. (Världskulturmuseet website, 2012)
>
> [We use a definition of the concept 'world culture' that takes as point of departure a global, holistic and individual variability and reciprocity. It describes a global movement towards an existence in our planet that becomes increasingly interconnected and adopts common forms, but that also awakes counter reactions, for example through increased nationalism and isolationism. Methodologically, we use the concept as an approach where we depart from the idea that culture is always in the making and that we can give relational knowledge and perspectives to local and global cultural utterances – historically and in the present.] (translation by the author)

Digital Practices: Catering for Diverse Audiences

In its website, the Museum of World Culture uses an array of different platforms to create spaces for diversity. Some of the platforms are more traditional for museum websites, while others are truly experimental. I discuss below the museum's use of databases and crowdsourcing. As in the case of the MOL, the museum makes an effort to provide tools for lay and expert audiences, as well as providing resources for local and global visitors.

Searching the Collection

Collection-oriented websites are built around a database that is organized and indexed following the museum's curatorial practices. Such websites require a larger investment in time and resources, as it is necessary to digitize the collection and prepare it to be presented and searchable online. Museums and the documentation and heritage sector have made large investments over the years to make their collections available and cross-referenced through such kinds of websites. Online meta-databases are one way for this to happen. These databases may work between museums or between museums and other public or private archives. In many countries there is growing government pressure to make archives accessible and preferably integrated. Museums are expected to take part in these forms of collaboration and funding is often tied to it.

One example of such large meta-database projects was 'Carlotta', an information system shared by State museums in Sweden. The Museum of World Culture in Gothenburg was one of the institutions using this system. Through Carlotta, the Museum of World Culture provided an expert-oriented way of searching through its collection (this was only available in the Swedish version of the website).

Upon entering Carlotta, the user was presented with some options for selected objects ('object of the week' and 'object of the month'), a help page with tips about how to conduct a search, and links to simple and advanced search pages.

When using a system such as Carlotta, however, there was little room for free exploration. The searches clearly worked best for researchers and specialists who knew what they were looking for. This can be illustrated by the searches for Kuna art in the Carlotta database when I first visited the system in 2010. The Museum of World Culture holds a large collection of artefacts from the Kuna Indigenous of the Atlantic coast of Panama. When I tried to search for the word 'Kuna'[1], on the simple search page, the database returned two results. With the advanced search, it returned one result. The page included a more general search field on the top, and when I typed 'Kuna', this search returned 1284 results. It seemed that if a specialist was searching for a particular type of Kuna artefact, the advanced search produced very accurate results, but when doing general searches, the results would be either scarce or overwhelming. When typing 'Mola' (a specific type of Kuna artefact), however, the results were much more relevant and precise. Again, Carlotta was very handy for researchers who knew exactly what piece of the collection they wanted to find, but it was a little off-putting for those who were after suggestions about what could be interesting for them from the collection.

As of 2013, the Museum of World Culture still offers Carlotta and also a simple search motor on its website, which yields a list of results which can be hard to navigate.

I attempted a new search for 'Kuna' in the system in 2013, and found 1263 results. There were few ways to filter the results, the main problem continuing to be the lack of tools to quickly make sense of the type of content found.

However, since 2008 change has been on the way with Carlotta and other systems used in Swedish museums (such as Carpe Cultura, D'Art, MIS, Primus, Sofie, TMS and more). A meeting was held at this time in which the various providers agreed to work together in the development of a long-term project led by the Riksantikvarieämbetet, called K-samsök (Riksdag 2009). K-samsök's purpose is to gather in a single system information about collections from the network of museums as well as from actors from outside the sector. K-samsök, translated in English as SOCH (Swedish Open Cultural Heritage), combines data from Carlotta, MuseumPlus and Primus (the two other main database systems in use in the museum sector in Sweden) in a single space, which then feeds the data into Europeana, the large portal of cultural heritage in Europe.

The system was launched in 2011, and there are notable changes in terms of the collection experience for users. For example, for users who want to have some form of structural involvement with the collections, the website has an API which allows the technically savvy to create their own mashups. Also, all metadata in K-samsök is licensed under a Creative Commons 0 license (CC0), a license that puts the metadata in the Public Domain. This is not the case for images, which may have restricted or open access. In general, however, the system's goal is to make the content as open as possible to the public, to provide metadata in a generous manner so as to motivate increased use – and therefore maintain the relevance – of cultural heritage (Swedish National Heritage Board 2013).

In fact, Carlotta uses data from K-samsök for its results, but it restricts the search to information to a specific museum's database. However, the Museum of World Culture also offers a list of alternative ways to search the collection, which make visible connections to other museums in the Swedish network, as well as to other cultural institutions in Europe. One of these services is Kringla, which aggregates metadata from K-samsök and Europeana, maps from Google Maps and photographs from Panoramio.

Searching for 'Kuna' in Kringla yields fewer results than searching through Carlotta, but the advantage is that it is possible to filter those results in a number of ways. For instance, one can select a time period, a region, a type of document, and in which museum the artefact is located. Once inside a document, the system offers opportunities to get involved with the creation of metadata (for registered users). Users are invited to log in and add links to related images or articles in Wikipedia or Wikimedia Commons, as well as add related objects.

Kringla also gives results for Europeana. In the Europeana website, it is possible for users to save their searches and create their own tags for objects, but these are not publicly available. In that sense, the website does not go as far as the Brooklyn Museum's Posse Tagging Service discussed previously.

Summarizing the approach of the Museum of World Culture to collection search, as far as the main website is concerned, the control over information is still firmly in the hands of the museum. However, the museum is opening up to user-generated content by offering a connection to external services such as Kringla. Nevertheless, across all these sites (Carlotta, Kringla, Europeana), user-generated content remains external to the content that bears the mark of authenticity provided by the museum. The system may prove sustainable in that it provides clear rules for participation, tight control and mechanisms to boost the quality of this participation. It lags behind, however, in trying to incorporate non-expert knowledge or assistance in the filtering process. These are both features that, due to the exponential increase of data, might be not only necessary but almost a prerequisite in the future management of cultural databases.

Incorporating Digitally-Born Collections

In addition to the way in which the Museum of World Culture manages traditional collections, it has recently become involved in more experimental types of online collections. In May 2012, in partnership with the Expressions of Humankind Foundation, the museum launched a project entitled 'A Day in the World'. This project invited photographers (both amateur and professional) from all over the globe to submit their photographs of one day, 15 May.

The thing to note about this collection is the lack of differentiation between photographs produced by 'professionals' and 'amateurs'. The Expressions of Humankind group of curators curated all images, so there was no direct input from the participants in this process. The exhibition invited participation in the form of provision and reflection, but was not innovative in terms of structural involvement. However, the Aday.org website states that features such as making one's own selections will be added in the future. It is also worth noting that this collection has not been incorporated in the official database of the museum, and that Aday.org currently hosts it.

In Conclusion

The Museum of World Culture maintains the trend observed at the Museum of London in keeping full control of what is defined as its official collections. However, this museum has started to experiment with richer opportunities for participation via the incorporation of links in services such as Kringla (which the museum does not own, but which it promotes). In addition, it has started to create opportunities for provision that go beyond traditional collection practices (such as in the 'A Day in the World' exhibition).

While the museum's mandate and desire is to encourage dialogue amongst diverse audiences, online this is not yet evident. The museum runs numerous workshops and events on-site, but in terms of online dialogue there is not yet much activity. The museum maintains a blog, but it has few comments on it. The blog therefore does not seem to work as an important platform for dialogue with the public.

In effect, the closest the museum has come to creating opportunities to establish a globewide nexus online (one of the goals pointed out previously) is through efforts such as the 'A Day in the World' exhibition. If the museum were to meet its mission both off- and online, these activities would need to be expanded and enhanced.

The next chapter focuses on the issue of diversity, with a comparative study of museums and galleries in Sydney and Panama City. Emphasis is placed upon in-depth analysis of the contexts in which exhibitions have emerged in these two cities. These contexts are intertwined with various moments in technological changes affecting museums at these locations.

Endnote

1. The official name since 2010 is Guna but I kept to the better-known denomination for this experiment. The Guna General Congress approved a change from 'Kuna' (a term coined by foreigners) to 'Guna' (G is a sound closer to Guna pronunciation); interview with Anelio Merry, Guna Congress of Culture, 2012.

Chapter 8

Comparing Off- and Online Aboriginal, Indigenous and 'Ethnic' Representations in Museums and Galleries in Sydney and Panama City

In this chapter we explore and compare museums off- and online in two cities, Panama City and Sydney.[1] In both cases we ask: what place do Aboriginal, Indigenous and 'ethnic' groups have in their museums, off- and online? And how can we understand or even compare the way in which museums use digital and social media in these cities? To answer these questions, we provide a thorough and in-depth examination of the contexts in which museums have emerged and operate, and intertwine these contexts with the digital practices they have fostered.

We have chosen these two cities for the way in which their museums illuminate some particular form of tension, contest or change, and some particular solution. They highlight especially well tensions in representations of diversity (we use diversity here as 'the multiple aspects of a single subject, the many cultural forms of a particular time or place, the various people in the world both now and then', see Lohman 2006: 14). Both places bear witness to the impact of colonization upon original populations and to the plight of contemporary migrants. Thus, they help to illustrate two forms of diversity: diversity in the form of Aboriginal and Indigenous groups, and diversity in the form of 'ethnic' groups (we acknowledge that many groups can be contained – and constrained – by words such as 'Aboriginal', 'Indigenous' or 'ethnic', and where possible, we use the names that groups themselves have chosen).

The particular solutions we find at these locations to the question of diversity and the way technology is used to address it shed light upon some persistent features of museums, features that transcend geographical, political and technological boundaries. One such feature is the museum's role in reflecting expressions of power. Expressions of power are visible in distinctions drawn between 'us' and 'others' in off- and online exhibitions, in assumptions of what a museum is for or what it should be like, whose history it should tell, in the style of museum websites, what those museums contain (or exclude), who staffs them or has the role of curator, the audiences they aim at or attract, and the perspectives of those who found or fund museums: whether their goal is to help forge a single national identity or to include some acknowledgment of diversity, and furthermore, whether including 'diverse groups' may also be a mechanism for strategic exclusions. As we shall see, museums and galleries in Panama City and Sydney share very similar features in the emergence of their museums, the reasons behind the growth of their collections, and to an extent, their take on national identity. In the discussion to follow, the tensions, contests, change and solutions that we find in these two cities, and that have been more recently expressed in their uses of digital technologies, will allow us to explore frameworks for comparison grounded in the idea of institutions, values and artefacts as durable structures that extend across particular situations and help to shape them (Nardi 1996: 83).

Following the DHS framework that was presented earlier, we take a predominantly chronological approach to discuss contexts. We begin with an introduction to the birth of museums in both locations, and how they reflected connections to colonial powers. We then turn to more recent times – more specifically from the 1970s to 2008. During this period, a number of major policy shifts felt in both cities were reflected in museum representations of Indigenous people and of new arrivals in the form of immigrants and refugees. We combine the discussion of these contexts with an examination of digital practices and museum approaches to the Internet and to digitization in both locations.

This chapter departs from the previous cases in that technology is presented as secondary to the situation of museums. We believe this better reflects the real position that websites and social media have within the broader workings of museums and within the social and political contexts in which these institutions perform their mission. While this may seem at odds with the emphasis in other chapters in the book, we think it is important to present technology also within this larger perspective, so as to highlight how the impact and influence of websites and social media on museums and their communities should not be exaggerated.

People Who 'Matter'

Pedrarias Dávila, General Captain and Governor of Castilla del Oro (the name the Spanish Crown gave to a region extending from the Gulf of Uraba to the Belen River, between today's Colombia and Costa Rica), founded the first settlement of Panama City in 1519, on the site of an Indigenous village of the same name. Over two centuries later, in 1788, the British First Fleet founded Sydney upon arrival at Sydney Cove. Both Panama City and Sydney then went through political change from colonial status to independence. Panama declared independence from Spain in 1821, and after a short-lived union with La Gran Colombia (a coalition of Latin American states led by Simón Bolívar that was formed after the wave of independence from Spain in the region during the nineteenth century) became a republic in 1903. The colonies in Australia became a Federation in 1901 and adopted a parliamentary system, though they never completely parted from Britain. The foundational histories we have outlined here synthesize what has long been the standard official narrative. This is one in which, until very recently, Aboriginal and Indigenous populations that lived in these cities prior to, during, and after colonization were omitted, or their importance barely recognized.

Australia was legally regarded as 'empty' (a 'terra nullius', see Mabo v. Queensland, 175 CLR 1, 1992) until as late as 1992. Aboriginals were often described as 'nomadic', as having no attachment to place, no recognizable names for who they were or where they came from, and definitely no ownership of the land. There was then no recognition – as there currently is – that Aboriginals had a strong attachment to place, strong links between place and identity, and a strong but different form of ownership, expressed in phrases such as 'this is where I come from but the country owns me'. There was also little interest in Aboriginal names for the Sydney area and the people who lived there: an interest that is now more prominent.

Indigenous culture was present in foundational histories of Panama from early on, yet the focus was solely on the Pre-Columbian period. The story was told through gold and ceramic archaeological artefacts, and also through idealized stories of resistance against Spanish colonizers. In the main, however, Indigenous groups were relegated to the category of extinguished transient populations. One explanation of this omission of surviving Indigenous populations from foundational post-independence history may be the low status that colonial society assigned to living Indigenous populations. Another explanation, provided by Coba (2005: 14), is that the widespread mestizaje (the interracial breeding between

Indigenous, Spanish and Black populations) would make it difficult to promote an Indigenous-based identity in Panama, in contrast to places such as Mexico, which had a much stronger background of Indigenous heritage (Aztec and Maya civilizations). In any case, Indigenous culture did not become a core component of Panamanian national identity upon independence from Spain. Also, although mestizaje shows us that ethnic segregation during the colony was in practice not as strict, concerns with ethnicity and 'purity' were an important part of the social organization of the colony. These concerns lay behind the creation of a class system based on intricate divisions of people according to their 'lineage' (a system that is still very much in place in contemporary Panama). The remains of colonial infrastructure in Casco Antiguo attest to the strength of these class divisions: a wall marked the boundaries of land for lower and upper classes (see Castillero Calvo 1994: 206 and Tejeira Davis 2001: 29). In fact, the class system that was created during the colony is one of the most resilient features of Panamanian society, and over the centuries has seemed immune to the efforts of various parties to overcome it.

In both Sydney and Panama City, omissions went far beyond a place in history. Aboriginal and Indigenous populations were marginalized from civilian life. In Australia, Aboriginals also fell outside the corps of 'citizens' (they did not gain the right to vote until 1967) and were definitely considered to be outside the group of people who 'mattered'.

Similarly, in the first national censuses in Panama (1911 and 1920), Indigenous populations were bulked together and an estimate was drawn based on the volume of the rest of the population (Coba 2005: 27). The first Republican Government in Panama considered the Indigenous as uncultured, savage, and in need of being 'introduced to civilized life' (Anales de la Convención 1904: 438). Furthermore, in some cases policy resulted in the extinction of Indigenous peoples. This was the case with groups of the central province of Coclé after the implementation of Law 59 of 1908 (see Coba 2005: 16).

Aboriginals and Indigenous people were not the only ones excluded. In Australia, the British brought with them – and sustained – a strong distinction between 'free settlers' and 'convicts'. The larger parts of the population in Sydney at that time were 'convicts': people found guilty of various crimes in England, Wales, Ireland and Scotland and sentenced to 'transportation' to the new outpost. Between 1788 and 1868, 164,000 were transported: men and women, adults and children. The new outpost was intended from the start to be a site for 'transportation'. That move took some of the strain off England's already overcrowded prisons. It also provided available labour for the buildings that were needed, for the work of any farming, and for domestic help. There is now some degree of acknowledgment that many have ancestors some distance back in the family tree who were convicts at least for a short time (many were granted 'tickets of leave' and most stayed, with the possible granting of land a strong incentive). The difference between one Australian state and another was for some time often described as a difference in the extent of its convict population. People in the state of South Australia, for example, have often described their state as built only by 'free settlers'. In contrast, the state of Tasmania was widely regarded as one where the original colonial population consisted almost entirely of convicts. That sense of origins, plus competition for resources, control over trade and status, contributed to the slow emergence of the Federation of States (1901).

In Panama, the Spanish brought African slaves and also Indigenous slaves from other parts of the continent. Jaén Suárez (1998: 4) has noted that the slave trade was intense between the sixteenth and eighteenth centuries: more than 90,000 African slaves crossed Panama on their way to plantations in other parts of South America, many of whom were bought in Panama City (Jaén Suárez 1998: 5). These groups would be excluded from the narrative of Panamanian identity upon independence, since in spite of mestizaje, the dominant elite preferred to trace their family tree to Spanish merchants and explorers.

In effect, both groups (the Aborigines and convicts in Australia, and the Indigenous and Africans in Panama) were excluded from the group of people who 'mattered': the people whose concerns were dominant or even considered when it came to topics such as the nature of museums or where power should lie.

What then were the first concerns of those who 'mattered'? These included surviving, making money in some way or other, being granted land, and displaying or achieving the status of 'gentry'. In Australia, as more cities and states began to develop, a major concern became who could claim to be the first or 'premier' state. In Panama, as the Spanish empire weakened, the focus was upon achieving economic and political independence.

How could museums emerge from such a background? At both locations, they seem to have emerged first as a demonstration that the 'outpost' was in fact a civilized society and that its people had interests that went beyond trade and control over land, and also as expressions of membership in the international community of civilized, independent nations.

Museum Origins

The first plans for a museum in Australia were put forward long before Federation, in 1821. It was to be in Sydney but would be called the Australian Museum. Its establishment did not come from public policy, but was instead proposed as part of the proper activities of citizens of a particular class and status (Branagan 1979: 6).

The Australian Museum was established in the 1830s with the State contributing land, the costs of construction, and the salary for a curator. The contents of the museum, however, depended heavily on the 'concerned gentlemen' who donated most of the material and paid for collecting expeditions. The museum contained a mix of natural history and Aboriginal collections; it will come as no surprise that natural history was prominent. The inclusion of Aboriginal material was included as curiosities and based largely on interest from overseas in a 'dying race' (Strahan 1979: 11).

Added to the inclusion of Aboriginal material was also an interest, at least within the groups working toward a museum, in maintaining bonds to Britain and to what was seen as civilized Europe. In museums, this bond was maintained by their playing a dual role. People in Sydney were both creators of their own collections for the colony and providers of goods and 'curiosities' to England in particular. In Australia (and we will see later on that this was also the case in Panama), there was a healthy trade to Europe with collecting expeditions often funded abroad (Strahan 1979: 3).

The precedents for a National Museum of Panama go back to a period of dissatisfaction with the union with Colombia, which saw influential thinkers and politicians such as Justo Arosemena grapple with the issue of a national identity. Museums in North America had seen intensive development from the end of the eighteenth century, and the model of a natural history museum as bastion of education and scientific progress was well established by the 1870s (Lopes 2003). The same model was proposed in Panama in 1878, through a private initiative that ultimately failed (Méndez Pereira 1915: 288; Camargo de Cooke 2003: 165). When Panama became a republic, the idea was rekindled. One of the first actions of the new government was to allocate funds for the creation of the Museo Nacional. Law 52 of 20 May 1904 designated that 3.25 million pesos were to be invested in public infrastructure in several provinces, and this included the creation of a National Museum and Library (Sánchez Laws 2009: 56). In 1906, President Manuel Amador Guerrero inaugurated the Museo Nacional (Gonzáles Guzmán 1976). The creation of this museum was only a small part of the ambitious plan to establish buildings to demonstrate Panama's commitment to the republican ideal. A National Theatre and Presidential Palace were also commissioned to Italian architect Genaro Ruggieri, who designed these as a series of neoclassical governmental buildings.

It was argued that through its display of the country's natural richness, the Museo Nacional would help Panama towards into agricultural and industrial development (Gonzáles Guzmán 1976). Thus, and similarly to Sydney, the first collections consisted of 'desiccated birds, mammals, desiccated reptiles, fish, insects, native wood, archaeological objects and plants' (Gaceta Oficial 1916, in Sánchez Laws 2009: 58). From 1909 onwards, however, new objects entering the collection included 'pieces of jewellery and ceramics from aboriginals of the American Continent, objects from the period of the Spanish domination, and national products' (Gaceta Oficial 1916, in Sánchez Laws 2009: 58). Yet the growing activities of overseas museums and their 'treasure hunters' presumably fuelled the collection of these items by the nascent Panamanian government. During this period, a number of 'archaeological investigations' were conducted, resulting in the export of many Pre-Columbian pieces to museums in Europe and the United States. Early inclusions of Aboriginal and Indigenous artefacts in museums in Panama City and Sydney reflected then no sense of social inclusion or the possession of power for these groups.

In Panama, interest in contemporary Indigenous culture grew during the mid-twentieth century, and Indigenous groups became major protagonists in the city's museums (especially in the Museum of the Panamanian Man). At the beginning of the twenty-first century, groups such as the Gunas (formerly known as Kunas) would create museums to express their take on national identity. Their presence and activities became especially strong online and through social media.

In Sydney there have also been moves toward an acknowledgement of Aboriginals as the first inhabitants of Sydney, together with an acknowledgement of their continuing presence, their attachment to place, their version of history, their continuing production of material that attracts international attention, and the need for their inclusion in any account of what is 'Australian' and of Australian origins. Yet changes in physical exhibitions have not been followed up in the same degree with online initiatives.

How those changes came about, and the specific forms they took, are best illustrated by a period of major amendments, starting with the 1970s. The same period also saw sharp adjustments in the acknowledgment, within museums and within public policies, of immigrants and refugees. Those two directions of change were not identical and we shall start by considering each separately. Both, however, bring out many of the same issues, and both raise questions about the nature and bases of change.

The 1960s: Challenging the Status Quo

Let us set the stage very briefly for the Australian case. The 1960s saw the start of non-Aboriginal protest over the treatment of Aboriginal Australians. In 1965, Freedom Riders (a mix of Aboriginal and non-Aboriginals) protested in many Australian towns against the segregation of white and black Australia. In 1967 Aboriginals were finally given the right to vote and were counted in the census (Curthoys 2002).

A change of government to Labour in 1972 led in 1975 to the passing of a Racial Discrimination Act and the creation of a dedicated Aboriginal Arts Board as part of the Australia Council for the Arts. Land Rights claims and Acts followed. These included, for example, the passing over of traditional lands such as that surrounding Uluru (previously known as Ayers Rock) and the land's listing as a World Heritage Site under the then new UNESCO convention for World Heritage.

A perception of Australia as white and as essentially 'British' in its origins, however, did not disappear or lose its dominance in this period. For example, 1988 brought with it the Bicentenary of British colonization of Australia. It was marked by a re-enactment of the First Fleet's arrival and by an emphasis on the founding fathers. Aboriginals pointed out that these 200 years were for them times of loss and mourning. The dominant mood among non-Aboriginals, however, was one of celebration and a sense that here were the country's origins.

Within museums in Australia at this time there was overall little recognition or representation of Aboriginals' perception of history. The clearest mark of recognition occurred in an art gallery. The Australian National Gallery (a gallery placed within a city – Canberra – that is the Federation capital and has its own local government) commissioned a work containing 200 Aboriginal commemorative poles marking each year of colonization (poles of this kind mark a death). The set of poles was displayed at the 1988 Biennale of Sydney, and is now on permanent display at the Australian National Gallery with the title 'The Aboriginal Memorial'.

Over time, a shift in public perception of history and the increasing politicization of Aboriginal groups contributed to a mind-shift in government policy and museum practice. 1992 saw a Labour Prime Minister openly acknowledge that the responsibility for Aboriginal poverty and marginalization stemmed largely from non-Aboriginal attitudes and policies (see Keating 1992). 1993 saw the Australian Museum Association publish a paper with the title 'Previous Possessions, New Obligations' (see Council of Australian Museum Associations 1993). It called for museum reform regarding Indigenous representation and, particularly, for care in relation to sacred and secret material and to human remains. A 2001 report noted that many museums had become more open to Aboriginal participation and even curatorial responsibility but there was a long road to go (Dolan 2001).

The shape of Panamanian identity also took a new direction between the 1960s and 1970s. The populist military regime of General Omar Torrijos attempted to establish Panamanian identity as the composite of Spanish, Indigenous and African heritage. Torrijos' military dictatorship and its cohort of scholars resuscitated the idea of Panamanian national identity as stemming from the isthmuses' geography. This idea had been in vogue prior to separation from Colombia. Dr Reina Torres de Araúz, a Panamanian anthropologist trained in Argentina and director of the National Museum between 1969 and 1970, was a key figure in this process. She pushed for a definition of 'Nation (as) a conglomerate founded in geography and supported by the political entity of State' (1983: 167). She also had a prominent role as architect of the new network of museums that would emerge from the restructuring of the National Museum from 1975 onwards. Panamanian national identity was redefined in this period as coming from the Hispanic-Indigenous group, and eminently racially and culturally hybrid (Sánchez Laws 2009: 70). These changes were imposed at the highest level. In the 1972 Constitution, Chapter IV on National Culture declared that the State had to 'recognize and respect the ethnic identity of national Indigenous communities, and . . . carry out programs to develop the material, social and spiritual values of each of their cultures' (National Institute of Culture 1978: 25).

In the Panamanian museum sector, a massive restructuring took place. This included the creation of the Museum of the Panamanian Man. In it, Torres de Araúz's own anthropological investigations of contemporary Indigenous groups of the Isthmus of Panama became the backbone. It is worth noting the very different origin of changes in the Australian and Panamanian museum sectors. While in Australia changes came from the exercise of democracy, in Panama, they came from a military backed intelligentsia.

The push for ethnic diversity in the Panamanian museum sector would seem at odds with stereotypical ideas of the functioning of military regimes. However, when taking into account that the new conception of 'ethnic diversity' had components of exclusivity (the Spanish descendant elite and any group that could be associated with US colonialism was undesirable in the new mix), the push seems less at odds. From the start, the military regime framed previous governments as corrupt and elitist, led by a Spanish descendant elite that cared little for the rest of the population (see Sánchez Laws 2011). General Omar Torrijos, leader of the 'Revolutionary Government', as the military chose to call themselves, created a profile of populism that sought to empower previously discriminated groups (such as the Indigenous), in the hope that these groups would support and give credence to the military's permanence in power. In addition, Torres de Araúz was concerned with a dislocation of the State that Indigenous groups such as the Gunas (who had successfully revolted against the Panamanian government in 1925, see Sánchez Laws 2011: 30) could promote. This was another important reason to try to integrate Indigenous populations into the official narrative of Panamanian identity provided by museums.

It should be noted that the topic of diversity faded out of discussions in the heritage sector after the end of the dictatorship. Ethnic diversity as a positive feature of Panamanianness was, however, later rekindled during Martin Torrijos' (Omar Torrijos' son) administration (2004–2009), especially through the hiring of 'marketing experts for multicultural environments' as political strategists (see Flores and Batista 2008).

1990s on: Alternative Physical and Digital Spaces for Aboriginal and Indigenous Presence

In Australia, one of the first museums to have an online presence was the Australian Museum, which opened a website in 1994 (Skates and Firminger 1998). Other museums started to follow suit, and in 1996, the Australian Federal Government commissioned a report on the digitization of museum collections. Amongst the concerns voiced in this report was the need to protect national identity online. In his presentation of the report at the Museums and the Web 1998 Conference, Smith summarizes the issue:

> Now consider the size of the digital archives being developed in North America and Europe for on-line consumption and the integrity of digital archives that will be offered on-line by the likes of The British Museum and the Smithsonian. The non-native Australian content held and digitized by Australian museums will be overwhelmed by sheer weight of the digital offerings emanating from the Northern Hemisphere and by world-recognized centers of academic excellence. As researchers in Australia shift their mode of research increasingly to on-line sources they will find most of their non-Australian content coming from these bountiful overseas

> sources, which in turn will render the physical holdings of non-Australian content accessed less and less.
>
> Should museums therefore continue to collect, hold and/or digitize non-native content? Shouldn't they concentrate their resources on collecting, digitizing and adding value to content native to their land, heritage and culture? If they don't, who will? (Smith 1998)

Against this background, in 1998, the Australian Museums Online (AMOL, later Collections Australia Network CAN) website was launched, originally stemming from the Working Group of the Cultural Ministers Council's Heritage Collections in 1993 (Kenderdine 1999). The AMOL project invited museums and galleries in Australia to contribute with information about their five most significant items. The project was especially interested in supporting small and regional museums, which were indeed the most enthusiastic users given the benefits in terms of support for the digital preservation and dissemination of collections that the project represented. The project became an online virtual community, offering workshops, seminars and regional museum collaboration opportunities (Kenderdine 1999). In addition, the AMOL project sought to level the playing field between large city museums and their regional counterparts so that no particular institution had higher prominence than another.

These online projects, however, did not highlight in particular the need to address Aboriginal heritage. In the main, Aboriginal presence in Sydney was (and continues to be) more marked through commercial galleries that include Aboriginal art, Aboriginal buskers at the central ferry quay, and Aboriginal artefacts (predominantly fake copies) in the many souvenir shops than in museums.

From the late 1980s to the 1990s, an Aboriginal presence began to surface in the art gallery circuit. One example was the Boomalli Aboriginal Artists Cooperative, part of a number of small arts outlets in the city, created in 1987. A second was the Art Gallery of New South Wales (AGNSW) large Indigenous Gallery – the Yiribana Gallery – founded in 1994 (see Official City of Sydney Website).

The Yiribana Gallery is marked by an interesting history. The big burst in contemporary Australian Aboriginal art in the forms that are currently best known (acrylic paint on canvas with a wide range of colours) began in the 1970s. At that time the Gallery was predominantly interested in bark paintings in earthy colours. From the Gallery's point of view, the bark paintings represented 'true Aboriginal art' with a long history and a continuing presence. The new forms were originally rejected as belonging to the 'commercial' world. Their first appearance was in an exhibition created by the curator for the Gallery of Contemporary Art. In 2011, however,

Hetti Perkins, the curator for the Yiribana Gallery, left the museum, arguing that the Art Gallery of New South Wales as a whole had stagnated in its support for indigenous art with no new major exhibitions taking place.

In a letter to the AGNSW, Perkins argued that the Yiribana Gallery had 'remained unchanged for almost twenty years' despite having 'strongly advocated for the refurbishment. . . to bring it up to the standard of other spaces' (Perkins, cited by Morgan 2011).

A third example of the surfacing of Aboriginal presence in Sydney reflects especially well some of the debates about versions of history and museum representations in the late 1980s and 1990s. This is the Museum of Sydney, conceived in the bicentennial year of 1988. The site was originally seen as important because it was where the first Government House had been built. On that basis also, the Historic Houses Trust was appointed as the developer of the museum. From the very start, however, there was controversy over the story it was to tell. In line with changes in policy and Aboriginal protest, the museum plan developed by the Trust gradually shifted from celebration to 'contact'. The Trust also came to acknowledge the variety of meanings the site held for different people (Historic Houses Trust, cited by Ireland 1996: 100).

Tracy Ireland, at the time archaeologist with the Department of Planning, Heritage Division, commented that this move towards a mixed message 'immediately alienated the Friends of First Government House' (Ireland 1996: 100) and led them to protest against the plans of the Trust. For them the site was not only about the creation of nation and the attachment to the Commonwealth, but also about the acknowledgement of convict and working-class history (Ireland 1996: 100).

The Trust abandoned the statue of Governor Phillip and, following an open competition, chose for the entrance of the museum a contemporary installation designed and executed by two women artists. The installation is called Edge of the Trees and was created by Janet Laurence (non-Aboriginal) and Fiona Foley (Aboriginal).

This installation, placed outside the museum and visible at the street level, consists of tall, undecorated poles. Carved into them are spaces that contain objects of meaning for the settlers and for Aboriginals. Included also were recorded voices that represented people from the past, both Aboriginal and settlers, as well as a number of names. Especially powerful for Aboriginals were the names of Aboriginals who represented resistance to total control by the new arrivals. In the words of David Prosser, the museum's curator of Aboriginal Studies, this installation 'represented our history – the untold history'. He saw as especially important 'the inclusion of the names of the "warriors of the first people of the Sydney area" – people such as Pemulway, Tedbury and Patya – as well as the "warriors of the first fleet". Until now, these revered ancestors have been virtually excluded from Australian history lessons, or if they are mentioned they are given cursory acknowledgement' (Prosser 2000: 97–98).

Despite the inclusion of names, however, the installation was relatively subtle in its message. A shift to more explicit storytelling appeared in 1999 with the opening of the Cadigal Place Gallery. This gallery included objects used by the local people as well as early personal stories of warriors such as Pemulway (sometimes referred to as Pemulwoy) (Goodnow 2006: 155–56). Contemporary stories from descendants were also included. These stories make it clear that the original owners have not simply faded away.

During this period the themes that were receiving attention online were again stories of discoverers and adventurers arriving at the Australian continent, such as the Duyfken Replica website, launched in 2002, which presented a replica of the Dutch vessel *Duyfken* and told the story of its 1606 journey from Indonesia to Queensland (Towler et al. 2002).

Yet this contrasts with the discussions that were taking place at the time about the role of museums online. For example, Australian researcher Fiona Cameron argued that museums online had the task of exposing interpretive frameworks and explaining 'the fact that object interpretations change and as such should no longer be presented as definitive accounts carrying the ultimate authority' (Cameron 2003). Indeed, a wave that favoured polysemy and contestation of previously sacrosanct narratives had begun to gain strength in Australia.

In 2004, the Questacon National Science Centre in Canberra launched its first web exhibition, Burarra Gathering Online, which was the virtual extension of Questacon's first Indigenous-based exhibition, Burarra Gatherings. The online version was a remarkable attempt at creating a community-museum partnership for the development of an online exhibition, where approval from Burarra Elders was sought at all stages of the project (Crane 2004).

The nature of the debate and the scarcity palpable online in terms of the representation of Aboriginal culture and heritage might well have been different in current times. In 2007 a Labour government headed by Kevin Rudd was elected. One of Rudd's first actions was to officially say 'sorry' to Australian Aboriginals for the treatment they had received from European Australians: an action that the previous Prime Minister – John Howard – had consistently refused to take.

In Panama, the 1980s and 1990s saw the end of the military dictatorship. With it, a new wave of changes in official museums ensued. This wave of changes involved the creation of new museums in Panama City, which also brought changes in the city landscape. One such case was the Museum of the Inter-Oceanic Canal, which was placed in the middle of the then decaying (and now heavily gentrified) Old Cask area. Another was the MARTA, a new museum symbolically placed in the former Canal Zone (a territory controlled by the US Government as part of the management of the Canal, and fully returned to Panama in the year 2000). The MARTA was the product of a failed project for a children's museum that had stood empty for two years due to lack of funding to develop its exhibitions. In 2006, the wife of the newly elected president Martin Torrijos, Vivian de Torrijos, ordered the relocation of the exhibitions of the then closed Museum of the Panamanian Man into the new building. The exhibitions at the Museum of the Panamanian Man, Dr Reina Torres de Araúz's œuvre and one of the few locations where contemporary Indigenous culture was on display, were dismantled, and a great deal of the original concept was dismissed. All the dioramas that had been used in the previous museum were put in storage, and a few of the Pre-Columbian pieces were put on display at the new museum. The MARTA became about the life of Dr Torres de Araúz, with small sections of the Pre-Columbian ceramics collection and a few pieces from the collection of monumental stone figures from the Barriles site remaining. The reasons for this change of focus were unclear, but the MARTA clearly reflected the impact of political swings upon the museum sector in the country. The changes, in sum, came to signify the State's marked abandonment of the representation of Indigenous culture. When asked in 2006 about possible reasons for the lack of inclusion of contemporary Indigenous culture in the new MARTA, Guillermina de Gracia, then sub-director of Historic Patrimony, cited a prevalent racism and discrimination that made it hard to present to the Panamanian public the idea that both their ancestors and their contemporary culture are linked to Indigenous peoples. For De Gracia, the public's lack of care for the Indigenous collections at MARTA was a reflection of the fact that 'Panamanians do not feel Indigenous' (see Sánchez Laws 2011: 35). In terms of digital media, the Instituto Nacional de Cultura (INAC) launched an online directory of its museums in the 2000s. This directory worked as an online brochure of locations, type of collection, opening hours, and description of the buildings. In the main, descriptions of the various museums followed the established narrative of Spanish conquest, with little regard given to the particulars of Indigenous heritage.

Although at street level Indigenous culture is very present in Panama, mainly in the form of souvenirs or stylizations of Pre-Columbian motifs in the architecture or imagery, after the 1990s the presence of Indigenous culture within museum exhibitions diminished drastically. Alternative spaces emerged for the display of Indigenous culture, though mostly outside of Panama City. One such space was the community museums of Guna Yala.

In contrast to Australia, in Panama the Gunas had won rights over land as early as 1925, when a revolution led to the recognition by the Panamanian state of the political autonomy of the Guna people over a territory and archipelago in the Atlantic coast of Panama. By 2008, a quarter of Panamanian territory was legally the property of Indigenous communities, all within the legal regime of Comarcas, basically territorial divisions established through a study of historical antecedents, geography or economic features (Sánchez Laws 2009: 150).

In spite of these conquests, in terms of having a place in official representation the situation was very different. Since the 1990s, the Congreso General Guna had lobbied, to no avail, for the inclusion of their culture in museums in the form of state support for a museum project. The project for a museum about Guna culture began to crystallize through external agents, such as the Museum of World Culture in Gothenburg and the National Museum of the American Indian, which provided members of the Congreso with opportunities for exchange and training. Simultaneously, delegates from the Union of Community Museums in Oaxaca, Mexico, got in touch with the Congreso and presented the idea of community museums. It became obvious that the most expedite and efficient manner of going about creating the desired Museum of the Guna Nation was to sidestep government and create it with Guna General Congress means. The Museum of the Guna Nation opened in 2007, and two additional museums were inaugurated on other islands of the archipelago. Alongside the physical museum, the online networking activities were vital in establishing the credibility of the project, and in expanding its outreach.

The situation of official museums has not changed much of late, although there have been a few attempts at temporary exhibitions focusing on contemporary Indigenous culture. One example was the exhibition of *molas* (a Guna textile) presented at the Museo del Canal Interoceánico. In December 2009, the Museo del Canal Interoceánico hosted a temporary exhibition of 200 *molas* from the collection of Fundación José Félix Llopis. This was the first time that *molas* had been the core of an exhibition at a major museum in the city.

Another example was an exhibition entitled Caminos de Maiz, organized by private stakeholders and hosted at the Museum of Contemporary Art. The exhibition had as its goal to make visible Indigenous culture, in the context of the 2003 Centennial celebrations of the creation of the

Republic of Panama. Alexandra Schjelderup, director of Enredarte and creator of Caminos de Maiz, wanted to confront the Panamanian mestizo audience with contemporary Indigenous culture, to expose, share and provoke self-criticism, and also to propose an alternative to the more 'mainstream culture' activities taking place as part of the celebrations (Schjelderup 2003: 70). Both exhibitions, however, were only temporary interventions. During the decade, the representation of Indigenous culture in museums in Panama City continued to be short sections dedicated to Pre-Columbian culture.

By the mid-2000s, however, a host of Indigenous and 'Ethnic' museum initiatives had begun to flourish online. This was the case of the Museum of the Guna Nation, which was linked to the webpage of the Congreso General Guna, and through it, to the publications of the Koskun Kalu Research Institute.

The Patronato Panamá Viejo also published an online archaeological register where visitors to the website could browse the collection and look at the results of current archaeological investigations. The website also provided an online tour of the ruins via a map, and downloadable publications from its scholarly journal *Canto Rodado*. While the Patronato Panama Viejo was a pioneer in exploring the use of social media to expand their outreach, they continued to use the new platforms in a unidirectional communication flow fashion. This is visible in their blog, which serves as an improved news outlet, and which at the moment does not contain any substantial dialogue with the public. This is due largely to a lack of staff capable of focusing exclusively on online activities.

Developments off-and online have been made in both cities over time and with changing political interests. Indigenous peoples may be now seen as more a part of people that 'matter' in both the museum national narratives. In Sydney at least, they remain represented, however, predominantly through the exhibition of artwork rather than in broader exhibitions on social and economic issues, both off-and online.

Multicultural Policies and 'Ethnic' Representation

A further minority or form or diversity, 'ethnic' diversity, highlights the need to understand the context within which museums emerge and operate, involving also issues of inclusion and exclusion in national narrations.

In 1901, an Immigration Restriction Act was part of the Federation of Australia. What is now termed the 'White Australia policy' continued to limit the number of non-white immigrants to the country during the period 1901–1973. The post-1945 period saw an increase in non-British, but white, immigration. Most of these new arrivals came from various parts of Europe, many with a history of being refugees or having been displaced.

The World War II years were a period of exclusions in Panama, prompted by strong racist policies. Article 23 of the 1941 Constitution prohibited migrants from black races, yellow races and races from India, Minor Asia and North Africa (Pérez, Ghandi and Shahani 1976: 204).

For the Chinese and West Indian migrants who had come to work for the Canal construction at the beginning of the twentieth century, the new Constitution resulted in forced departure. Families who had been in the country for decades were robbed of their small businesses and expelled. Others chose to hide their ethnic background (for example, a Chinese migrant with the surname Siu changing his name to Sánchez) to avoid being detected.

In both Sydney and Panama City, however, the post-war period saw marked shifts in attitudes towards migrants. In Panama, after the deposition of Arnulfo Arias Madrid, a project to reform the 1941 Constitution was put in motion. On 1 March 1946 a new Constitution that consecrated the equality of rights for both nationals and foreigners was adopted (Pizzurno Gelós and Araúz 1996: 324). In the 1970s, however, the Panamanian dictatorship started a renewed campaign for the consolidation of a national identity, a campaign that again was markedly racist. The target group on this occasion were US and European migrants. Torrijos' government promoted the mestizo version of Panamanian national identity. As argued previously, this was also a way of classifying US migrants as intruders, and of portraying the displaced political elite as descendants of previous intruders, the Spanish.

The extent of the shift on the part of the Australian State at the time is indicated in particular by some changes in legislation in 1975. The Australian Labour government passed a Racial Discrimination Act. One of its effects was to make selection based on race illegal. Asian immigrants then increased in number, with one particular change being the arrival of large numbers of Vietnamese refugees (the name Nguyen is now one of the ten most frequent names in the Sydney telephone directory). The government aim was always to include these new groups within the labour force: a form of inclusion that the people in these groups also valued. The anticipation was that in time they would 'become Australian'. They would retain some of their characteristics. The presence of differences would be accepted, but on the whole the new arrivals would increasingly 'fit in', acquiring the values and practices of the groups already in place and not offering any serious challenges to them.

One assumption that emerged in Sydney was that diversity in ethnicity was a phenomenon that began only after the end of World War II. Ethnic diversity was then not part of any story of origins. In fact, there were from the start numerous people born in other British colonies but who were not white. Some were sailors; others were convicts. Later waves included a large Chinese population, stimulated by the discovery of gold in the 1850s (something similar, and during the same period, occurred in Panama due to the California Gold Rush). Not all of these arrivals stayed in Australia and some were actively discouraged from doing so. Anti-Chinese legislation restricted their long-term stay, the setting up of businesses and, in particular, family reunion.

In Panama, the assumption could be stated as follows: that the political climate demanded that European or North American arrivals should be removed from the story of the nation. Ethnic diversity did make it into the official representations of national identity after World War II, but this diversity was limited to populations of African slaves, Indigenous and American Spanish (as opposed to European Spanish).

Comparing our two cities within the optic of 'ethnic' diversity, several important features about the representation of this form of diversity begin to surface.

The first feature is the way in which ties to colonial powers were treated in these two cities. In Australia, ties to Britain are still at the core of the country's official structure. Australia is part of the Commonwealth of Nations, and England's Queen has been until today regarded, at least officially, the person to whom loyalty and allegiance are owed. Being Australian still means for many being white with a British history. Nonetheless, in the 1970s, there was a sense that the country could move toward a stronger recognition of diversity in values and practices, with a greater tolerance or acceptance of differences. Emerging also was the sense that the country could even take pride in its capacity to allow diversity. The mark of the nation would then be its 'multiculturalism' rather than its homogeneity or its insistence on one set of values and practices. Multiculturalism became 'a dominant national ethic' (McShane 2001: 123). Unlike the threat of 'black armband history', the perception of the country as multicultural was seen initially as presenting little threat to the established concept of nation or its national core.

In Panama, by contrast, ties to Spain were removed from the core of national identity. All efforts were directed towards telling the story of the consolidation of independence. Several strategic reasons lay behind this attitude, amongst them the need to portray everything external as a threat to Panama's fight for control over the Canal in the 1970s, and a need to assert the country's neutrality after the reversion of the Canal. Being

Panamanian meant being mixed, although it had to be the right type of mix. After reversion in 2000, a push for a broader 'multiculturalism' emerged. Several media campaigns celebrating migrants were launched (for example, the 'Panamix' government funded publication in 2006). It could be said that 'multiculturalism' also became the dominant ethic in Panama, though perhaps mainly because of economic considerations attached to the handling of the Canal.

In terms of online representations, the website of the Society of Friends of the West Indian Museum of Panama (SAMAAP) was a pioneer in this regard. The SAMAAP website provided a host of links to associated networks and articles from SAMAAP print publications. After 2008, however, these features were eliminated and the website became geared towards making the visitor contribute monetarily by joining SAMAAP. Yet the activities of SAMAAP and associated stakeholders truly crossed physical boundaries through their online networking. Aside from SAMAAPs own website (Samaap.com), the activities of SAMAAP were disseminated through websites such as *Etnia Negra de Panama* (DiadelaEtnia.homestead.com). Managed by SAMAAP member Anthony McLean, this website provided alternative timelines of the history of Panama, detailed biographies of members of the West Indian community, and information on the various efforts of SAMAAP and other associations to expand the reach of the Afro-Panamanian community's work against discrimination. Similarly, through *PanamaCouncilNY.com*, the Panama City Council of New York, which attempted to gather around it Panamanian diasporas in the US (New York has the largest concentration), also promoted the activities of the SAMAAP and functioned as a research centre on issues of black ethnicity in Panama. Although online SAMAAP might be proposing the coalescence of black minorities and the Panamanian society in general around a project against discrimination and in favour of a more inclusive society, these concerns have not been made explicit at the permanent exhibition at the West Indian Museum of Panama.

The second feature consists of some limits, at the major museum level, to the representation of 'multiculturalism'. A few museums in Australia included stories that extended beyond Anglo-Irish convicts and officers. The Australian National Maritime Museum in Sydney's Darling Harbour included the theme of broader immigration through its Passengers Gallery (Witcomb 2003b). In its original incarnation the National Museum of Australia in Canberra also had a gallery devoted to immigration, both historical and contemporary. Contemporary exhibitions were often 'safe expressions' of non-Imperial heritage (food, crafts, etc.). Some consisted of 'community spaces' that would contain temporary 'ethnic' exhibitions.

The Museum of Sydney offers temporary exhibitions that cover a variety of 'ethnic' groups with a focus on their current interests. The Powerhouse Museum houses The NSW Migration Heritage Centre that collaborates with individual museums in the creation of 'migrant' exhibitions. The activities of the centre, which as the Museu da Pessoa is conceived as a virtual museum, have included the 2010 exhibition *Tracking The Dragon: A History Of The Chinese In The Riverina*. The project was developed in collaboration with the Museum of the Riverina, Wagga Wagga and Centre, and it sought to explore the public and private lives of Chinese-Australian migrants. In 2012, the new NSW Government commissioned the document *Multicultural Advantage 2012–2015*, in which it was stated that it would seek 'to further reap the great social and economic benefits of (multiculturalism)' by developing 'multicultural hub/s in a specific location/s' which 'could include a migration museum' (New South Wales 2012). Commenting on the Multicultural Advantage 2012–2015 document, John Petersen, Manager of the Migration Heritage Centre, stated that

> The feasibility study of the Multicultural Advantage 2012–2015 policy would again open the discussion for a migration museum as an option – and indeed a new means for community interaction of different peoples – and draw upon the partnerships and substantial volunteer and professional efforts of heritage workers in culturally diverse communities to record regional heritage legacies of collections, places and associated memories of migration and settlement. (Petersen n.d.)

At the time of writing, however, the plans for such a museum have not moved forward.

The Museo del Canal Interoceánico in Panama City covers Chinese and West Indian migrations, and the Museum of the West Indian deals with migrants from this specific group. However, no separate museum was established to cover immigration history in a broad sense in either Sydney or Panama City. Within Sydney there was no specific new museum devoted to immigration.

The third feature is the emergence of some broader forms of immigration in galleries and arts centres. One example was developed at the University of Western Sydney in collaboration with the Migration Heritage Centre. This was 'Generate: Youth Culture and Migration Heritage in Western Sydney'. This exhibition focused on the mobility of youth within the urban landscape. The past then is a 'cultural background' (predominantly Middle Eastern and Asian). The present is life in Australia and particularly that in suburban Sydney.

A second example, this time in Sydney's city centre, was the work by Guan Wei, a Chinese-Australian artist. Guan Wei has worked in particular with issues of connectivity and multiple belonging. In a 2007 exhibition at the Powerhouse Museum, he created murals and added objects based on the real and imagined journeys of the Chinese explorer Zheng He (1371–1432). At the centre of the exhibition was an object, a small figure of the Chinese God of Longevity, unearthed in Darwin in 1879 and attributed to a possible arrival by Zheng He to the Northern coast of Australia some 350 years before James Cook. Guan Wei took this object as a starting point to create an imagined Chinese view of pre-colonial Australia, challenging official national histories that give pride of place to the British narrative.

In Panama City, another artist with Chinese heritage, GuXiong, provides a third example. As part of ciudadMultipleCity, a series of public art interventions during the 2003 Centennial celebrations, GuXiong traced the lives of Chinese migrants to the city from the first arrivals during the construction of the Trans-Isthmian Railroad. The project, entitled 'Soy quien soy' (I am who I am), consisted of a series of enlarged photographs hung along Avenida B, a street crossing Panama City's Chinatown. The photographs were the product of interviews carried out with members of the Chinese community in Panama, and were inscribed with 166 testimonies in Traditional Chinese, Spanish and English.

In Conclusion

The features we have outlined above raise questions about the stability of change, the limits to change, and the directions of change. Attention to two forms of diversity – Aboriginal and ethnic – has brought to the surface both differences and similarities. One difference is the extent to which the recognition of diversity is equivalent in our two examples. Some expressions of 'ethnic' diversity are privileged above others. 'Ethnic' artists and 'ethnic' representations within Sydney and Panama City are unlikely to be regarded as unique, especially if they represent only aspects of heritage.

With this chapter, we have attempted to offer insights into the ways in which policies flow onto representations and into the ways in which the privileging of particular groups and their histories prompts the marginalized representation of other groups. It is in this manner that we find comparisons both possible and enlightening. Often, the discussions about museum digital technologies and online media bypass considerations of multiculturalism and diversity, of social inclusion, and of the broader social, political, cultural and economic contexts that shape the work and practices of museums, off- and online. Yet, as has been attempted in this chapter, an understanding of these contexts is fundamental in assessing the reasons behind gaps in representations of the digital heritage of a number of groups. As can be gleaned from the history presented above, official representations change slowly, yet changes in technology have made the option of self-representation much more feasible for Aboriginal, Indigenous and so-called 'ethnic' communities. The cases of the Guna online activities and the Society of Friends of the West Indian museum in Panama City attest to this. These communities have greatly benefited from the accessibility of dissemination channels that social media provide. Yet in Australia, Aboriginal heritage dissemination online still seems to be firmly in the hands of various government and regional non-Aboriginal stakeholders.

In the next Part IV, Futures, Chapter 10 presents a case in which the traditional balance of power presented above is temporarily subverted by the digital colonization of the National Museum of Australia via mobile locative and social media technologies.

Endnote

1. Professor Katherine Goodnow, Department of Information Science and Media Studies, University of Bergen (retired), conducted the research on Sydney's physical museums and galleries.

Part IV: Futures

Chapter 9

Augmenting the Garden of Australian Dreams at the National Museum of Australia

This chapter is about the challenges and opportunities that designing a mobile media, large-scale collective creativity project posed for a community of content creators (university students), researchers and digital officers at the National Museum of Australia.[1]

The Garden of Australian Dreams is an open space at the centre of the National Museum of Australia. It contains a walkthrough map of Australian geography, culture and history conveyed through layers of graphics, text, sculptures and landscaping. A shallow pond, establishing a geographic frame of reference where one footstep equates to fifty kilometres on the continent, borders the coastal outline of the top end of Australia. The two main layers are a map with places and roads on it, and a map of aboriginal language boundaries that symbolically interweave 'the Great Australian Dream' (the belief in Australia that home and land ownership are the hallmarks of one's success in life) with the aboriginal 'Dreaming' (Australian Indigenous stories of creation that speak about the relationships between land, animals and people). Other layers include maps of vegetation, soil and geology, explorer tracks, electoral boundaries, a weather map from Australia Day 1998, the Dingo-proof fence, and the Pope's line that divided the world between Portuguese and Spanish interests in the fifteenth century, and is now the West Australian border.

There are also conceptual and abstract references, such as the word 'home' written in different languages, plantings of oaks to represent immigration, and references to famous Australian painters and paintings (Weller 2002).

No signage or explanatory text is provided at the Garden of Australian Dreams. The architect's intention was to leave the meaning of the Garden

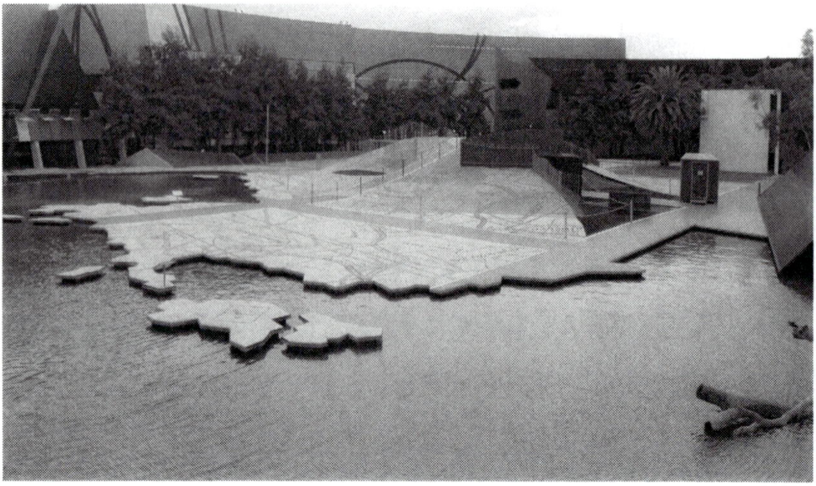

Figure 9.1. The Garden of Australian Dreams

open to multiple readings. Instead, trained guides roam the space answering visitor's queries, explaining the history, and telling stories sparked by various references and features.

Between January and May 2012, my colleague Stephen Barrass and I facilitated a collaborative design and peer-review process with 150 students from the Cross-Media Production unit at the University of Canberra, in collaboration with the National Museum of Australia (NMA). The project began in late 2011 through a conversation with Catherine Styles, the Education Officer and Media Manager at the National Museum of Australia, where we proposed to use mobile media to overlay extra information on the text panels in one of the museum galleries. Wi-Fi was to be installed in the outdoor courtyard at the centre of the museum, which led to further discussion about geo-located media that could be used to overlay digital stories in the area. Our project became therefore to augment National Museum of Australia's Garden of Australian Dreams using mobile media technologies such as GPS and Augmented Reality (which are digital overlays created in the physical space by using the mobile's camera).

Our proposal was to augment a selection of the symbolic elements in the garden with a layer of geo-located mobile media (GPS points in a map that can be seen through the mobile device) and a layer of Augmented Reality media (3D objects that can be overlaid on top of the physical space via the mobile's camera). The idea was to design a digital experience that could engage visitors with the hidden meanings in the Garden of Australian Dreams' symbols that architects had embedded in the open space. We were aware of the interpretive problems the garden posed to visitors, and thought that a digital layer of interpretation could help bridge the built and symbolic environments present in the garden. At a basic level, we wanted to connect the symbolic elements in the Garden of Australian Dreams to the objects referred to in the collection in the National Museum of Australia. During the design process, we also realized that the digital media overlay provided an opportunity for our students to augment the Garden of Australian Dreams with their own personal stories and memories.

Due to the scale of the project, the management of the peer produced material became one of the most important challenges. The large number of elements that the students generated was difficult to handle in the open platforms chosen to display this content in the mobile devices. Evaluating this content in terms of interface design, technical issues and curatorial concerns became the biggest task.

Collective Creativity and Peer Production

Three concepts guided our design choices during the project: peer production, collective creativity and collective intelligence. This section provides a short background to these concepts.

'Peer production' was coined to describe the 'free software' movement. As Benkler (2006) points out, peer production has been driven by personal interest and social capital, rather than by contracts or marketing. For example, in producing 'free software', thousands of volunteer programmers worked together to develop the source Linux operating system (Benkler and Nissenbaum 2006). Yet in spite of the 'personal capital' spirit of the effort that Benkler notes, the coordination of massive production by widely dispersed individuals who were working mostly online and in isolation depended not only on their will to participate, but also on the availability of sophisticated technical infrastructures. Revision control systems were implemented to automatically manage the relationships between different versions of the various modules. This modular framework and revision system enabled the integration of individual contributions at different levels of granularity, and provided coherence to the whole project.

'Collective creativity' has to do with the emergence of large-scale collaborative projects online facilitated by increasing access and ease of use of media production equipment. The design of socio-technological frameworks within which others can express their creativity is an important new role for artists and designers involved in community driven arts and collaborative media projects (Sanders 2001). The availability of 'prosumer' (professional consumer) equipment has put professional quality video, audio and editing capabilities into the hands of consumers (although this does not necessarily mean that professional skills are included in the package). The combination of lower barriers to production, higher Internet bandwidths, and a free software movement that has enabled the easy creation of online social environments, have enabled the emergence of ad-hoc collaborative projects at a much larger scale, thus fostering new forms of collective creativity. One example is the use of green screen special effects by the founders of Wreckamovie.com. Although considered 'old technology', green screen special effects were previously difficult to produce without professional equipment. The ability to produce special effects at home on a computer led a group of Finnish filmmakers to peer produce a feature length sci-fi parody of *Star Trek*, which they released for free on the Internet in 2005. In order to facilitate their peer production process, they built the Wreckamovie.com social platform. Wreckamovie.com was used for the self-selection of roles and integration of modular parts at different granularities. This community of filmmakers has since produced several more feature length films using the peer production model of self-selection, distribution, decentralization and a shared objective to create a free cultural good. More than 300 projects are now underway on the site. As in the case of the Linux operating system, however, and as pointed out by Hjorth (2014) in her analysis of the Wreckamovie community, despite the utopian rhetoric around a level playing field based purely on enthusiasm, the community does have a social hierarchy according to a 'karma' widget that rates activity and contributions, and the number of 'likes' each members receives. Collective creativity has been generated through games, contests and networks, but Yu et al. also suggest that systems that foster social learning are a promising direction for the future (Yu et al. 2012).

'Collective intelligence', which involves solving complex problems through a massive collective effort, has been purposefully harnessed for scientific discovery in 'serious games' such as Foldit (a 'protein folding' online game) where gamers solved the structure of a retrovirus enzyme that had stumped scientists for more than a decade. Another example of collective intelligence in action is an Alternate Reality Game (ARG) called the Beast. The game was conceived as an online viral marketing campaign for Spielberg's sci-fi film *A.I.* in 2001. An online discussion group on Yahoo, called the Cloudmakers, formed to share clues about the puzzles in the game. The group grew to include more than 7,000 members who 'brought together a diversity of skills ranging from cutting edge spectral analysis to a unique and unrivalled knowledge of historical events and world literature . . . and a whole lot more' (http://www.cloudmakers.org/). The Cloudmakers solved three months' worth of puzzles in three weeks. In order to stay ahead of their audience, the writers, known as 'puppeteers', began to include material from the Yahoo lists into the story, creating a feedback loop with their audience.

More recent examples have further developed the distinctive aspects of collective intelligence and participatory audiences, and there has been a change in emphasis in the definition towards a focus on an audience contributing to the 'additive comprehension of an extendable story world' (Jenkins 2011). Yu et al. distinguish the open-endedness of this kind of participatory content creation from other crowdsourcing tasks. The authors analysed a variety of online collective activities, such as Foldit, Wikipedia, GalaxyZoo and Crowdfunding, in terms of routine or non-routine tasks, and aggregated or emergent outputs. Aggregated outputs are simply the sum of the parts, while emergent outputs occur when the integration of parts produces something novel, like in Foldit (Yu et al. 2012). Through this classification, these authors assign hierarchies between the various forms of online collaboration. For example, the quadrant of activities that involve non-routine tasks and have emergent outputs is distinguished from other forms of collective intelligence and labelled as collective creativity.

Social widgets (interface buttons such as 'star ratings', 'likes', 'thumbs up', and other ranking buttons) are also examples of crowdsourcing collective intelligence. This 'peer curation' challenges the traditional reliance on experts to judge quality and aesthetics in the media and in the arts. One example is the Brooklyn Museum's 'Click! A Crowd Curated Exhibition' discussed in previous chapters.

The recurring topic in ideas such as 'peer production', 'collective creativity' and 'collective intelligence' is how to create effective architectures of participation. These ideas also bring us back to the previous discussion about forms of public engagement and how they may play out online. These architectures of participation should ideally support the collaborative production and, more importantly, the curation of contributions. In our examples, some architectures of participation emerge organically and 'on site', that is, while the project is being generated, while others are carefully planned in advance.

In the next section, we describe our large-scale collaborative project, and discuss our findings in light of the various concepts presented above and their implied design choices.

Gathering a Collective of Creators

The project was run as part of the unit of Cross-Media Production, Bachelor of Media Arts at the University of Canberra. In this unit, students examine the forms, cultures and practices of cross-media or hybrid production, where producers use multiple technologies, media forms and modes of audience interaction to deliver a single work. They consider and evaluate the relationships between media elements and participatory audiences that characterize such works, and develop a critical understanding of current practice and theory in cross-media production. They apply that understanding by working in collaborative teams to integrate networked, linear and interactive elements into prototype cross-media projects.

We were offered an online testing space through the Australian Broadcasting Corporation (ABC), which had a project entitled MyTribe whose goal was to explore new forms of engagement and learning with media online. 150 students from the Cross-Media Production unit at the University of Canberra participated in the design of a collaborative interpretation of the Garden of Australian Dreams. In the initial stage of the design process, a guide presented official explanations of various symbolic elements to the students. The NMA also provided a gallery of high-quality images the students could use in their designs.

The students were asked to go to the Garden of Australian Dreams in their own time and document elements that they found interesting, as follows:

1. Walk around and find out what is there.
2. While walking around think about a Journey through the space that could be connected to form a story of some kind.
3. Select at least 5 waypoints along the Journey – graphic, sculptural, geographic, sonic, etc.
4. Document each waypoint using any or all of photos, sound recordings, sketches and notes.
5. Take focused, close up, evenly lit photos of each waypoint that can be used for image-based search and recognition using Google Googles or Layar Vision.
6. Take a note of the location and/or GPS coordinates of each waypoint. (Moodle documentation 2012)

The students were then required to upload this material to the Australian Broadcasting Corporation Pool website, a collaborative online space created by Australian Broadcasting Corporation, which is also used for teaching. As opposed to the closed system available at the university for student online work ('Moodle', an open source educational software system), Pool is open to the public; all our student activities were visible.

For this reason, we required our students to use nicknames to protect their privacy, although the page we created in Pool for the Garden of Australian Dreams project was branded as a University of Canberra student project page. The students were able to upload pictures, sound and video, include text, and comment on each other's work. They were also able to geo-locate their content (by visiting the site and grabbing GPS coordinates from their mobile, or by using freely available Google Maps based GPS localization services), and to link it through the Pool website to an augmented reality layer in Layar, a mobile application for Augmented Reality content. Pool provided this layer. In a third stage, the students were introduced to Google Fusion Tables (a free service provided by Google that facilitates the creation of simple data visualizations such as scatter-plots, map based visualizations, bar charts and network graphs). Students could create personalized pins with their GPS coordinates, add an image, text and an URL to their pins, and display them in a map visualization. This map visualization was then embedded into an HTML5 web app (an application running on the mobile by using a browser), which the students could customize.

Once the students had uploaded all their content to Google Fusion Tables, we discovered that it was very difficult to navigate through all the content. The students produced about 400 items, and when we attempted to display all of them in a single application, it looked as cryptic and hard to navigate as the physical space! We then asked each student to select his or her own pins and create a 'personal journey' through the Garden of Australian Dreams. Some students decided on a sequential narrative, marking each point with a number.

After each student had created his or her own journey, we then proceeded to the evaluation process. We asked the students to look at each other's projects and to 'vote' on them. The idea was to get a list of the ten best journeys and aggregate these in an application that the National Museum of Australia could launch for the general public. For this activity, we conducted a Usability Evaluation workshop. In this workshop, the students were presented with a fictional scenario in which they had been contracted to produce the official Garden of Australian Dreams Portal for the launch of the My Garden of Australian Dreams exhibition at the National Museum of Australia, and would therefore need to employ methods of Usability Evaluation to iterate on their prototypes and those of their peers. The methods for user-centred design presented to students were use-case scenarios, expert heuristics and user testing.

Use-case Scenarios

Use-case scenarios involve asking the designer to think from the perspective of another person. This can allow many new insights into the many assumptions they have made about the initial design, and issues with the technologies involved. The students were asked to write three use-case scenarios that respond to the question: 'How do you think visitors to the Garden of Australian Dreams would like to use a mobile web app?' Each scenario was a paragraph describing a possible activity at the garden with a mobile app. Students wrote the first best-case scenario from their own first-person perspective, 'as a designer who is interested in the possibilities of mobile media and storytelling in AR' (Moodle documentation 2012). The second scenario had to be from the perspective of their mother, 'who has gone to Garden of Australian Dreams to see your work on a sunny afternoon' (Moodle documentation 2012). And a third scenario had to be written from the perspective of a child of ten years from another country who has come on holiday with their parents, and is leading them around the Garden of Australian Dreams.

Student A identified technical challenges and also described preferences in terms of type of user:

> a strong Wi-Fi connection to make browsing Layar easy. . . .weather should be slightly cloudy so that use of the device would be easier e.g. there would be no sun glare on the screen causing the users vision is impacted negatively. . . all of the webapp content should be placed correctly, so not to cause any confusion and to keep continuity and also that all links were working and up to date. (Moodle documentation 2012)

Student B made general design suggestions and attempted to connect these to potential users:

> Having the web app for my mum would be a great benefit as it would allow for her to see my information throughout the garden without having to ask me what things are. It is also a great invention for my mum as my web app easy to use because she is not very tech savvy. It is also a great invention as she is able to see our families/and my own personal interpretation of each way point which would give her an insight of what the garden has to offer everyone on a personal level. . . Based on our experiences, as web app designers our group believes that having a web app for these different scenarios would increase the fun children would have in the Garden of Australian Dreams. For mothers it would make information easier to access if there were nobody to ask or answer their questions about the garden. For personal use, having that information there would mean we would be able to explain it if we took family or friends to visit the Garden of Australian Dreams. As a group we would change the initial web app design to make it more appealing to

a public audience. We would make the map zoomed in more along with the points of each journey for vision impaired users. (Moodle documentation 2012)

The above excerpts show how these students placed themselves within multiple perspectives – as potential users, as museum stewards, as media designers – above all wanting to contribute to improving the space of the museum without hesitating to claim a certain amount of ownership of this space.

Expert Heuristic Evaluation

Expert heuristic evaluation requires experts in the field to critique an existing design and suggest improvements based on their experience with similar applications and products (Preece et al. 2002). Students were asked to form into groups of three in a fictional situation where they were a new Cross-Media design studio starting up in Canberra. They were then asked to compare their use-case scenarios and discuss how Garden of Australian Dreams Portal v1.0 would work with these scenarios. In this situation, they were asked to act as experts, and assess how could their applications could be changed to fit better, based on their experience as web app developers. Each group had to write a summary proposal for My Garden of Australian Dreams v2.0 based on the scenarios.

A group of students acting as an 'agency' provided the following concrete technical recommendations:

> Our proposal for Garden of Australian Dreams v2.0 · Standalone APP for IPAD (Called GOpAD) that fits the style guidelines of the museum · Augmented reality (Need IPAD 2 or 3 because they have a camera, or IPhone 4 or 4s) optimized for this use (tour) · 3 different settings that change the tone and density of the journey, kids, teens and adults · treasure hunt in the Garden of Australian Dreams . . . information compared to cartoons/animations – way finding and a final RPG style score to make it competitive and unlock things as they walk around. Interactive Gamerfication.

The students were successful in identifying and articulating answers to issues with technical aspects of the application's design. Students also showed an awareness of the latest developments in mobile media technology, to an extent that might not have even been accessible to digital officers at the museum. One of the advantages of such a large technology-based collaboration is precisely the expanded knowledge exchange and multiple avenues which lead to solutions or alternatives to technology challenges. In terms of the success of this kind of collective creativity project, the compounded technology expertise was an important asset, and one that the museum could profit from much more if it were to incorporate similar initiatives as part of their permanent digital media research.

User Observation

Heuristics capture expert knowledge but that knowledge is still inherently subjective and based on a whole lot of implicit assumptions and untested hypotheses. According to Nielsen (2012), by observing five users in context interacting with a digital artefact, one can identify 70 per cent of problems that were never anticipated. This method is called 'discount usability' because it is much cheaper than a laboratory study with 100 users, and less risky than beta testing on your actual audience who may never come back. In this activity, the students were asked to imagine they were like psychologists or anthropologists recording observations of behaviour. Again they worked in groups; one member of the group was the User, and the other two acted as Observer 1, who recorded the user's spoken dialogue, and Observer 2, who recorded the number of button clicks and key presses, number of errors, and the time taken to complete subtasks and the total task. Observers were asked to avoiding telling the User how to do things. The User's task was to start from the Garden of Australian Dreams Portal, and from there navigate through the My Journey Web Apps of Observer 1 and Observer 2, whilst speaking aloud their thoughts as they progress (Lewis and Rieman 1993). They should also speak aloud the text of Journey items. After each Journey they should summarize their understanding of it. The following two questions were provided:

1. Did the user testing uncover different problems and issues or were they the same as those in the expert heuristic evaluation?
2. Based on your combined observations, how would you improve the WebApp to improve the performance in the task? (Moodle documentation 2012)

Students then had to upload their results to their Pool page.

Student G provided a thorough report of user observation:

LeeceyLou: I liked browsing through others' journeys/web apps, especially since I hadn't been through these journeys before. Both of the journeys I visited Citrusurfer and Artshesaid had substance and provoked my interest, resulting in a positive experience. Obviously I found the web apps easy to use, as I am now very

> familiar with that environment. The whole process went smoothly, the only hiccup being a broken link from the Garden of Australian Dreams portal web app to the Artshesaid web app. Easily fixed though!
> **Spoken Dialogue (Citrusurfer):** What's your web app called? What's your icon look like? Ok which part of Garden of Australian Dreams is your icon? Ah the clicky thing isn't working, what the heck? I can't click on it! What if it breaks? None of these are working I can't click on any of them near the dream house? Ok. I'm looking at the first waypoint now I'm reading the waypoint. Where did the waypoints go? Waypoint number 2! Number 3. That is number 4. And this is the last one, if it actually wants to work. Ok. So I assume your journey is about all over different experiences and places you've been and places you want to go. Ok what's your web app? Where's your icon? Thank you that was very informative. And that didn't work. What's going on with your link? Ok I'll just read what's here. Ok, I hope this works. All right I'm reading the second waypoint. I dunno which one I just viewed. Reading a different one now. Next one. Cool, now up to the last one. Awesome So I kind of knew what your journey was about anyway but it was cool seeing it. I like how you interpreted everything visually rather than metaphorically. (Moodle documentation 2012)

Afterwards, Student G performed an analysis of these records as follows:

> User Observation 1. Discuss how well the user performed the task, and what you observed in the process.
>
> She had trouble clicking on any of the links. She then eventually zoomed out to fix the problem but she took a while to find Citrusurfer's waypoint due to my lack of communicating the location properly. Once she found the link it was all-good from there. She read the waypoint and once she was done she found Artshesaid's waypoint. There was no link to the web app but after being informed of the URL she was able to easily navigate her way through the web app.
>
> 2. Did the user testing uncover different problems and issues or were they as predicted in the expert heuristic evaluation?
>
> She had difficulty controlling the map as predicted in the heuristic evaluation and also discover Artshesaid's missing link. Other than that there were no major issues.
>
> 3. Based on your combined observations, how would you improve the Web App to improve the performance in the task?
>
> To improve the web app I would make navigation clear and introduce the function of searching for a particular app to make navigation easier instead of looking at each waypoint through the clutter. A search bar would make a world of difference, maybe even a section with key words to find each way point or a list of the waypoint next to the map that will show where each waypoint is when you hover/click on it. (Moodle documentation 2012)

The benefit of peer creation is that it is much easier to find subjects to test digital platforms with. These user observations were invaluable for the students to identify further design issues, and it is often this kind of testing that becomes both difficult and costly for museums. Yet these students, as they were the creators of the digital platforms, were more than willing and interested in providing feedback and in analysing together any potential problems with their apps.

Final Filtering of Content

After the student evaluation activities were performed, the project coordinators were still left with large amounts of data that could not be easily displayed in the mobile app. The next task became to find mechanisms to narrow down the number of elements to be displayed, from 400 objects to 50 (collectively selecting 10 journeys).

Students were asked to 'favourite' journeys from their peers, using the ABC Pool social rating functions. They could not vote for their own journey, but they could select three other journeys.

The top journeys from this process were then distributed amongst an expert panel consisting of a curator, an official from NMA, the instructors and guest lecturers who had participated in explaining the Garden of Australian Dreams to students. The panel then created a list of ten journeys that were filtered into a new Layar channel for display in the mobile device.

We asked the students to imagine, design and evaluate their mobile applications in relation to the actors involved (users), the context (the physical space of the garden and the situation in which the application would be used), as well as aspects of the outcomes of their design choices. We were not, however, seeking a 'quality' judgement from the students in terms of meta-analyses of the contexts of their work. Our goal was much more limited, in that we sought to design exercises that would heighten the student's awareness of the context and users that would be involved with their design.

At this point, the involvement of students in the evaluation process became limited, and they were only able to view the selected journeys later on but not to make any amendments or comments on the final results of the selection process. In this part of the process, curators from the National Museum of Australia and guest speakers worked as a panel to make selections of content.

The screenshot in Figure 9.2 provides an example of the MyTribe page and the final mobile web app developed during the project.

As the results from the use-case scenarios show, students' appreciation of technical issues was highly developed. During this activity, students effectively reflected on the design challenges present in the environment.

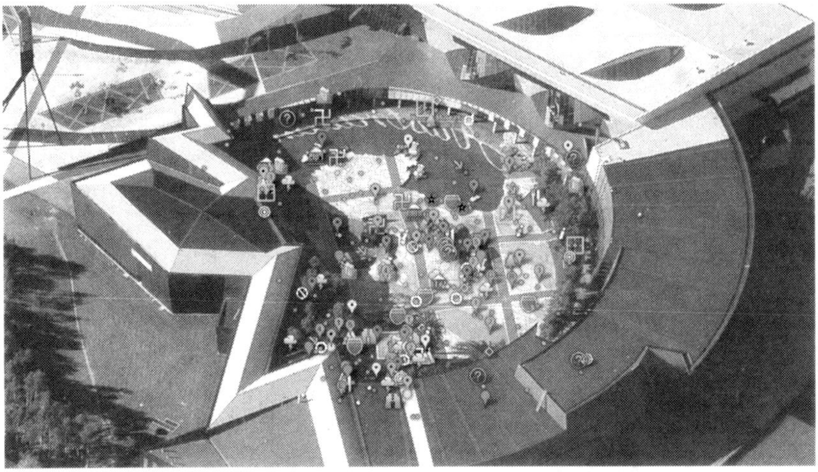

Figure 9.2. Geo-located Points of Interest in a Garden of Australian Dreams web app (all student points).

Map data ©2014 Google Imagery ©2014, CNES/Astrium, Digital Globe.

However, they were less successful in imagining issues that could arise for specific users, although they were able to consider more or less stereotypical types of users.

Ideally, these issues would have led to a discussion of use-case scenarios in class. However, since the evaluations were posted on the Pool website after the face-to-face workshop, the task of having to find each evaluation in a system not tailored for online teaching would be a complex one for tutors; this meant that feedback on these issues was limited.

The expert heuristic evaluation activity had better results in that students were able to articulate their recommendations as 'experts' concisely. At this point of their university degree, the students had acquired a good vocabulary to manage design challenges from a technical point of view. When contrasted with results from the use-case scenarios, it is clear that the educational challenge is in connecting these students to a community, in enabling them to put themselves in the shoes of others, rather than just concentrating on the technical aspects of design.

In relation to user observations, these seem to have helped students to identify new issues with the web app. For example, Student G began to see that a major problem with the app was navigation and the uncomfortable sense of being lost in a journey. Student G was then able to suggest improving searchability. Instructors should have had the opportunity to discuss further with Student G what was present in the transcript, but having the student responses and analyses posted on the Pool site after the in-lab exercise prevented the possibility of providing this kind of feedback. The sheer number of responses and students would have made the task very difficult in the classroom as well. One option to address this problem would have been to perform a task in which students peer reviewed each other's results, but as they lacked the appropriate background in design research methodology (which is both beyond the scope of the Cross-Media unit and beyond the scope of their bachelor's degree), this may have had counterproductive results.

From the above discussion several lessons can be extracted:

1. Prepare for content filtering. More than the coordination of discrete production tasks, the greatest challenges in large-scale digital media based peer productions are content filtering and cataloguing. In fact, progression from the production of the first few elements in a largely distributed project to a medium or large amount of elements happens extremely quickly and at an exponential rate!
2. Emphasize the importance of understanding the audience. In our case, users/producers were much more comfortable and skilled in creating material and evaluating it under technical webdesign criteria, than in evaluating it from the perspective of what other users might experience. It was hard for the students to place themselves in the shoes of other users. This suggests that training in evaluation should happen before production, and would perhaps help to improve the quality of material produced, and make the filtering task easier for participants and more robust for the project.
3. Use peers. Providing online feedback on evaluation tasks on a large scale is difficult when the number of instructors and their allocated time is limited. An alternative to the classroom model of teachers providing expert feedback is to shift the responsibility to peers, something that MOOCs (Massive Online Open Courses) are experimenting with (see, for example, the evaluation practices of Coursera, Udacity and other such sites). The issue then becomes the perception of appropriateness of feedback in a situation where students are expecting this feedback to come from teachers, and may have lower expectations of the kind of learning they might achieve from peer feedback.
4. Focus on system architecture. In a large-scale peer production, the organizers of production may profit more by spending the most amount of time creating a robust architecture for filtering and cataloguing content than using the majority of their time resources in creating the production activity. A simple production activity, as we

saw in this project, can lead to enormous amounts of data, so ensuring enough participation does not seem to be the major issue.

In Conclusion

This project showed that museums attempting large-scale peer productions need to invest the majority of resources in creating a robust architecture for evaluation (of the interfaces, of the content), prioritizing the creation of shared understandings of how to filter and categorize data once it is produced, and reducing the complexity of both evaluation and production tasks so that they can be distributed to peers, since as the project grows bigger, even the smallest task will become a very onerous process for a reduced number of expert evaluators.

As an exercise in collective creativity, the project was only partially successful, since at the end, a very small group was in charge of making the final selection. We think that an architecture where the final decision about content remained in the hands of the collective would require a different institutional setting. Thus, for future experiences, establishing solid collaboration pathways with host institutions should be a primary step in these types of collective creativity projects, for example by clearly outlining and agreeing upon the kinds of filtering that the institution can perform in the final outputs from participants. The task of managing content filtering and ranking so that they remain in the hands of a majority of participants could also be incorporated as part of the preliminary collective design discussion.

In contrast to the cases of the Museum of World Culture and the Museum of London, the National Museum of Australia has in this instance allowed a digital colonization of its institutional space. Through this activity, the museum has broken new ground in creating opportunities for digital participation, as it lets users decide form, function and content within a physically localized, digital layer of the museum. Provision opens up to personal stories that probably would not have been accessible for the museum outside of a peer-produced project. Access lies beyond the control of the museum, as the community is able to reappropriate collections and the physical space itself to create new personal narratives. Yet again, and as would be the case within the museum, the biggest challenge continues to be the sustainability of such endeavours. After the completion of this project, and after the final curation was taken over by museum officials, the responsibility of continuing to host and maintain the platforms created by the students vanished. The main hosting provider, ABC Pool, decided to close the platform after two years because it was no longer commercially profitable. While some of the content creators continue to maintain their personal stories, most of these projects were lost with the closure of Pool. Again, while the promise of enlarged participation sounds appealing and brings to mind ideas of expanded public engagement, in reality participation without responsibility for maintenance can quickly become futile.

The following chapter presents a different take on the use of digital technologies in museums. Explorations of the uses of new technologies go beyond the screen and into the realm of hybrid novel artefacts that blur the boundaries between digital and physical.

Endnote

1. The project described in this chapter was conducted in collaboration with Stephen Barrass, Associate Professor in Media Arts and Production, University of Canberra. A different chapter on this research has been previously published in S. Barrass and A.L. Sánchez Laws, *Experience and Evaluation in the Collective Creation of a Public Digital Exhibition*, in L. Candy and S. Ferguson (eds), Interactive Experience in the Digital Age, Springer Series on Cultural Computing, Springer, 2014.

Chapter 10

Cultural Interfaces to Environmental Data at the Questacon National Science Centre, Australia

The increased amount, sophistication and accessibility of large environmental data (static or real-time sensor based input) is creating new opportunities to investigate novel displays of these data. This chapter discusses a project to investigate the presentation of this information to the public. The project was a partnership between the Digital Design and Media Arts Cluster at the Faculty of Arts and Design, University of Canberra, and the Questacon National Science and Technology Centre in Canberra. The purpose of the project was to explore ways in which data about the energy consumption of the Questacon building could be used to present environmental issues around the topic of energy efficiency. The project involved research and the production of 'cultural interfaces' (interfaces that appropriate heterogeneous sources of data to tell a story from the perspective of cultural practices) with data derived from the physical environment: the building's structure, energy consumption, climate and the environmental effects of visitors themselves. The aims were to visualize this data in a novel way that promoted exploration and discovery by Questacon visitors; to reveal important narratives of the built environment through interactive data visualizations; to provide insight into the design of tangible interfaces to physical environmental data in a science centre context; to develop knowledge of the aesthetics of environmental data; and to create new understandings of forms of non-expert engagement with environmental data (visitors' experiences). This involved the exploration of touch, touchless and other digital and physical interfaces. A series of prototypes of interactive systems, some for online use and some for use in the physical space, gathered and represented the variety of environmental data from the Questacon building.

The Questacon National Science Centre building in Canberra, Australia, is full of life: the life surrounding it in the external environment, the life that passes through it with every visit, and its own material life as expressed by its electricity consumption, temperature and air quality features and dynamics. For most visitors, however, this life goes unnoticed. Busy with the hundreds of artefacts on display, young children and adults may be blind to the rich life and energy cycles that surround them. There is an opportunity therefore to create a mediated experience that can entice visitors into exploring these cycles.

Examples of this kind of project include the work of architect and theorist Alex Haw's AtmosStudio 'luminous architectural surveillance' in LightHive (2009), where LED lights were used to display real-time data from the movements of people inside London's Architectural Association (Hanrahan et al. 2009). ART+COM 'data sculptures', exhibitions about sustainability and climate change with tangible interfaces such as Level Green (2011) where the goal is to make accessible complex environmental facts and figures, are another point of reference. However, an even more important example is the 'Idea of A Tree' from Mischer'Traxler in Vienna. This project is an abstract tangible representation of environmental data in the form of a solar-based mechanical apparatus that dyes and wraps a thread around a large spindle in response to the ambient lighting conditions (Argyriades 2009; Pinto et al. 2011). Beyond these prototypes or one-off exhibitions, the California Science Centre designed by Renzo Piano is entirely dedicated to showing how a physical building can be environmentally friendly and efficient.

Environmental data representations normally found in the Australian context consist of proprietary 'dashboards' that display graphs and statistics (for example as trend graphs of air quality, temperature levels, or household electricity consumption on a weekly, monthly or yearly basis, etc). An important goal of our project was to find alternatives to the types of interfaces. Instead of these highly legible displays, we were interested in the cultural role that more playful or abstract displays may have in the communication of scientific facts about the environment. We had a very broad definition of 'public', although we were aware that the primary audiences for these displays were families with small children.

The project employed a 'hands-on' iterative design process that was interdisciplinary and practice-based. An experimental phase initially focused on environmental analysis and conceptual development before moving on to prototyping.

Questacon provided three different sets of data: temperature, electricity consumption and air quality. The datasets were from different times of the year so it was not possible to make direct comparisons. We formulated the problem as follows: how do we turn a table of values into something meaningful for the public?

We decided that displays that presented statistical analyses of the data would be of interest to a more expert public that could make virtual visits, or the segment of the public who might be involved in policy (e.g. other institutions in Canberra's parliamentary triangle which are also working on improving the energy efficiency of their buildings). However, for exhibition displays, these types of interfaces were not a priority.

An overarching concept was developed that included the creation of five distinct themes: public engagement, play, sensory experience, mobile experience and social media dissemination.

Public Engagement

As discussed in the introduction, public engagement can include a flow of communication from the organization towards its communities; a flow from communities to organization via consultation; and a two-way flow implied in various forms of participation. In terms of the public engagement module for this project, it was conceived primarily as a communication module where the organization made data available to the public. The module sought to harness the potential of public data applications freely available online. The application chosen was Xively (formerly known as Pachube or Cosm.com), a cloud application that lets users create feeds that help them to visualize data sent from sensors. The graph generated via Xively would show a decrease in the electricity consumption of the Questacon building over a period of a year.

However, the idea of this public engagement module went beyond communication. Through the use of Xively, the goal was to connect several institutions in a single feed, and to have them establish a dialogue with each other about the sustainability and energy initiatives they pursued, as well as the results they were obtaining, so that visitors were able to contrast and compare electricity, air quality and water usage parameters between buildings. As would be expected this module would have required an enormous effort in promoting the adoption of such open data approaches to internal meters. Even within Questacon, this was hard to achieve. The organization was using a private vendor for the management of these datasets, and it was not possible to easily release a feed online from them.

Play

The second module developed sought to use novel touchless interfaces such as the Microsoft Kinect, building on the idea of Serious Games and Educational Games. A gestural interaction space shows the inner life of the Questacon building. Children learn about relationships between temperature, air quality, electricity consumption and their own activities through a playful, immersive and highly reactive interface that tells the story of energy efficiency and sustainability. The space allows children to reveal and explore different layers of the building that would otherwise remain hidden to them. These include the building's electrical wiring, water system, air conditioning ducts, insulation and other structural materials. Visualizations show streams of electricity, water, heat and CO2 based on real-time data from sensors in the building and its weather station. Children can 'dive' into the data in the 3D space, and swim through particles. Their movements are tracked and shown as heat maps in the visualization.

These interfaces sought to explore ways of approaching these datasets where the organizing principle was the idea of 'play' instead of 'search'. In their work on the visualization of large cultural datasets, Ennis-Butler, Hinton and Whitelaw (2011) have spoken about Shneiderman's 1996 Visual Information Seeking (VIS) approach, which recommends 'Overview

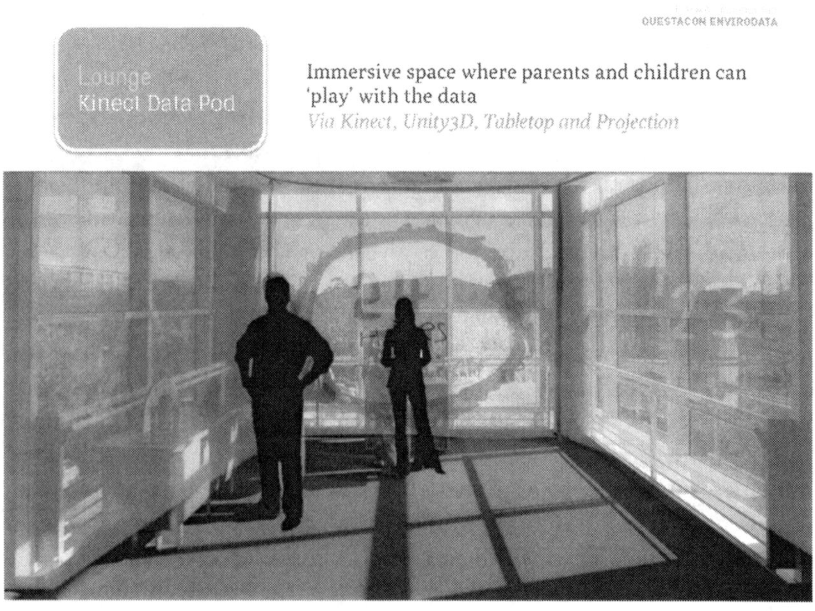

Figure 10.1. Dataviz concept – Stephen O'Connor

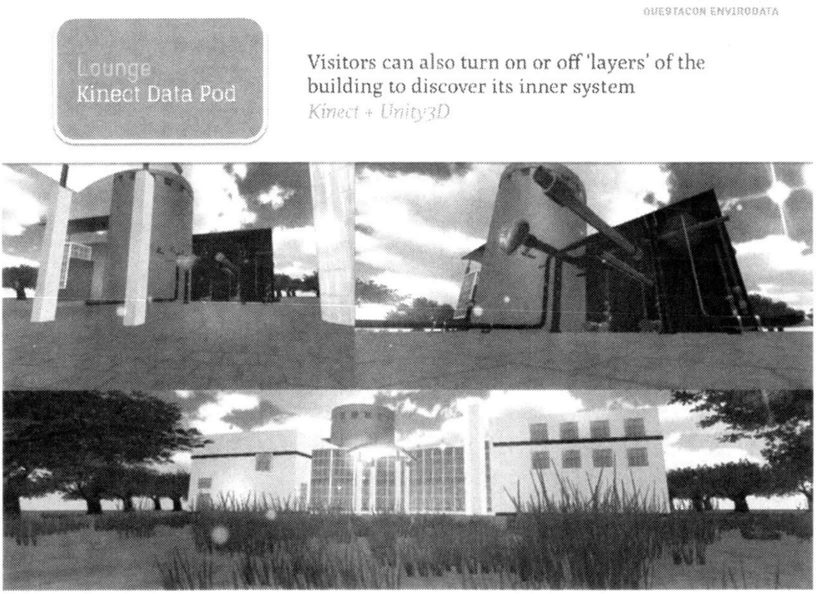

Figure 10.2. Kinect immersive game space – concept Ana Sánchez Laws

first, zoom and filter, then details on demand'. Within this view, presenting the entire dataset in first view was important in order to provide users with an instant impression of what was to be found there. In addition, creating simple ways to focus attention and go deeper into the data was another important design goal. In terms of the idea of play, Ennis-Butler, Hinton and Whitelaw (2011) follow Huizinga in discussing the activity in terms of creating a space that is safe, separate and pleasurable, and where the laws of everyday life do not apply. Furthermore, and following Callois, they discuss how play can be divided into *ludus*, where a strong structure with defined rules is in place, and *paidia*, where there are no rules at all (Ennis Butler et al. 2011).

In our proposed interfaces, the highly legible chronological interface fell within a *ludus* conception, while the more abstract interaction proposed in the interface with data as matter within the building would lean towards a *paidia* conception of play. In both cases, the goal was to make children use the datasets primarily as toys. These toys would, however, reveal important concepts about the inner functioning of the Questacon building.

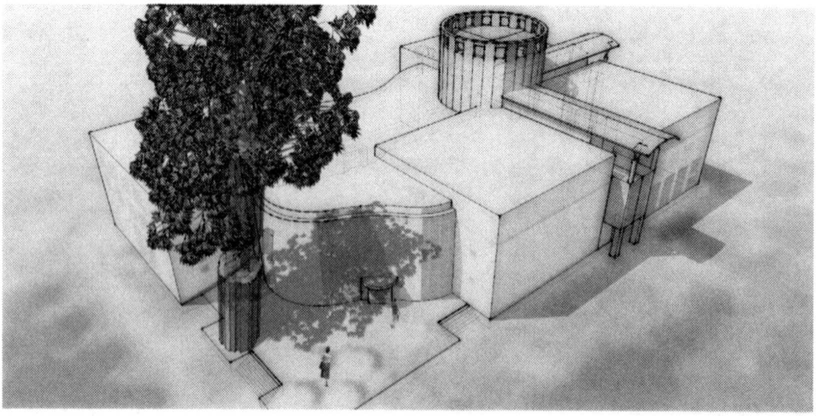

Figure 10.3. 'VAWT Tree', vertical wind axis turbine – concept Ana Sánchez Laws

Sensory Experience

We developed a sonification prototype, and two sculpture prototypes. The first sculpture prototype was an attempt at representing 'fields of energy', using magnetism as the driving force, and the second was an anesthetization of a Vertical Axis Wind Turbine (VAWT).

Exploring these prototypes and sculptures implied a process in which data would go back to an analogue format. This way, the boundaries between digital and physical were blurred and subverted. Information which originally came from the environment was transformed in a first cycle into datasets, which were then taken back to the physical environment as novel objects. The transformation, while lossy, would remain close to the original information, thus providing a layer of authenticity in the new objects.

Mobile Experience

Our concept for a mobile experience of the data was an Augmented Reality Telescope. When looking through a microscope, medical researchers or biologists are not interested in the microscope itself, but in what they can understand about a biological phenomenon. In this conception, untrained eyes gain less from looking through that microscope, in the sense that there is no specific knowledge being acquired to solve a problem. The same may be said of environmental science, where sensed data helps model and make predictions about changes in the environment for the purposes of assessing risk and responding to future

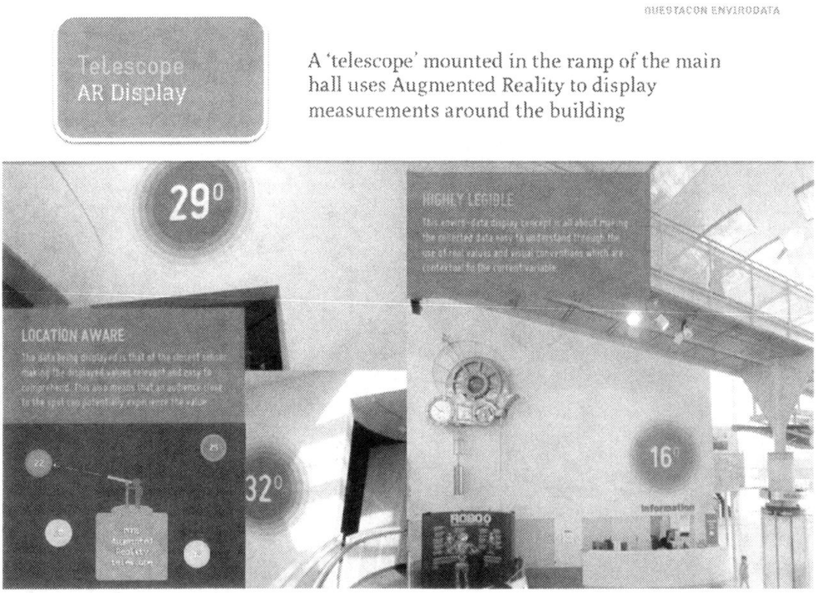

Figure 10.4. Augmented Reality Telescope shows temperature in various parts of the building – concept Stephen O'Connor

conditions. For an untrained person, data coming from environmental sensors may be meaningless. However, the aesthetic pleasure derived from looking at stylized representations of environmental data may be a way to invite the public to discover more about the scientific interpretation of the data.

For Questacon visitors, primarily children, the aesthetic and sensory gains may be a prerequisite for any later engagement with the problem-solving tasks of the environmental scientist or the environment-aware adult. Nevertheless, there is the risk that such an activity will create a 'shield', a barrier that in fact detaches from the impact of this sensing and understanding upon the environment itself.

Social Media Dissemination

We also created a film that shows the Questacon building and its surrounds. This was a poetic exploration of the forms of the built environment, the interplay between light and shadow, between interior and exterior environments, accompanied by a text that highlighted the current work that Questacon is doing to manage its energy consumption.

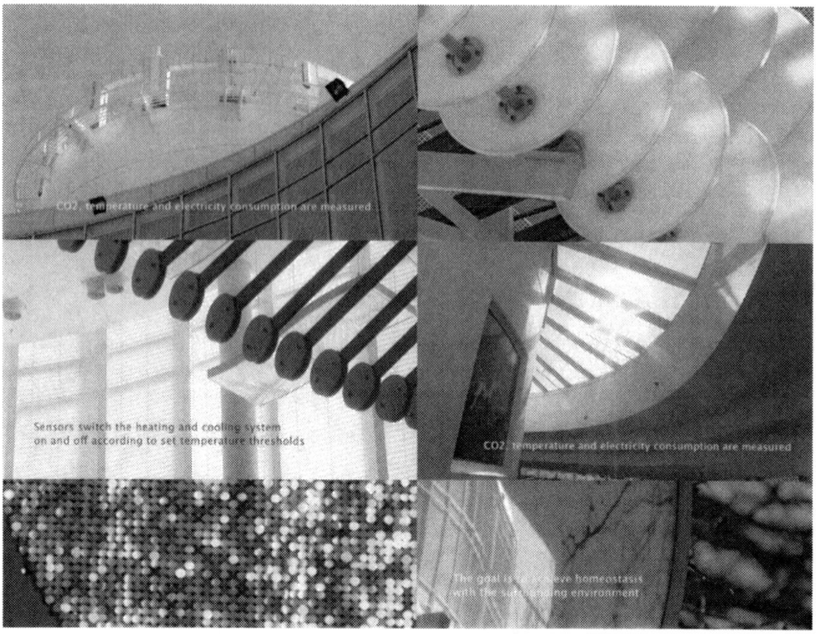

Figure 10.5. Poetic film exploring the inner and outer environments of Questacon – concept and realization Ana Sánchez Laws

We also created a draft framework that would help us to understand when we were 'upcycling' or 'downcycling' the datasets (Munroe, Hatamiya and Westwind 2006; Steinhilper, Hieber and vd Osten-Sacken 1997; Steinhilper and Hieber 2001).

Within this framework, the public engagement activities had the highest potential to achieve the intended outcome of informing and encourag-

Table 10.1. Upcycling and Downcycling data

Impact	Upcycling	Downcycling
Social	Communicating the need to focus on energy consumption	No awareness raising value
Economic	Augmenting efficiency in other buildings	Having no impact in longer term energy conservation action
Political	Public data	Enclosure/exclusion
Cultural	Aesthetic Symbolic	Ugliness, invasiveness
Environmental	Expressing underlying sustainability principles	Consuming more energy than the potential benefits
Intellectual	Producing knowledge	Producing misinformation or becoming noise

ing the public to become more involved in urban sustainability issues. The novel objects we prototyped could function as initial hooks into the topic, but would fall short of presenting a more intelligible message. In terms of interfaces that used play as a starting point, the problem of the dilution of the message or misinterpretation needed to be addressed.

In Conclusion

In this project, we sought to explore alternative ways of presenting large and complex datasets for an audience of science centre visitors. The prototypes embodied a desire to abandon searches as the preferred method of access to digital material, and to favour concepts such as play and mobility, as well as highlighting analogue to digital cycles that could be established between interfaces and data. Social media platforms that helped share environmental data (Cosm/Xively) were seen as an important tool for dissemination and public engagement, but throughout the project it became apparent that this particular possibility was the most demanding of all potential activities, since it required the release of potentially sensitive information from the institution. Other forms we explored of representing these environmental data (data sculptures, 3D visualisations, films) were more aligned with what the institution normally does (objects in the exhibition which show a physical or biological phenomenon). The issue is whether these more standard formats would in fact contribute to broadening the outreach of the message of sustainability and environmental awareness that Questacon wanted to send to the community, or whether the institution was again limiting itself to the public that already knew and cared for its work.

Within the scope of the project, it was not possible to go onto the next stage of testing the reception of the various prototypes. For other institutions wanting to repeat similar experiences, this step is essential to be able to understand the true impact of their outreach initiative.

Conclusion

The development of channels of communication between museums and their various stakeholders has been a major concern for museums in the last few decades, as these institutions move away from a focus on the conservation of material culture towards a focus on their role as forums for the dissemination and negotiation of knowledge. Museums use social media to take on new roles, seek new audiences and become sites of debate and discussion, even allowing multiple interpretations of the objects they hold.

This chapter provides a short reflection upon the four main topics the book has set out to deal with: participation, sustainability, trust and diversity in the context of museum digital media.

New Forms of Participation

Concerns with issues of gender, ethnicity, class and power in social structures and their implications for democracy building have driven a large amount of recent scholarship on museums. The emergence of digital media has raised concerns as to how to understand the dialogue and connections that digital media are affording museums.

It is currently argued that museum social media can help to increase participation (access, creative reworking of collections, debate) by working as platforms to build trust, allowing for post-visit feedback, and in general communicating with museum visitors in a two-way fashion. Since the last part of the twentieth century and the beginning of the twenty-first, a large number of theorizations about museums have dealt with the organization's social role and mission, and with shifting focus from the organization to the communities it is meant to serve. The discussion has very much centred on institutional voice and authority and issues of participation. Indeed, the creation of a sense of community comes from participation in a variety of ways, and a museum's web presence may enhance that participation through the use of social media.

As has been shown in the examples in this book, museums are using social media to explore new flows of information and public engagement, from communication to consultation to participation and structural involvement. Social media make visible cases where participation is structural, by letting us see if the community of users has been involved in the curatorial process or decisions made about an exhibition or museum activity, but the question remains as to how this structural involvement online feeds back into institutional practices offline. It seems though that if structural involvement occurs online, it is because the institutional culture of the museum allows it from before, as it is often the case that the more open the museum is to allowing visitors to take part in decisions at the physical museum, the more it will be willing to do the same online. Also, social media will demand constant follow-up and an understanding between museum leadership and staff in charge of these media about the type of communication they are trying to foster.

A number of museums have embraced social media's call for broader public engagement. Many examples in this book show the numerous efforts and resources museums are devoting to this task. Social media amplifies the web as a place to make connections between people, who then have started to connect their collections of valuable possessions in many creative, challenging, organic webs of knowledge. Armies of enthusiastic amateur curators and collectors are eagerly participating in the online preservation, conservation and dissemination of heritage at a scale and pace greater than ever before. In this landscape, museums are redefining themselves as hubs for community building.

The paradigm shift in museums' views of the World Wide Web from a place for storage space towards a place for encounter is becoming a reality. The key issue in this shift is the redefinition of the museum-community relationship, and the changes in power structures this may involve.

Digital Sustainability

The above points to an enormous growth of the generation of culture and heritage in digital forms. A large amount of culture now lives and evolves online, and ideally, museum technology needs to support generational bridges for this emerging heritage. As highlighted throughout the book, a pressing question for museums in this regard is the sustainability of digital heritage. It has been noted that in documents such as the National Library of Australia's 'Guidelines for the preservation of digital heritage' for UNESCO's Memory of the World Programme, issues regarding the participation of a broader range of stakeholders in aspects of digital heritage were not salient in discussions about what to do to protect or disseminate heritage. The document reflects the assumption that museums will continue to be the main custodians, both off- and online. This situation seems nevertheless to be in flux.

As with New Museology in the twentieth century, social media call for a rethinking of the role of museums in the twenty-first century. This involves asking how museums, national institutions, international bodies and the media define digital heritage through practices, policies, funding and public opinion in ways that address limitations imposed on the public's participation, limitations which in turn may no longer fit with the public's expectations.

The role of museums needs to be expanded so that it includes the 'contemporary experience' as part of the preservation of digital heritage. In this regard, social media can be an important asset. The question is one of moving from an exclusively institution-controlled view of heritage to one where responsibilities are horizontally shared between institution and community. Social media are part of a culture in which voices of 'authority' are increasingly being challenged. As discussed when dealing with the issue of trust online, museums must now address how to incorporate the voices of a variety of stakeholders without diminishing the public trust in the institution. The question becomes which voice – are there still some groups that get preferential treatment, are there groups that continue to be excluded from taking a more involved part in museum activities? – and in this sense, how social media change museum communication practices and frameworks for engagement – do social media help promote a more open culture at the museum, or do they on the contrary provide grounds for more restricted participation from the public?

For non-linear experiences such as social media interactions, it is necessary to question whose experience should be preserved, and the problem of the subjectivity of the interactive experience. When preserving games, artworks, multicomponent systems (e.g. interlinked systems for display, haptics and sound which may be triggered by human interaction), whose point of view do museums choose, and why? In this sense, we see a return to the problem of authenticity, the authority and credibility of museums, and the emerging challenges of expert vs. non-expert control over the experience.

Trust and Community-Building, On- and Offline

Social media technologies provide a unique opportunity to make visible the museum's networks of social relations online. As argued by

Haythornthwaite (2005), investments in technological infrastructure help institutions to make visible latent ties of common interests amongst their stakeholders (for example, when institutions invest in communication channels such as social media). From the experiences presented throughout the book, it can be concluded that providing platforms for the collaborative creation of heritage has become a core activity of museums, and that a very diverse range of museum stakeholders has joined in to a much greater extent and with far more evident power the common enterprise of the communication of heritage. This change must be received with the warmest of welcomes; it hopefully points to a future in which museums will continue to play an important role in creating and maintaining community.

As pointed out before, the legitimation of a given version of history or culture by museums is at times a point of conflict when one considers what the web and social media might bring. A decision has to be made as to whether to be transparent about debates and contestations about heritage online, and when and how to include multiple interpretations coming from online audiences. The abuse of trust under the cloak of Internet anonymity is a real threat, yet audiences seem to be more inclined to return the trust the museum bestows on them. No doubt the dynamics will continue to change, but it is important for museums to recognize that establishing and maintaining trust will be one of the vital tasks of their online activities.

Diversity

When looking at the content of the large conferences which deal with questions regarding digital technologies in museums, the lack of contributions addressing the issue of diversity is alarming. In a global environment, questions of identity and inclusion should be as much in the forefront of museum online activities as they are in their physical museum routines. It seems though as if the message of The New Museology and the awareness it brought to the sector in terms of the social, economic and political forces involved in the representation of culture have yet to be included in the language of digital heritage. One important contribution in this area is by Skartveit and Goodnow (2010), who have undertaken solid groundwork in beginning to address imbalances of power visible in museum digital practices. For example, these researchers warn us of the potential tokenism implied in relegating difficult issues affecting minority groups to an almost invisible URL. They also highlight, however, how the Internet, and especially social media, has helped smaller groups to create networks that can bypass official limitations in the dissemination and preservation of their heritage.

In a different piece of research on the heritage of recent migrants (unpublished), I have investigated Braithwaite's work on 'weapons of the weak' (2004), which may be very relevant for the issue of diversity in digital heritage. Braithwaite discusses how so-called weak groups can create conditions that advance their causes in contexts where they interact with very powerful actors. For Braithwaite, when weak groups recognize the power of networked governance, where power is distributed through multiple nodes and actors other than the traditional central stakeholders can attain power, they can harness the power of enrolling experts and placing them in strategic positions. Following on from this work, increasing support for a more diverse digital heritage may require three strategies:

a) Turning the quest to salvage a specific heritage item into a larger cause that can appeal to other groups
b) Using inclusive and strategic networking to enrol experts and other influential actors, which Braithwaite (2004: 312) describes as 'creating a galaxy of networked power'
c) Placing the new networks in nodes of governance and fora that can impact the decision-making processes concerning their heritage.

Throughout the examples provided in this book, it is clear that some groups are successfully adopting these strategies in their quest to gain visibility and recognition of their heritage via digital means. Hopefully this book also represents a step forward in providing a solid base for initiatives where diverse groups, curators and digital technologists create healthy and thriving galaxies of networked power for the safeguarding and enjoyment of digital heritage.

References

Alonzo, F., F. Garzotto and S. Valenti. 2000. '3D-Temporal Navigation and the Web: How to Explore a Virtual City along Multiple Historical Perspectives', *Museums and the Web 2000 Conference. Selected Papers.* http://www.archimuse.com./mw2000/papers/garzotto/garzotto.html.

Anales de la Convención. 1904. *Proyecto de Ley 3(55), 15 de julio de 1904.* Panama: Biblioteca Nacional Ernesto J. Castillero R.

Anderson, D., and G. Britain. 1997. *A Common Wealth: Museums and Learning in the United Kingdom.* London: Department of National Heritage.

Anderson, M.L. 1997. 'Introduction', in K. Jones-Garmil (ed.), *The Wired Museum: Emerging Technology and Changing Paradigms.* Washington DC: American Association of Museums, 11–32.

Argyriades, M. 2009. 'LEVEL GREEN – The Concept of Sustainability'. Yatzer. http://www.yatzer.com/LEVEL-GREEN---The-Concept-of-Sustainability.

Australia ICOMOS. 1988. *Guidelines to the Burra Charter.* Burwood: Australia ICOMOS. http://australia.icomos.org/wp-content/uploads/Guidelines-to-the-Burra-Charter_-Conservation-Policy.pdf.

Baier, A. 1986. 'Trust and Antitrust', *Ethics* 96(2): 231–60.

Barlow, J.P. 1996. *A Declaration of the Independence of Cyberspace.* Davos: Electronic Frontier Foundation. https://projects.eff.org/~barlow/Declaration-Final.html.

Barthes, R., and S. Heath. 1977. *Image, Music, Text.* London: Fontana Press.

Benkler, Y. 2006. *The Wealth of Networks: How Social Production Transforms Markets and Freedom.* New Haven, CT: Yale University Press.

Benkler, Y., and H. Nissenbaum. 2006. 'Commons-based Peer Production and Virtue*', *Journal of Political Philosophy* 14(4): 394–419.

Bennett, T. 1995. *The Birth of the Museum: History, Theory, Politics.* London: Routledge.

Berners-Lee, T. 1989. *Information Management: A Proposal.* Meyrin: CERN.

Bernstein, S. 2008. 'Where Do We Go From Here? Continuing with Web 2.0 at the Brooklyn Museum', paper presented at the Museums and the Web 2008 conference, Toronto, 31 March.

———. 2009. 'Crowdsourcing the Clean-Up with Freeze Tag!', *bloggers@brooklyn museum.* http://www.brooklynmuseum.org/community/blogosphere/2009/05/21/crowdsourcing-the-clean-up-with-freeze-tag/.

———. 2011. 'Should I Stay or Should I Go?', *bloggers@brooklynmuseum.* http://www.brooklynmuseum.org/community/blogosphere/2011/09/07/should-i-stay-or-should-i-go/.

Billings, S. 2011. Social Media Dialogue. Scott Billings Blog. Originally written for Museum Next 14 (unavailable), n.p. http://www.scottbillings.co.uk/social-media-dialogue/.

Bowen, J.P. 2010. 'A Brief History of Early Museums Online', *The Rutherford Journal* 3: n.p. http://www.rutherfordjournal.org/article030103.html.

Box, K. 2014. 'Social Scholar: Using Social Media in Museums, Archives and Libraries', *SAS Blogs*, 5 September. http://blogs.sas.ac.uk/2014/02/06/social-scholar-27-february-using-social-media-in-museums-archives-and-libraries/.

boyd, d.m. 2004. 'Friendster and Publicly Articulated Social Networking', *Extended Abstracts of the 2004 Conference on Human Factors and Computing Systems*, pp. 1279–82.

Branagan, D.F. 1979. 'The Idea of a Museum', in R. Strahan (ed.), *Rare and Curious Specimens: An Illustrated History of the Australian Museum*. Sydney: The Australian Museum, 1–6. http://australianmuseum.net.au/uploads/documents/27103/rare_and_curious_specimens_complete_lowres_web.pdf.

Braithwaite, J. 2004. 'Methods of Power for Development: Weapons of the Weak, Weapons of the Strong', *Michigan Journal of International Law* 26(1): 298–330.

Brooklyn Museum. 2008. *Exhibitions: Click! A Crowd-Curated Exhibition: Top Ten Compared*. Brooklyn, NY: Brooklyn Museum.

Brundtland, G.H., and UN World Commission on Environment and Development. 1987. *Our Common Future*. Oxford: Oxford University Press.

Bruns, A. 2008. *Blogs, Wikipedia, Second Life, and Beyond: From Production to Produsage*. New York: Peter Lang.

Byrne, D.R., H. Brayshaw, T. Ireland and N.S. Wales. 2003. *Social Significance: A Discussion Paper*. Sydney: NSW National Parks and Wildlife Service.

Camargo de Cooke, M. 2003. 'Entre Penas y Glorias: 100 Años de Museos en Panamá', in R. Miró Grimaldo, A. Castillero Calvo and I. Gólcher (eds), *Panamá, itinerario de una nación*. Panama: El Hombre de La Mancha, 165–84.

Cameron, D.F. 1968. 'A Viewpoint: The Museum as a Communications System and Implications for Museum Education', *Curator: The Museum Journal* 11(1): 33–40.

———. 1971. 'The Museum, a Temple or the Forum', *Curator: The Museum Journal* 14(1): 11–24.

Cameron, F. 2003. 'The Next Generation – "Knowledge Environments" and Digital Collections', paper presented at the Museums and the Web 2003 conference. Retrieved on 13 September 2014, http://www.museumsandtheweb.com/mw2003/papers/cameron/cameron.html.

———. 2007. 'Beyond the Cult of the Replicant: Museums and Historical Digital Objects – Traditional Concerns, New Discourses', in F. Cameron and S. Kenderdine (eds), *Theorizing Digital Cultural Heritage: A Critical Discourse*. Cambridge, MA: MIT Press, 49–75.

Cameron, F., and S. Kenderdine. 2007. *Theorizing Digital Cultural Heritage: A Critical Discourse (Media in Transition)*. Cambridge, MA: MIT Press.

Castells, M. 1996. *The Rise of the Network Society: The Information Age: Economy, Society, and Culture*, Volume I. Oxford: Blackwell Publishers.

Castillero Calvo, A. 1994. *Arquitectura, Urbanismo y Sociedad, La Vivienda Colonial en Panamá, Historia de un Sueño*. Bogota: Editorial Presencia.

Challborn, C. 2005. 'Wiki Products: A Comparison', *The International Review of Research in Open and Distance Learning* 6(2): 1–5.

Chan, S. 2009. 'Working with Wikipedia – Backstage Pass at the Powerhouse Museum', *Fresh & New(er)*. http://www.freshandnew.org/2009/04/working-with-wikipedia-backstage-pass-at-the-powerhouse-museum/.

———. 2011. 'More on Mobile Tech Impacts in Museums (extended Mashable remix)', *Fresh & New(er)*. http://www.freshandnew.org/2011/09/more-on-mobile-tech-impacts-in-museums-extended-mashable-remix/.

———. 2013. 'Considering Museum Collections as 8-bit Versions of History', *Fresh & New(er)*. http://www.freshandnew.org/2013/03/museum-collections-8-bit-version-history/.

Cheddie, J. 2012. 'Embedding Shared Heritage. Human Rights Discourse and the London Mayor's Commission on African and Asian Heritage', in R. Sandell and E. Nightingale (eds), *Museums, Equality and Social Justice*. London: Routledge, 270–80.

Clark, K. 2008. 'Only Connect: Sustainable Development and Cultural Heritage', in *The Heritage Reader*. London: Routledge, 82–98.

Coba, E. 2005. *Los pueblos indígenas de Panamá: Diagnóstico sociodemográfico a partir del censo del 2000.* Santiago: United Nations. Retrieved from the Economic Commission for Latin America and the Caribbean website, 30 November 2010, http://www.eclac.org/publicaciones/xml/7/22277/LCW20-panama.pdf.

Copenhagen Museum Website. 2012. *Væggen*. http://vaeggen.copenhagen.dk.

Council of Australian Museum Associations (CAMA). 1993. *Previous Possessions, New Obligations: Policies for Museums in Australia and Aboriginal and Torres Strait Islander Peoples*. Melbourne: Council of Australian Museum Associations.

Council of Europe. 2005. *Council of Europe Framework Convention on the Value of Cultural Heritage for Society*. Retrieved on 5 September 2014, http://conventions.coe.int/Treaty/EN/Treaties/Html/199.htm%3E.

Crane, G. 2004. 'Burarra Gathering: Sharing Indigenous Knowledge', paper presented at the Museums and the Web 2004 conference. Retrieved on 13 September 2014, http://www.museumsandtheweb.com/mw2004/papers/crane/crane.html.

Currall, Steven C., and A.C. Inkpen. 2008. 'On the Complexity of Organizational Trust: A Multi-level Co-evolutionary Perspective and Guidelines for Future Research', in R. Bachmann and A. Zaheer (eds), *Handbook of Trust Research*. Cheltenham: Edward Elgar.

Curthoys, A. 2002. *Freedom Ride: A Freedom Rider Remembers*. Sydney: Allan and Unwin.

Davis, H. 2006. *Search Engine Optimization. Building Traffic and Making Money with SEO.* Sebastopol, CA: O'Reilly Media, Inc.

Digital Preservation Coalition. 2008. *Digital Preservation Handbook*. York: Digital Preservation Coalition.

Dolan, J. 2001. 'Making Policy Practice: Previous Possessions, New Obligations in Western Australian Community Museums', *Open Museum Journal* 3: Policy and Practice (May).

Drotner, K., and K.C. Schrøder. 2013. *Museum Communication and Social Media: The Connected Museum*. London: Routledge.

Duxbury, N., and M.S. Jeannotte. 2010. 'Culture, Sustainability and Communities: Exploring the Myths', *Oficina do CES. Working Paper No. 353*. Coimbra: Centro do Estudos Sociais. http://www.ces.uc.pt/myces/UserFiles/livros/614_CES%20Oficina_353.pdf.

Ellison, N.B. 2007. 'Social Network Sites: Definition, History, and Scholarship', *Journal of Computer-Mediated Communication* 13(1): 210–30.

Ennis Butler, B., S. Hinton, and M. Whitelaw. 2011. 'Playing with Complexity: An Approach to Exploratory Data Visualisation' (WWW Document). Australian Council of University Art & Design Schools. Retrieved on 13 September 2014, http://

acuads.com.au/conference/2011-conference/article/ben-ennis-butler-sam-hinton-and-mitchell-whitelaw/.

Evans, M., K. Knight, D. Boden, N. MacGregor, S. Davies, N. Serota, D. Fleming, R. Sheldon, and J. Glaister. 2001. *Renaissance in the Regions: A New Vision for England's Museums*. London: Resource, The Council of Museums, Archives and Libraries.

Fiske, J. 1982. *Introduction to Communication Studies*, Studies in Communication. London and New York: Methuen.

Fleming, D. 2011. 'Museums and Social Responsibility', *ICOM News* 1 (February): 9.

Flores, L., and J.L. Batista. 2008. 'Los asesores electorales, del anonimato al protagonismo', *La Prensa* (24 August). Retrieved from the La Prensa website, 29 May 2011, http://mensual.prensa.com/mensual/contenido/2008/08/24/hoy/panorama/1493061.html.

Forte, A., V. Larco, and A. Bruckman. 2009. 'Decentralization in Wikipedia Governance', *Journal of Management Information Systems* 26(1): 49–72.

Foucault, M. 1970. *The Order of Things*. New York: Pantheon Books.

Fukuyama, F. 1995. *Trust: The Social Virtues and the Creation of Prosperity*. London: Hamish Hamilton.

Fylkeskommune, H. 2010. *En smak av sosiale medier*, Hordaland Fylkeskommune. Retrieved 5 September 2014, http://www.hordaland.no/Hordaland-fylkeskommune/Kultur/Fylkesbiblioteket1/Arkiv-fylkesbiblioteket/2010/Februar/ABM-kurset-Ein-smak-av-sosiale-media-i-gang-i-Hordaland/%3E.

Gaceta Oficial. 1916. Ley 8 del 23 de Octubre de 1916, *Segunda época* 12(2467): 6 November, Panama.

Gallagher, R. 2007. 'Camera Tossing Live'. Exhibition at the Torrance Art Museum, 31 March–26 May. Los Angeles, CA: Torrance Art Museum. http://projects.ryangallagher.name/cameratoss/gallery/show/web.php.

Gambetta, D. 1987. *Were They Pushed or Did They Jump? Individual Decision Mechanisms in Education*. Cambridge: Cambridge University Press.

Garden, M. 2012. 'Defining Blog: A Fool's Errand or a Necessary Undertaking', *Journalism* 13(4): 483–99.

Gelsthorpe, D. 2012a. 'Geology Curation Masterclass, Live Q&A', *Palaeo Manchester*. http://palaeomanchester.wordpress.com/2012/05/18/geology-curation-masterclass-live-q-a/.

———. 2012b. 'Type Specimens', *Palaeo Manchester*. http://palaeomanchester.wordpress.com/2012/06/22/type-specimens/.

Giaccardi, E. 2012. *Heritage and Social Media: Understanding Heritage in a Participatory Culture*. London: Routledge.

Giulianotti, R., and R. Robertson. 2004. 'The Globalization of Football: A Study in the Glocalization of the "Serious Life"', *British Journal of Sociology* 55(4): 545–68.

Gonzáles Guzmán, R. 1976. 'Estado Actual de los Museos en Panamá', Sunday issue of *El Panamá América* (14 September), n.p.

Goodnow, K. 2006. *Challenge and Transformation: Museums in Cape Town and Sydney*, Museums and Diversity. London: UNESCO.

Goodnow, K., and H. Ackman (eds). 2008. *Scandinavian Museums and Cultural Diversity*. Oxford: Berghahn Books.

Goodnow, K.J., J. Lohmann, and P. Marfleet. 2008. *Museums, the Media and Refugees: Stories of Crisis, Control and Compassion*. Oxford: Berghahn Books.

Grimen, H. 2009. *Hva er tillit?* [What is trust?]. Oslo: Universitetsforlaget.

Gyöngyi, Z., and H. Garcia-Molina. 2005. 'Link Spam Alliances', paper presented to the 31st International Conference on Very Large Databases.

Hanrahan, S., et al. 2009. '"Interface: Virtual Environments in Art, Design and Education", a Report on a Conference Exploring VLEs in Art and Design Education', *Arts and Humanities in Higher Education* 8(1): 99–128.

Haythornthwaite, C. 2005. 'Social Networks and Internet Connectivity Effects', *Information Communication and Society* 8(2): 125–47.

Hess, C., and E. Ostrom. 2007. *Understanding Knowledge as a Commons: From Theory to Practice.* Cambridge, MA: MIT Press.

Hinton, S. and M. Whitelaw. 2010. 'Exploring the Digital Commons: An Approach to the Visualisation of Large Heritage Datasets', *Electronic Visualisation and the Arts* (EVA 2010), London.

Hinton, S., and L. Hjorth. 2013. *Understanding Social Media.* London: Sage.

Hjorth, I. 2014. *Networked Cultural Production: Filmmaking in the Wreckamovie Community.* PhD thesis. Oxford: Oxford Internet Institute, University of Oxford.

Hoem, J. and T. Schwebs. 2010. *Tekst2null. Nettsamtalenes spillerom.* Oslo: Universitetsforlaget.

Hooper-Greenhill, E. 1991. *Museum and Gallery Education*, Leicester Museum Studies Series. Leicester: Leicester University Press.

———. 1992. *Museums and the Shaping of Knowledge.* London and New York: Routledge.

———. 1994a. *Museums and Their Visitors.* London and New York: Routledge.

———. 1994b. *The Educational Role of the Museum*, Leicester Readers in Museum Studies. London and New York: Routledge.

———. 1995. *Museums, Media, Message.* London and New York: Routledge.

House of Lords, 2000. *Science and Technology - Third Report*, Parliament of the United Kingdom, London. http://www.publications.parliament.uk/pa/ld199900/ldselect/ldsctech/38/3801.htm.

Hughill, M. 2011. 'Social Musings: The First Month of a New Plan'. Australian Museum Blog. Sydney: Australian Museum. http://australianmuseum.net.au/blogpost/web-2u/social-museumdia.

ICOM. 2010. 'Round Table Santiago do Chile ICOM, 1972', *Cadernos de Sociomuseologia Centro de Estudos de Sociomuseologia* 38(2010): 13–21. http://revistas.ulusofona.pt/index.php/cadernosociomuseologia/article/download/1640/1305

Immigration Museum in Melbourne website. Retrieved 5 February 2013, http://museumvictoria.com.au/immigrationmuseum/.

Ireland, T. 1996. 'Excavating National Identity', in S. Hunt (ed.), *Sites – Nailing the Debate: Archaeology and Interpretation in Museums.* Sydney: Historic Houses Trust of New South Wales.

———. 2012. *Conversation with A. L. Sánchez Laws.* Canberra: University of Canberra.

Jaén Suárez, O. 1998. *La población del Istmo de Panamá.* Madrid: Ediciones de Cultura Hispánica, Agencia Española de Cooperación Internacional.

Jenkins, H. 2009. *Confronting the Challenges of Participatory Culture: Media Education for the 21st Century.* Cambridge, MA: MIT Press.

———. 2011. 'Transmedia 202: Further Reflections', *Confessions of an Aca/Fan, the Official Weblog of Henry Jenkins.* http://henryjenkins.org/2011/08/defining_transmedia_further_re.html.

Johnson, L., et al. 2011. *The NMC Horizon Report: 2011 Museum Edition*. Austin, TX: The New Media Consortium.

Jones-Garmil, K. 1997. *The Wired Museum: Emerging Technology and Changing Paradigms*. Washington, DC: American Association of Museums.

Kalay, Y., T. Kvan and J. Affleck. 2007. *New Heritage: New Media and Cultural Heritage*. London and New York: Routledge.

Karp, I. 1992. 'Introduction', in *Museums and Communities: The Politics of Public Culture*. Washington DC: Smithsonian Institute Press, pp. 1–17.

———. 2006. *Museum Frictions: Public Cultures/Global Transformations*. Durham, NC: Duke University Press.

Karp, I., and S. Lavine. 1991. *Exhibiting Cultures*. Washington DC: Smithsonian Institution Press.

Keating, P. 1992. Copy of speech 'History of the Stolen Generations'. Retrieved 5 February 2013, http://www.stolengens.org.au/index.php?option=com_content&view=article&id=62:former-prime-minister-paul-keating-speech-at-redfern-park-1992&catid=36:our-history&Itemid=73.

Keith, C. 2010. *Agile Game Development with Scrum*. Boston: Addison-Wesley.

Kelly, L. 2009. 'The Impact of Social Media on Museum Practice', paper presented at the National Palace Museum, Taipei.

———. 2010. 'How Web 2.0 is Changing the Nature of Museum Work', *Curator: The Museum Journal* 53(4): 405–10.

Kenderdine, S. 1999. 'Inside the Meta-center: A Cabinet of Wonder', paper presented at the Museums and the Web 1999 conference. Retrieved 13 September 2014, http://www.museumsandtheweb.com/mw99/papers/kenderdine/kenderdine.html.

Klein, B. 2008. 'Cultural Heritage, Cultural Diversity and Museums in Sweden: Some Critical Reflections', in K. Goodnow and H. Ackman (eds), *Scandinavian Museums and Cultural Diversity*. Oxford: Berghahn Books.

Krug, S. 2006. *Don't Make Me Think: A Common Sense Approach to Web Usability*. Berkeley: New Riders.

Kumar, A. 2011. 'User Stories – Agile – Scrum'. Arun Kumar's Blog. Retrieved 6 April 2015, https://arunkumarhn.wordpress.com/2011/12/15/user-stories-agile-scrum/.

Lagerkvist, C. 2008. 'The Museum of World Culture: A "Glocal" Museum of a New Kind', in K. Goodnow and H. Ackman (eds), *Scandinavian Museums and Cultural Diversity*. Oxford: Berghahn Books.

Lemaire, R., and H. Stovel. 1994. 'Nara Document on Authenticity', paper presented to Nara Conference on Authenticity.

Lessig, L. 2008. *Remix: Making Art and Commerce Thrive in the Hybrid Economy*. New York: Penguin Publishing Group.

Lewis, C., and J. Rieman. 1993. 'Task-Centered User Interface Design', in *A Practical Introduction*. Boulder, CO: self-published shareware e-book. http://hcibib.org/tcuid/.

Lidchi, H. 1997. 'The Poetics and the Politics of Exhibiting Other Cultures', in S. Hall (ed.), *Representation, Cultural Representations and Signifying Practices*. London: The Open University, SAGE Publications.

Light, H. 2005. 'Changing Headsets: The Impact of Museums on Social Thinking'. Australia-Israel Hawke Lecture. Adelaide: University of South Australia. http://w3.unisa.edu.au/hawkecentre/events/2005events/2005ai_lecture_Light.asp.

Lister, M., et al. 2003. *New Media: A Critical Introduction.* London and New York: Routledge.

Lohman, J. 2006. 'Introduction to the Series', in K. Goodnow, *Challenge and Transformation: Museums in Cape Town and Sydney.* Oxford: Berghahn Books, 12–13.

Lopes, M.M. 2003. 'Museus e Educação na América Latina: o modelo parisiense e os vínculos com as universidades', in G. Gouvêa et al. (eds), *Educação e Museu: a construção social do caráter educativo dos museus de ciências.* Río de Janeiro: FAPERJ, Editora Access, 63–82.

Lukensmeyer, C.J., and L.H. Torres. 2006. *Public Deliberation: A Manager's Guide to Citizen Engagement.* Washington, DC: IBM Center for the Business of Government.

Lury, C. 2008. 'Cultural Technologies', in T. Bennett and J. Frow (eds), *Handbook of Cultural Analysis.* London: Sage, 570–86.

Macdonald, G.F., and S. Alsford. 1997. 'Conclusion: Toward the Meta-Museum', in K. Jones-Garmil (ed.), *The Wired Museum: Emerging Technology and Changing Paradigms.* Washington DC: American Association of Museums.

Marstine, J. 2011. *Routledge Companion to Museum Ethics: Redefining Ethics for the Twenty-First Century Museum.* Abingdon, UK and New York: Routledge.

Marty, P.F., and K.B. Jones. 2012. *Museum Informatics: People, Information, and Technology in Museums.* New York: Taylor & Francis.

Mason, R. 2003. 'Fixing Historic Preservation: A Constructive Critique of "Significance"', *Places: Forum of Design for the Public Realm* 16(1): 64–71, ArtFull Text (H.W. Wilson), EBSCOhost, viewed 8 August 2012.

Matos, J.S., K. Worcman, and R. Henriques. 1999. 'Museum of the Person: A Brazilian Experience of Virtual Museum', paper presented at the Museums and the Web 1999 conference. Retrieved 13 September 2014, http://www.museumsandtheweb.com/mw99/papers/worcman/worcman.html.

McCarthy, C. 2007. 'Before "Te Maori": A Revolution Deconstructed', in S. Knell, S. McLeod and S. Watson (eds), *Museum Revolutions: How Museums Change and Are Changed.* London: Routledge, 117–33.

McLean, K. 1999. 'Museum Exhibitions and the Dynamics of Dialogue '. http://www.findarticles.com/p/articles/mi_qa3671/is_199907/ai_n8833602/print.

McLeod, C. 2011. 'Trust', in E.N. Zalta (ed.), *The Stanford Encyclopedia of Philosophy.* http://plato.stanford.edu/archives/spr2011/entries/trust/.

McQuail, D (ed.) 2007, *Mass Communication*, SAGE Benchmarks in Communication, Vol. 4. London: SAGE Publications Ltd. doi: http://dx.doi.org/10.4135/9781446262467.

McShane, I. 2001. 'Challenging or Conventional? Migration History in Australian Museums?', in D. McIntyre and K. Wehner, *National Museums: Negotiating Histories,* Conference Proceedings. Canberra: National Museum of Australia, the Centre for Cross-Cultural Research and the Australian Key Centre for Cultural and Media Policy, 122–23.

Méndez Pereira, O. 1915. *Historia de la instruccion publica en Panamá.* Panama: Tipografía Moderna.

Migration Museum in Adelaide website. Retrieved 5 February 2013, http://www.history.sa.gov.au/migration/about.htm.

Miles, R. 1982. *The Design of Educational Exhibits.* London: Routledge.

———. 1986. 'Museum Audiences', *International Journal of Museum Management and Curatorship* 5(1): 73–80.

Ministerio de Cultura de España. 2011. 'El Museo Reina Sofía y la esfera pública digital'. http://www.mcu.es/principal/docs/MC/culturaEnRed/2011/CeR_publicadigital.pdf.
Moore, K. 2000. *Museums and Popular Culture*. London: Continuum.
Moore, R.W., J.F. Jaja, and R. Chadduck. 2005. 'Mitigating Risk of Data Loss in Preservation Environments', *Proceedings of the 22nd IEEE / 13th NASA Goddard Conference on Mass Storage Systems and Technologies*, 11–14 April. Monterey, CA: IEEE Computer Society, 39–48.
Morley, D. 1980. *The Nationwide Audience*. London: British Film Institute.
Mosoddik, B. 2009a. 'Museum of London and Social Software: the Conclusion of Effectiveness of Social Software on Museum', *The Working Life of Museum of London Blog*. London: Museum of London. http://blog.museumoflondon.org.uk/museum-of-london-and-social-software-the-conclusion-of-effectiveness-social-software-on-museum/.
———. 2009b. Interview with Heng Wu. London: Museum of London.
Moyes, N. 2011. 'A Social Media Plan for a Museum'. Moyes Noise (blog). http://nick-moyes.blogspot.com.au/2011/02/social-media-plan-for-museum.html.
Müller, K. 2002. 'Museums and Virtuality', *Curator: The Museum Journal* 45(1): 21–33.
Munroe, T., L. Hatamiya, and M. Westwind. 2006. 'Deconstruction of Structures: An Overview of Economic Issues', *International Journal of Environmental Technology and Management* 6(3): 375–85.
Munster, A., and A. Murphie. 2009. 'Editorial – Web 2.0: Before, During and After the Event', *Fibreculture Journal* 14: n.p. http://fourteen.fibreculturejournal.org.
Museum and Gallery Services, Queensland. 2014. *FREE Social Media Training*, Museum and Gallery Services Queensland. Retrieved 1 September, http://www.magsq.com.au/01_cms/details.asp?ID=980.
Nardi, B. (ed.). 1996. *Context and Consciousness: Activity Theory and Human-Computer Interaction*. Cambridge: MIT Press.
National Institute of Culture. 1978. Cultural Policy in the Republic of Panama. Madrid: UNESCO. Retrieved from the UNESCO website 7 December 2010, http://unesdoc.unesco.org/images/0003/000328/032826eo.pdf.
Neale, M. 2001. 'Future Shots. Prominent Australians Share their Thoughts on Museums of the Future', *Humanities Research* 8(1): 68–70. http://press.anu.edu.au/wp-content/uploads/2011/02/HRJ2001.pdf.
New South Wales. Community Relations Commission for a Multicultural NSW (issuing body). 2012. *Multicultural Advantage 2012–2015: Citizenship and Communities Portfolio*, 2nd edition. Sydney: Community Relations Commission.
Nielsen, J. 2012. 'Why You Only Need to Test With 5 Users, 2000', *Jakob Nielsen's Alertbox*. www.useit.com/alertbox/20000319.html.
Nootebom, B. 2008. 'Forms, Sources and Processes of Trust', in R. Bachmann and A. Zaheer (eds), *Handbook of Trust Research*. Cheltenham: Edward Elgar.
Official City of Sydney website on Aboriginal Sydney: Barani. Retrieved 5 February 2013, http://www.cityofsydney.nsw.gov.au/barani/themes/theme3.htm.
O'Reilly, T. 2005. 'What is Web 2.0. Design Patterns and Business Models for the Next Generation of Software'. http://oreilly.com/pub/a/web2/archive/what-is-web-20.html?page=1.
Ostrom, E. 2005. *Understanding Institutional Diversity*, Princeton Paperbacks. Princeton, NJ: Princeton University Press.

Parks, M.R. 2011. 'Social Network Sites as Virtual Communities', in Z. Papacharissi (ed.), *A Networked Self: Identity, Community, and Culture on Social Network Sites*. New York: Routledge, 105–23.

Parry, R. 2007. *Recoding the Museum: Digital Heritage and the Technologies of Change*, Museum Meanings. London and New York: Routledge.

———. 2011, 'Transfer Protocols: Museum Codes and Ethics in the New Digital Environment', in J. Marstine (ed.), *Routledge Companion to Museum Ethics: Redefining Ethics for the Twenty-First Century Museum*. London: Routledge, 316–31.

Patronato Panamá Viejo. 2006. *Panamá Viejo, de la aldea a la urbe*. Panama: Editorial Patronato Panamá Viejo.

Pérez, A. de, A Gandhi, and R. Shahani. 1976. 'Evolución histórico demográfica de la comunidad hindostana de Panamá', in Biblioteca de la Nacionalidad (ed.), *Panamá, sus etnias y el canal*. Panamá: Autoridad del Canal de Panamá, 189–212. http://bdigital.binal.ac.pa/bdp/tomoXXXP1.pdf.

Petersen, J. n.d. 'Distributed Collections, Decentralised Partnerships, Community Participation in a Virtual Museum - New Arrivals'. Retrieved 13 September 2014, http://amusine.typepad.com/new_arrivals/distributed-collections-decentralised-partnerships-community-participation-in-a-virtual-museum--1.html.

Pierroux, P., I. Krange, and I. Sem. 2010. 'Bridging Contexts and Interpretations: Mobile Blogging on Art Museum Field Trips', *MedieKultur. Journal of Media and Communication Research* 27(50): 18.

Pinkerton, B. 1994. 'Finding What People Want: Experiences with the WebCrawler', paper presented to the Second International World Wide Web Conference.

Pinto, R., et al. 2011. 'Bees: New Creative Agents'. Proceedings of the 2011 Conference on Designing Pleasurable Products and Interfaces. New York: ACM, article 3, n.p.

Pizzurno Gelós, P., and C.A. Araúz. 1996. *Estudios sobre el Panamá Republicano (1903–1989)*. Colombia: Manfer S.A.

Preece, J., Y. Rogers, and H. Sharp. 2002. *Interaction Design: Beyond Human-Computer Interaction*. New York: John Wiley & Sons.

Prosser, D. 2000. 'Last Words from the Protagonists: The Curator of Aboriginal Studies David Prosser', in D. Dysart (ed.), *Edge of the Trees: A Sculptural Installation by Janet Laurence and Fiona Foley from the Concept by Peter Emmett*, Exhibition catalogue. Sydney: Historic Houses Trust of New South Wales, 97–98.

Reed, D. 2002. 'Leveraging Community with the Internet'. SynEARTH Archives. http://futurepositive.synearth.net/2002/page/18/.

Rellie, J. 2006. 'Ten Years On: Hopes, Fears, Predictions and Gambles for UK Museums On-line', paper presented to the Museums and the Web 2006 conference in Toronto.

Richardson, J. 2008. 'How to Create an Innovative and Pioneering Marketing Campaign', Museum ID, n.p. http://www.museum-id.com/idea-detail.asp?id=3.

———. 2009. 'Creating a Social Media Plan', *MuseumNext*. http://www.museumnext.org/2010/blog/creating-a-social-media-plan.

Riksdag, S. 2009. 'Kraftsamling -museisamverkan ger resultat, del 1', [Collecting power – the work of museums gives results], *vol. Statens offentliga utredningar* [State Public Studies] 2009: 15. http://data.riksdagen.se/fil/3D8F78DA-9520-4B5D-BEF4-A9DB5FFEE1F2.

Ross, C. 2009. Interview with Heng Wu. London: Museum of London.

Rousseau, D.M., et al. 1998. 'Not So Different After All: A Cross-discipline View of Trust', *Academy of Management Review* 23: 393–404.

Rowe, G., and L.J. Frewer. 2005. 'A Typology of Public Engagement Mechanisms', *Science, Technology & Human Values* 30(2): 251–90.

Rushkoff, D. 1994. *Cyberia: Life in the Trenches of Hyperspace*. San Francisco: Harper Collins.

Russo, A., J.J. Watkins, L. Kelly, and S. Chan. 2006. *How Will Social Media Affect Museum Communication?*, paper presented at Nordic Digital Excellence in Museums (NODEM), Oslo, Norway. http://eprints.qut.edu.au/6067/.

Sánchez Laws, A.L. 2009. *Panamanian Museums: History, Contexts and Contemporary Debates*. Bergen: University of Bergen.

———. 2011. *Panamanian Museums and Historical Memory*. Oxford: Berghahn Books.

Sandell, R. (ed.). 2002. *Museums, Society, Inequality*. London: Routledge.

Sanders, L. 2001. 'Collective Creativity', *LOOP: AIGA Journal of Interaction Design Education* 3: 1–6.

Schjelderup, A. 2003. 'Agradecimientos', in *Caminos de maiz*. Exhibition catalogue. Panama: Enredarte, 70.

Shachaf, P., and N. Hara. 2010. 'Beyond Vandalism: Wikipedia Trolls', *Journal of Information Science* 36(3): 357–70.

Simon, N. 2007. 'Human + coLAB Experiment Post Mortem', *Museum 2.0*. http://museumtwo.blogspot.no/2007/10/human-colab-experiment-post-mortem.html.

———. 2010. *The Participatory Museum*, Museum 2.0. Santa Cruz: Self-published. http://www.participatorymuseum.org.

Skartveit, H.-L., and K.J. Goodnow. 2010. *Changes in Museum Practice: New Media, Refugees and Participation*. Oxford: Berghahn Books.

Skates, A., and P. Firminger. 1998. 'Demonstrations', paper presented at the Museums and the Web 1998 conference. Retrieved 13 September 2014, http://www.museumsandtheweb.com/mw98/abstracts/skates.html.

Smith, S. 1998. 'Digitising Collections: The Redefining of Museums', paper presented at the Museums and the Web 1998 conference. Retrieved 13 September 2014, http://www.museumsandtheweb.com/mw98/papers/smith_s/smith_s_paper.html.

Smithsonian Institution. 2009. 'Experience Brief – Attributes'. SI Web and New Media Strategy Wiki. Washington, DC: Smithsonian Institution. http://smithsonian-webstrategy.wikispaces.com/Experience+Brief+-+Attributes.

Sooke, A. 2011. 'The Problem with Google Art Project', *The Telegraph*. http://www.telegraph.co.uk/culture/art/art-news/8296251/The-problem-with-Googles-Art-Project.html.

Spadaccini, J. 2006. 'Radical Trust', *Ideum Blog*. http://ideum.com/blog/2006/08/radical-trust/.

Stam, D. 1993. 'The Informed Muse. The Implications of The New Museology', *Museum Management and Curatorship* 12: 267–83.

Starn, R.A. 2005. 'A Historian's Brief Guide to New Museum Studies', *The American Historical Review* 110(1): 68–98.

Stayton, K, 2008. 'Crowd-Curated or Crowd-Juryed?', *Bloggers@BrooklynMuseum*. http://www.brooklynmuseum.org/community/blogosphere/2008/07/23/crowd-curated-or-crowd-juried/.

Steinhilper, R., and M. Hieber. 2001. 'Remanufacturing: The Key Solution for Transforming "Downcycling" into "Upcycling" of Electronics'. *Proceedings of the 2001*

IEEE International Symposium on Electronics and the Environment. New York: IEEE, 161–66.

Steinhilper, R., M. Hieber, and vd Osten-Sacken, D. 1997. 'Decision Management Systems for Downcycling/Upcycling/Eco Design-Interdisciplinary Experiences Life Cycle Networks'. *Proceedings of the 4th CIRP International Seminar on Life Cycle Engineering*, 26–27 June 1997, Berlin, Germany. Berlin: Springer, 324–34.

Strahan, R. 1979. 'An Excellent Nucleus 1827–1835', in R. Strahan (ed.), *Rare and Curious Specimens: An Illustrated History of the Australian Museum*. Sydney: The Australian Museum, 7–14. http://australianmuseum.net.au/uploads/documents/27103/rare_and_curious_specimens_complete_lowres_web.pdf.

Surowiecki, J. 2008. 'Reflections on Click! by James Surowiecki'. New York: Brooklyn Museum Blog. http://www.brooklynmuseum.org/community/blogosphere/2008/08/08/reflections-on-click-by-james-surowiecki/.

Swedish National Heritage Board. 2013. *K-samsök*. http://www.raa.se/hitta-information/k-samsok/.

Tejeira Davis, E. 2001. 'The City, its People and its Architecture', in V. Spadafora and E. Tejeira Davis (eds), *Panama City's Old Quarter*. Panama: Ciudad City Publishers, 18–151.

Terranova, T. (2008). 'Cyberculture and New Media', in T. Bennett and J. Frow (eds), *The SAGE Handbook of Cultural Analysis*. London: SAGE Publications Ltd., 587–609. doi: http://dx.doi.org/10.4135/9781848608443.n29.

Timpson, C. 2010. 'Placing our Bets: Building a National Museum's Media Strategy from Scratch', in J.E. Katz and E. Lynch (eds), *Creativity and Technology: Social Media, Mobiles and Museums*. Edinburgh: Museums Etc.

Torres de Araúz, R. 1983. 'Apología de la Cultura Nacional', in J. Pereira de Padilla and R. Segura (eds), *Aproximación a la obra de Reina Torres de Araúz*. Panama: Instituto Nacional de Cultura, 163–67. http://bdigital.binal.ac.pa/bdp/aproxi4.pdf.

Towler, M., V. Hobbs, and D. Pigott. 2002., 'Here and There: Managing Multiply-purposed Digital Assets on the Duyfken Website', paper presented at the Museums and the Web 2002 conference. Retrieved 13 September 2014, http://www.museum-sandtheweb.com/mw2002/papers/towler/towler.html.

Trant, J. 2006. 'Trust, Audience and Community: Museums, Libraries and Identity'. Blog post. Silver Spring: Museums and the Web, Archive. http://www museumsandtheweb.com/blog/jtrant/trust_audience_and_community_museums_libraries_a.html.

Trant, J., and D. Bearman. 1997. *Museums and the Web: A Conference, a Community, and a Challenge*, Archives & Museum Informatics. http://www.archimuse.com/publishing/mw_97_intro.html.

UC Museum of Paleontology. 1994. *UC Museum of Paleontology*, Archive.org. Retrieved 21 April 1994, http://web.archive.org/web/19970606010526/http://www.ucmp.berkeley.edu/.

UNESCO. 1972. 'Round Table on the Development and the Role of Museums in the Contemporary World'.

University of Delaware. 2014. *Museum Studies at the University of Delaware*. Retrieved 5 September 2014, http://www.udel.edu/museumstudies/courses.html%3E.

Valtysson, B., N. Holdgaard, and R. Ling. 2010. 'The iPhone and its Use in Museums', in J.E. Katz and E. Lynch (eds), *Creativity and Technology: Social Media, Mobiles and Museums*. Edinburgh: Museums Etc.

Varines, Hd. 1985. 'Notes en forme d'avant-propos', in A. Nicolas (ed.), *Nouvelles muséologies*. Marseilles, FR: Muséologie Nouvelle et Expérimentation Sociale.

Vergo, P. 1989. *The New Museology*. London: Reaktion Books.

Wagner, I., D. Stuedahl, and T. Bratteteig. 2010. *Exploring Digital Design: Multi-disciplinary Design Practices*. London: Springer.

Walker Rettberg, J. 2003. 'Final Version of Weblog Definition'. Retrieved 28 June 2003, jilltxt.net/archives/blog_theorising/final_version_of_weblog_definition.html.

———. 2008. *Blogging*. Cambridge: Polity.

Webb, C. 2003. *Guidelines for the Preservation of Digital Heritage*. Paris: Information Society Division, United Nations Educational, Scientific and Cultural Organization.

Weller, R. 2002. 'Stepping Across a Continent', *Landscape Design* 308: 4–9.

Witcomb, A. 2003a, 'Editor's Introduction: The Other Side: Papers from the 2003 Museums Australia Conference [Online]', paper presented to Museums Australia, Perth.

———. 2003b. *Re-imagining the Museum: Beyond the Mausoleum*. London: Routledge.

Wolfensohn, J.D. 2000. 'Culture Counts: Financing, Resources, and the Economics of Culture in Sustainable Development', proceedings of the conference held in Florence, Italy, 4–7 October 1999, cosponsored by the government of Italy and the World Bank, in cooperation with the United Nations Educational, Scientific, and Cultural Organization.

World Wide Web Consortium (W3C). 2008. 'Web Content Accessibility Guidelines (WCAG) 2.0'. W3C Recommendation 11 December 2008. http://www.w3.org/TR/WCAG20/.

Wu, H. 2009. 'Interviews with Museum of London officials'. Fieldwork, University of Bergen.

Yu, L.L., J.V. Nickerson, and Y. Sakamoto. 2012. 'Collective Creativity: Where We Are and Where We Might Go', *Proceedings of Collective Intelligence*, No. arXiv: 1204.3890, n.p.

Zlotos, R. 2010. Interview with the author. Bergen: Hordaland Fylkeskommune.

Index